A FIGHTING CHANCE

ANDREW LORENZ

A Fighting Chance

The revival and future of British manufacturing industry

FOREWORD BY SIR FRANCIS TOMBS, CHAIRMAN OF ROLLS ROYCE AND T&N

Hutchinson Business Books

Copyright © Andrew Lorenz 1989

First Published in Great Britain by
Business Books Limited
An imprint of Century Hutchinson Limited
62–65 Chandos Place, London WC2N 4NW

Century Hutchinson Australia (Pty) Limited
89–91 Albion Street, Surry Hills,
New South Wales 2010, Australia

Century Hutchinson New Zealand Limited
PO Box 40–086, 32–34 View Road, Glenfield,
Auckland 10, New Zealand

Century Hutchinson, South Africa (Pty) Limited
PO Box 337, Bergvlei 2012, South Africa

British Library Cataloguing in Publication Data

Lorenz, Andrew
    A Fighting Chance: The revival and
    future of British manufacturing industry
    1.   Great Britain. Manufacturing industries
    I.   Title
    338.4'767'094'

    ISBN 0-09-174127-0

Typeset by Deltatype, Ellesmere Port
Printed in Great Britain by Mackays of Chatham PLC
Chatham, Kent

For Helen

CONTENTS

FOREWORD

For British industry the post-war years have been a turbulent period of change, characterized by widely differing government attitudes.

Until ten years ago, governments of both persuasions adopted an interventionist attitude and varying interpretations of the social contract theory. Combined with the growing power of trade unions at official and unofficial levels, the resulting climate was a hostile one for industry and saw a progressive deterioration in its international competitiveness.

The change over the last ten years has been enormous, with a seeming indifference on the part of government to the problems of manufacturing industry inherited from the past. The policy of benign neglect, supported by a condition that the fiscal climate had to be corrected particularly in relation to inflation, and combined with a decision to reduce the state-controlled sector of industry by privatization, has allowed industry to survive and to improve its competitive position.

During both periods, it is plain that government's appreciation of industry's problems was woefully lacking. In view of that, it is perhaps not surprising that the policy of the last decade has proved more successful, or that when temporarily abandoned, the results have not been praiseworthy.

This book examines the post-war tribulations of British industry in an interesting and detached way, illustrating its conclusions by a number of carefully constructed case studies. I feel sure that it will command the admiration of many industrialists and I hope that it will be read carefully by present and aspiring politicians.

Sir Francis Tombs

INTRODUCTION

First, a disclaimer. This book does not pretend to be an all-encompassing study of manufacturing industry in the 1980s. It aims to assess the themes and forces that made the decade the most momentous peacetime period in British manufacturing's twentieth century history. Its focus is not those areas of manufacturing where British companies were, and have tended to remain, internationally strong, but rather the regions of engineering, electronics, textiles, food and general manufacturing – 'industrials' on the Financial Times Index definition. These are the sectors whose fate will determine whether British-owned manufacturing has a prosperous future.

The experience of the companies most closely examined here – Dunlop and BTR, Avon Rubber and Weir Group, Cadbury Schweppes and United Biscuits, STC and GEC – stands for that of hundreds of other firms during the decade. This is their story, too – all the more dramatic since its dénouement remains uncertain.

All quotations are from interviews with the author, unless the source is otherwise stated. In some cases, I have protected the identity of the interviewee.

I offer my thanks to the very many people in or connected with industry and the City, without whose knowledge and advice over recent years I could never have attempted this book. I must express particular acknowledgement to The Scotsman and The Sunday Telegraph, for allowing me the freedom to range widely over the manufacturing field during the decade, and to The Sunday Times for giving me the opportunity to develop the subject.

My greatest regret is that my father, a manufacturing company director who possessed marvellous insight into the workings of British industry, is not alive to see the result of the interest he inspired.

Andrew Lorenz

CHAPTER ONE

MRS THATCHER'S INDUSTRIAL REVOLUTION

In 1986, an event was held in Britain which, at any time, in any other developed country, would have seemed quite nonsensical. 'Industry Year' was designed by its creators and sponsors – notably the venerable Royal Society for the encouragement of Arts, Manufactures and Commerce – to bring home to the British people the central importance of industry in securing their standard of living and future prosperity.

Industry Year was a mixed success, helping in what became its prime tangible aim – to build local links between companies and schools – but struggling for the organization necessary to achieve genuine national dissemination of its purpose.

Nevertheless, it did manage to involve a sizeable cross-section of the British public, from the Duke of Edinburgh (President of the Royal Society) to Robert Platt, an unemployed 17-year-old from Motherwell who participated in the Year's single largest event: a 4,000-strong rally in London's Royal Albert Hall organized by the Industrial Society.

Of all the entities with a stake in the future of British industry, only one maintained a low profile throughout the Year. Aside from a small Department of Trade and Industry grant towards the Industry Year budget, Mrs Margaret Thatcher's second Conservative government took little part in providing the national focus at which the Year's grassroots activities could aim.

Just as Industry Year was more potent as a symbol than as a fact, so the Government's lack of participation epitomized the Thatcherite doctrine of hands-off non-intervention which towered over British industry throughout the 1980s. The Thatcher approach, which produced a seismic change in industry tantamount to a second industrial revolution, was financed by a gift of nature – booming North Sea Oil revenues. But it was sustained with a quite remarkable consistency which owed nothing to providence and everything to the Prime Minister's sense of personal mission.

At various times, her determination set her at odds with a score of captains of industry, including Sir John Harvey-Jones of the chemicals giant ICI, Lord Weinstock of GEC and Sir Michael Edwardes of British Leyland. The Confederation of British Industry spent most of the decade, between election time restatements of its support for the Conservatives, warring with the Government about the effects of its policies on manufacturing industry. But Thatcher pressed on regardless.

Industrial strategy became two dirty words, since they reeked of interventionism and the bad old days of procrastinating compromise. Yet Thatcher's economic policies constituted the most effective industrial strategy of the century, breeding what became recognized as a new realism in industry and consigning to history the once-comfortable corporate life. A Confederation of British Industry (CBI)/British Institute Management survey of more than 500 managers in 108 companies, carried out in summer 1983, demonstrated the psychological impact of Thatcherism. It revealed an intriguing contradiction in attitudes: managers believed that they were getting more job satisfaction than before the recession, and that they were coping well in the prevailing tough conditions (in 1983, industry was only just starting to emerge from the slump of 1980–2). But they also felt that morale was generally lower than it had been before the onset of recession.

Concern about the then-low level of corporate profitability and about price competitiveness partly explained this paradoxical response. However, there was one overwhelming and ultimately encouraging inference: before the recession, managers had lived in an industrial Cockayne which had quite lost sight or sense of fundamental realities – of how far British companies were adrift of their overseas rivals. Now, they had woken up to the unpleasant reality. As recession survivors, their new resilience stood shoulder to shoulder with their sudden awareness of what they were really up against.

Subsequent events have tended to emphasize the positive face of this new realism. In the mid-1980s, British manufacturing industry arrested the slide in its share of world trade that had continued since 1960, abated only by occasional hiccups. After hitting a low of 7.6 per cent in 1984, Britain's share of exports by the major manufacturing countries increased to about 7.9 per cent in 1985, dipped back to 7.6 per cent the following year, then jumped to 8.2 per cent in 1987, and climbed further, to about 8.3 per cent, in 1988 (National Economic Development Office estimates, 21 March 1989.) This statistic is the obverse of the often-cited, widening balance of trade deficit in manufactured goods. While the trade deficit has clear ramifications for confidence in the economy, the world trade share figure, albeit approximate, may be a more accurate barometer to the health and wealth of the manufacturing sector.

The roots of this sustained recovery, albeit from a low base, were planted during the recession of 1980–2. Contrary to left-wing demonology, Mrs Thatcher did not create the British recession, which was triggered, like the rest of the world's, by the Ayatollah Khomeini's overthrow of the Shah of Iran and the ensuing second oil-price shock.

But Britain's recession was much more severe than that of other countries. In three years, unemployment increased by almost 80 per cent from 1.45 million in 1980 to 2.6 million at the end of 1982 – and went on spiralling thereafter. By the time Mrs Thatcher was re-elected for the second time, in June 1987, the number of jobs in manufacturing had dwindled from 7.1 million in May 1979 to 5.1 million – a loss of almost one worker in three.

The manufacturing output figures tell an equally dramatic story. Over the three years preceding the recession, output averaged a 1.2 per cent annual rise. In 1980, output dived by 8.7 per cent and the following year by another six per cent. Not until July 1987 did manufacturing output recapture its 1979 level.

At bottom, there was one simple reason why British industry's pain in the early 1980s was so great: Mrs Thatcher came to power dedicated to eradicating inflation from the British body economic. That single and overriding imperative determined that when the world recession struck, she and her hair-shirt Chancellor Sir Geoffrey Howe would not cushion the country from its impact by pumping money into the economy. Monetarism, given practical effect and objectives through their Medium Term Financial Strategy (MTFS) which was launched in the March 1980 Budget, aimed to squeeze inflation out of Britain's economic bloodstream by controlling the money supply. A prime instrument in this process were interest rates, which jumped sharply from 14 to 17 per cent shortly after the 1979 election and did not fall below 12 per cent until August 1982.

This was a shock in itself. But the knife was twisted into the soft underbelly of British industry, and then twisted again, by the potent combination of Britain's black gold mine in the North Sea, and misconceived economic policy.

The recession, induced by an oil price leap, struck just as Britain's oil reserves in the North Sea were entering their most fecund period. Crude North Sea oil production increased almost 50 per cent to 77 million tonnes in 1979, its largest annual jump en route to its mid-1980s peak. The output surge delivered more than £2 billion to the Exchequer – its first material chunk of oil revenues.

With United States oil reserves in secular decline, and other major developed countries lacking indigenous production, North Sea oil made Britain's currency a brilliant port in the international economic storm. Investors flooded into the pound, reversing a years-long trend of decline in its relative value. The peak against the American dollar came in late 1980, when sterling stood at almost $2.40, while in summer 1981 it reached more than 144 on its trade-weighted index against a basket of other currencies.

British manufacturers' cost-competitiveness suffered accordingly. Relative unit labour costs soared, first against the Americans, then compared with Europe. Late 1980 was the blackest hour, the period just before British manufacturing productivity started to gain ground on the overseas competition, offsetting the strong pound.

It was all too much for many British industrialists. Sir Michael Edwardes, who was trying to save British Leyland, Britain's only volume car maker, from the scrapheap, told the CBI November 1980 conference in Brighton that : 'If the Cabinet do not have the wit and imagination to reconcile our industrial needs with the fact of North Sea oil, they would do better to leave the bloody stuff in the ground.'

At the same conference, the CBI's new director-general, former Ford of Britain chief Sir Terence Beckett, made the celebrated remark that was to live with him and the CBI for much of the decade. On the eve of delivering his keynote speech, in pre-Agincourt Henry V mode, Beckett was circulating among the CBI troops. He happened upon a group of members from the West Midlands, the so-called heartland of manufacturing industry, who urged him to lay down the law. Next day, Beckett went for it, urging the CBI to use its 'bare knuckles' in a fight with the Government for the future of manufacturing. The call to arms backfired – several loyal Conservative members of the CBI resigned their membership, and the organization was tarred in Thatcherite eyes with the uncomfortable (for the CBI) brush of dissidence.

However ill-judged in political terms, Beckett's outrage at the carnage of recession was, in one respect at least, actually justified by the facts. Aside from its very deliberate refusal to reflate, the Government inadvertently deepened the slump by two signal pieces of economic mismanagement.

First, it honoured the extremely high 1979 public sector pay award made by the Clegg Commission appointed under the Callaghan Administration. In making the award, Mrs Thatcher kept an election campaign pledge, but the move stoked up inflation even further and thus made the counter-inflationary drive that much more severe.

The Clegg award was as nothing, however, beside Chancellor Howe's decision in his 1979 Budget to raise the Value Added Tax rate from eight to 15 per cent. This pushed up the cost of living at the very moment when the recession was taking hold. It was supply-side economics gone bananas, wilfully fuelling with one hand the inflationary fire that the Government was trying to extinguish with the other.

Thatcher, Howe and their confrères seemed to have little sympathy for the manufacturers. Almost the only thing about the MTFS that continually vexed the Prime Minister and her closest colleagues was the obstinate refusal of the money supply, defined in the early years as M3, to remain pinned within its intended target ranges.

The attitude that conditioned Thatcher's approach to industry was brought home to business people in her own Finchley, North

London constituency at a meeting early in the recession. This was an MP's surgery with a difference, because the surgeon took a verbal knife to the industrialists who were seeking some relief from their economic agony. In a withering riposte, the Prime Minister threw their requests for a loosening of the purse-strings back in their faces, accusing them of fomenting past inflation by handing out excessive pay rises in the face of exorbitant union wage claims.

Thatcher saw indolent British industry as the main threat to her objective of kicking the country's inflation habit. This fundamental precept was both the detonator that reduced the post-war industrial establishment to rubble, and the cornerstone of its reconstruction.

By routing out inflation, Thatcher blocked the road which had always allowed companies to take the easy exit. Increasingly, through the Seventies, Britain had become hooked on inflation as the engine of growth. The cost of living went up, so pay claims and awards went up, and prices were raised to finance the wage increases. As one manager noted in 1983: 'For many years, we lived on the fairy gold of stock inflation. We made stock profits and borrowed from the banks to provide cash for working capital. How wrong we were.' (*Financial Times*, April 1983). Inflation was the drug that remorselessly sapped industry's international competitiveness.

The Callaghan Government's successive years of pay restraint, otherwise known as the Social Contract with the Trades Union Congress, made no fundamental difference to this decline. Beneath the veneer of restraint on basic pay increases flourished a teeming mass of supposedly self-financing productivity deals which were anything but that. Manufacturing's cost-competitiveness declined by about 40 per cent in the Social Contract years (NEDO: British Industrial Performance), while average earnings increased by nine per cent in 1977 and by 15.5 per cent in 1979, when retail prices rose by 13.4 per cent.

The combination of the Clegg Commission pay awards and the VAT rise drove up earnings by 20.7 per cent in 1980 and prices by 18 per cent, but then the Thatcher medicine took effect. The rate of increase in average earnings fell to an annual low of 5.1 per cent at one stage in 1984, when retail price inflation was five per cent.

Employers were compelled to stand their ground on lower pay offers by the removal of their headroom to raise prices. As for the employees, it was fear – the fear of unemployment – which drove them to accept without a struggle. And not just on pay settlements. Through the Sixties and the Seventies, the strike had become almost as regular a feature of industrial life as clocking on. Vauxhall, the car maker, reckoned that by the late Seventies, one of its suppliers was on strike every day. Now all that changed. The number of strikes plunged from 2,703 in 1977 and 2,080 in 1979 to 1,330 in 1980 and a decade's low of 722 in 1988.

Against this backdrop, the face of the labour relations landscape was changed by a sustained act of Thatcherite industrial interventionism: the Employment and Trade Union laws introduced between 1980 and 1984 by successive Employment Secretaries Jim Prior, Norman Tebbit and Tom King.

Years of increasing union militancy, the so-called 'British disease', had reached their apogee in 1978/9's Winter of Discontent – the wave of strikes by tanker drivers, health and public service workers. Public reaction against the apparent anarchy of the strikes was undoubtedly a major factor that swept Thatcher to power. In letter and spirit, the new Government's first two union laws were inspired by the events of 1978/9. They radically narrowed the legal scope for strike action and conduct, by restricting such action to that concerned solely or mainly with wages and conditions; and by outlawing secondary picketing (the blockade of somewhere other than the strikers' workplace), exposing unions to fines or sequestration (confiscation) of their funds if they breached the law, making it easier for companies to sack strikers, and harder for unions to operate a closed shop.

The third Act went further, carrying the attack to the heart of the unions' own constitution in an avowed attempt to increase union democracy. It required regular elections of union executives by secret ballot and ballots to vote on union political funds – the unions' main financial link with the Labour Party. These provisions were of limited effectiveness, but far more significant was the section ordaining that unions would lose their legal immunity from action for damages if they failed to hold a secret ballot of workers before calling a strike. The Act did not go all the way and order such a ballot to be postal, but it nevertheless marked the end of the farcical 'show of hands' mass meeting that had persisted as the main strike decision-making method for a quarter of a century. As if to make the point, one characteristically chaotic strike-vote by mass meeting occurred at the luxury car company Jaguar, just as the new Act was coming into force.

With the union laws, the Thatcher Governments lived up to their constant refrain that they were in power to set the framework in which industry could flourish, but never to intervene in decisions which should be the responsibility of management alone. Apart from the early period of Edward Heath's 1970 Conservative Government, before the celebrated U-turn over State aid for Upper Clyde Shipbuilders, the Thatcherite view constituted a complete break with the practice of post-war governments.

For years, industrial strategy had combined grand but not always successful designs like those of the Industrial Reorganization Corporation in the 1966–70 Wilson Government, with the less edifying spectacle of eleventh hour horse-trading between ministers (notably the Prime Minister), employers and union leaders which ended almost invariably in evasion of the tough decision.

Thatcherism threw open the windows of Downing Street's previously smoke-filled rooms and blew the lingering smell of beer and sandwiches into history. Private sector companies had frequently been involved in the interventions of the – chiefly – Labour years, but it was the much-enlarged nationalized sector that had inevitably born the brunt of ruinous industrial politicking. Now it was the first major State sector strike of the Thatcher era that brought home the scale of the break with Britain's recent industrial past.

One Sunday early in the 13-week British Steel Corporation (BSC) workers' strike of 1980, Sir Keith Joseph, the Industry Secretary, was interviewed on London Weekend Television's Weekend World current affairs programme. Joseph was asked whether BSC's management and the leader of the main union involved, Bill Sirs of the Iron and Steel Trades Confederation, were about to meet, and what were the chances of a settlement. 'I don't know,' Joseph retorted, 'It's nothing to do with the Government.'

Whatever the truth of the matter – and the idea that the Government was not in touch with events during a major strike in a strategically important State industry took some swallowing –

Joseph's was an epoch-making image. The steel strike, the first of the giant public sector disputes of the 1980s which culminated in the 1984/5 miners' strike, was a watershed, not only for BSC itself, but for Government-industry relations.

Hindsight has emphasized what the strike meant, as British Steel has built a progressive improvement of its underlying performance on the foundations laid after the strike was defeated. But the essential contrast between the attitude of past governments and the Thatcher approach was hammered home at the time.

Steel epitomized the interventionism by both political parties that had dogged British manufacturers through the post-war years. It had been nationalized (in 1951), denationalized (in 1953) and renationalized (in 1967). It was a 1958 decision by Harold Macmillan to appease the Scottish lobby which landed the then-unnationalized industry with two strip mills: one, which was originally intended to be the only new plant, at Llanwern in South Wales; the other at Ravenscraig near Glasgow. Despite enjoying the temporary benefits of Ravenscraig's modern processes during the post-recession steel demand boom, at bottom, British Steel is still living with the over-capacity resulting from Macmillan's political move.

The Ravenscraig decision only hinted at the main evil of interventionism to which BSC became a prime witness during the Labour Government of 1974–79: the refusal to take tough decisions, which rendered the business increasingly uncompetitive and banked up the pain of eventual adjustment. In the face of mounting evidence that BSC had to raise efficiency by closing some operations and cutting its workforce, the Government did next-to-nothing. The reason was simple: from Prime Minister James Callaghan down, many Labour ministers and MPs had constituencies in or near British Steel works. Closures and redundancies were political impossibilities.

The Thatcher Government freed British Steel, and other management's, hands at the same time as exerting pressure on industry to improve its efficiency. Secretaries of State for Industry (Trade and Industry after the departments were merged in June 1983) came and went with disturbing frequency throughout the decade – Keith Joseph, Cecil Parkinson, Norman Tebbit, Leon Brittan, Paul Channon, Lord Young – but widely contrasting though their personalities were, the essential litany remained: management is up to the managers; government can only provide for them the right legislative and economic framework in which to operate.

In practice, the industrial strategy of forcing managers to stand on their own feet was abetted by a measure of covert interventionism. Taking the union laws as part of the framework, the most potent interventionist element was the effort to attract overseas, notably Japanese, companies to set up factories in Britain. This was a brilliantly conceived policy *'pour encourager les autres'*, aimed squarely at compelling native British companies to match the generally greater efficiency of the foreign firm setting up on their doorstep. Single union representation agreements, or entirely non-union deals; no-strike agreements; elimination of demarcation lines and more flexible working – all these and more were showcased by plants like the Nissan car factory in Washington, near Sunderland Airport in Tyne and Wear, and Yamazaki's machine tool works in Worcester.

The Government's policy did not come cheap: the Nissan project, its most spectacular coup, received £35 million in selective assistance, and stands to get another £90 million in total through regional grants – more than one-third of the plant's £350 million cost – as it gears up to output of 200,000 cars a year in the mid-1990s, then to a likely 400,000 by the year 2000.

Nissan fulfilled a long-lived dream in North-East England, which had always envied the West Midlands its car industry. It brought much-needed new jobs to a region decimated by steel, shipbuilding and coal mining closures. And it provided a new customer for British component suppliers – along with a fresh source of pressure on them to ensure the quality and reliability of their products.

Nevertheless, the Government's manifest incitement of 'inward' investment by foreign firms in Britain was sometimes contrasted by British companies with its apparent lack of interest in their own activities. This view was a small symptom of the more general disquiet felt by many industrialists about the Thatcher government. From their onset in attacks like those of Sir Terence Beckett and Sir Michael Edwardes at the CBI conference in 1980, these misgivings grew into a prevailing concern that the Government actually saw no future in manufacturing industry, believing that Britain could happily rely on the services sector.

This sentiment may have owed something to the psychological state of manufacturers bruised and battered by the recession, but it was not the product of industrialists' paranoia. As the recession drew to a close in 1982, a national debate developed about the respective merits of manufacturing and service industries. It was punctuated by the fashionable observation that with manufacturing jobs disappearing and the proportion of gross national product generated by manufacturing industry declining, Britain really could prosper as a service-dominated economy.

Some Government ministers appeared to lend credence to the services-only argument. According to the CBI, the first to voice such an opinion was John Wakeham, in August 1982. Wakeham, later Chief Whip but at that time a junior Treasury minister, averred that manufacturing was not important. Beckett immediately remonstrated with the Treasury and Sir Geoffrey Howe, then the Chancellor and on a visit to Canada, rang the furious CBI director-general from Montreal to assure him that Wakeham's view did not represent that of the Government.

However, the manufacturing versus services debate continued to gain currency in the country, and the issue between the CBI and the Government refused to lie down. In February 1984, the Department of Trade submitted a paper to the monthly meeting of Neddy, the National Economic Development Council, which was the only forum for tripartite economic discussion between the Government, employers and unions. The Trade Department paper claimed that overseas earnings from services in 1982 totalled 77 per cent of the earnings from export of manufactured goods.

Beckett strongly criticized the paper, and his arguments were supported privately by some Neddy officials. They pointed out that when interest and dividend receipts from overseas investments were excluded, the services contribution fell from 77 per cent of manufacturing earnings to 47 per cent. And that, excluding the services earnings which were manufacturing-dependent, the true proportion of earnings contributed by the service sector was only about 16 per cent.

For the CBI, the final straw followed when Nigel Lawson, then Secretary of State for Energy, remarked in a House of Commons debate that, while all sectors of the economy were important, he could not understand why some MPs attached selective importance to the manufacturing sector. In what still appears a remarkable step, even for a country with such an anti-industry culture as Britain, Beckett wrote to Lawson asserting the importance of manufacturing to the economy. He reported the correspondence to his members in the March issue of the CBI's monthly magazine, under what became the campaign's rallying call: 'Manufacturing Matters'.

The CBI director-general declared: 'I am concerned that one or two prominent figures have gone so far as to suggest that Britain's brightest future lies in becoming an up-market service station for our more successful overseas manufacturing competitors. The service sector is performing well. But manufacturing and services are interdependent . . .

'Our loss of market share in manufacturing is not inevitable. It stems largely from poor price and non-price competitiveness,' said Beckett, contending that non-price elements were the responsibility of industry, but 'the remainder stems from Government-imposed overheads and price-fixing within the nationalized industries, like energy prices.'

Beckett had half an eye on influencing the Budget later that month. What Lawson actually produced was a radical move to neutralize business taxation which aggravated the CBI and intensified manufacturing's persecution complex.

The Chancellor cut the standard rate of Corporation Tax from 52 per cent to 35 per cent, but announced the phasing out over three years of the capital allowances system under which a company could offset, for one year, the entire cost of its capital investment against its tax bill. The Treasury argued that the old allowances regime had encouraged companies to invest for the tax concessions, rather than to improve their commercial effectiveness, and that this explained why British industry's return on its capital – capital productivity – was inferior to that of its main overseas competitors.

Some industrialists agreed. Others saw yet another example of manufacturing being cut down to the level of the service sector, which stood to gain most from the tax changes because it was a relatively less heavy capital investor. The CBI forecast that Lawson's measure would choke a post-recession recovery in investment by the manufacturing sector, and cause a precipitous fall in investment – 'The Dip' – as the new rules took effect. Companies would be confronted with 'an unenviable choice of either slashing their investment plans or running into serious cash problems'.

Like many a spectre, 'The Dip' was a bogeyman who never materialized. Manufacturing investment did fall in 1986, but only by £250 million in almost £8.5 billion. It then resumed its climb back to pre-recession levels. In the second quarter of 1988, it reached the highest quarterly level ever recorded by government statistics.

A more real threat came from the Byatt Report, named after its author, the deputy chief economic adviser to the Treasury, which had been produced in December 1982 by an interdepartmental group of economists from the Treasury, the Trade and Industry departments, and the Overseas Development Administration section of the Foreign Office. Byatt was not published until 13 months later, in response to a Parliamentary Question. It then provoked an outcry from industrialists, who believed its thinking had taken secret and pernicious root in parts of Whitehall. One group, the Scottish Council for Development and Industry, said implementation of its proposals would 'amount to the wholesale de-industrialization of the United Kingdom'.

Byatt attacked the financial support given by British governments to capital goods exporters – those manufacturers of heavy construction and engineering equipment who competed for major projects such as power stations and bridges. Its conclusions were those of the archetypal free marketeers: the subsidies were very high – a total £640 million in 1981/2 – but lacked cost-effectiveness because they were not made conditional on efficiency improvements by their recipients. Moreover, 'the fact that other countries may support their capital goods exports . . . is not an economic argument for automatically doing likewise, even if UK firms would be competitive in the absence of the foreigners' subsidies'.

Under a different government, such arguments would have been dismissed as the irrelevant ruminations of ivory tower theoreticians. But in its present, highly sensitive state, British industry took them only too seriously. Neddy provided the rallying point for a counter-attack spearheaded by executives from GEC, John Brown and Davy McKee – all leading capital goods groups and beneficiaries of the Government subsidies. Their central point was straightforward enough: if Britain failed to match the international going rate for support, the foreigners would clean up and much of British industry would be out of a job.

The industrialists won their case: there was no Byatt brain-washing of the export subsidy system. But to an extent, it was a Pyrrhic victory. The Byatt debate forced the companies to defend their position; the following year, 1985, they tried to turn this successful defence into an offensive to win increased Government bilateral aid – the aid, targeted directly by one country to another, which gains most export business. The attempt failed, and three years later the companies were still complaining that Britain lagged behind its competitors in this area.

Byatt was a little-noticed signal which pointed to the new parameters for manufacturing established by the Thatcherite industrial revolution. The possibility, however remote, that such a sacred cow as support for exporters could be slaughtered showed how great was the upheaval of the old order, away from the factory floor that was already being transformed by the recession.

Other straws could be spotted in the wind of change. In 1984, the Institution of Mechanical Engineers organized a conference, the Cambridge Manufacturing Forum, which was attended by more than 100 senior executives of Britain's biggest engineering companies. The conference, titled 'Strategies for Survival and Success', was carefully designed to focus industrialists' recession-battered minds on the need to adjust their thinking to the different challenges of the post-recession phase.

An invitation to give the conference a keynote address was issued to Trade and Industry Department Secretary of State Norman Tebbit, and the signs that Tebbit would attend were so encouraging that his name was written into the conference programme. According to one of the organizers, the DTI attitude changed when discussion turned to what message Tebbit might deliver. The organizers suggested that the conference presented him with a wonderful opportunity to allay industrialists' fears about Government policy, and to declare his recognition of the vital role played by manufacturing in the economy. Tebbit did not address the conference. Kenneth Baker, then a junior Industry minister, came instead and did nothing to calm the executives' concern that their businesses were seen as 'sunset' industries, by regaling his audience with praise for 'Silicon Fen', the Cambridge electronics community.

In the prevailing atmosphere of recession-induced insecurity, it was little surprise that a sense of alienation developed in some industrial regions. One barometer of this effect was a series of 'dispatches from the front line' which appeared periodically in the *Financial Times*, written by the anonymous finance director of a medium-sized engineering company in the North-West. After a series of reports charting the post-recession battle to recover ground lost to overseas competitors, the author arrived at February 1986. He concluded his piece: 'Here in the North-West of England, despite all the optimistic noises being made by those who live and work south of Watford, we see industry generally slowly melting away like the Russian armies of 1917 . . .'

Sir John Harvey-Jones was all too conscious of Britain's industrial North. As chairman of the country's largest manufacturer, Imperial Chemical Industries, he had been forced by ICI's 1980 recession-induced slide to its first-ever quarterly loss to cut a swathe through the group's many factories. A humanitarian industrialist, Harvey-Jones was acutely aware of the pain he was inflicting on the Northern communities. That awareness made him all the more determined to see that ICI employees had not lost their jobs in vain. Apart from securing the recovery of his own company (under him, ICI fought back to match, and sometimes surpass, overseas competitors like the West German triumvirate of Bayer, Hoechst and BASF) Harvey-Jones was concerned to ensure that the cause of British manufacturing as a whole was taken to the nation's heart.

This mission informed his approach when he was asked by the BBC to give the Corporation's April 1986 Richard Dimbleby lecture, one of the few occasions during the decade when industry's case was argued on prime-time televison. Entitled 'Does Industry Matter?', the lecture was a compendious personal expression of the fears felt by many managers. Harvey-Jones started by castigating what he called

Britain's 'switch-off attitude to industry'. His talk then ranged across many features of industrial life, from status divisions inside companies, through the adversarial political system and the short-term attitudes of Britain's financial markets, to the future of science teaching in schools and the mutual dependence of manufacturing and science.

The core of the lecture, however, was a comprehensive assertion of the importance of manufacturing industry and a warning about its neglect by the nation. Britain could not pay its way in the world through service industries alone, he said. 'If we imagine the UK can get by with a bunch of people in smocks showing tourists around Mediaeval castles, we are quite frankly out of our minds. What's more, if that's the sort of future we offer our young, we shan't find them staying here to enjoy it,' Harvey-Jones declared.

'Images associated with the word "industry" not only fail to excite people, they actively repel them' although 'the Lowry image of manufacturing is false,' he told several million viewers. Manufacturing's share of national output was falling throughout the developed world, but over the previous 25 years, manufacturing's decline in Britain had been 60 per cent greater than the average. Even so, Harvey-Jones ended on a note of hope that Britain had a manufacturing future 'if we put our money on science and technology; if we can make the connection between invention and exploitation; if we enable our international companies to flourish and compete.'

By virtue of his television platform, the ICI chairman was speaking for British industry to a larger and wider section of the population than any other executive could address, at a pivotal time when the foundations of Britain's economic performance in the 1990s were starting to be laid. Yet there was one striking omission from the lecture: it contained no specific examination of current Government industrial policy, save for the observation that the Government should support fundamental research.

Between the lines, however, a message did emerge, partly from illusions of the 'if we enable our companies to compete' variety, and more pervasively, from the basic absence of any direct comment. It was as if Harvey-Jones had reined his views in to the point where the lack of reference to industrial policy communicated that there was a vacuum in Government strategy which permeated British industry as thoroughly as it underscored the Dimbleby lecture.

Harvey-Jones explained later: 'The omission was a deliberate one. One of the difficulties I have in speaking up is that it is known that I am not a supporter of the Government. It was merely that I was very anxious to try and avoid having the lecture dismissed as a political polemic.' The explicit case against the Thatcher Government's industrial policy had already been put, nine months earlier, in a report by the House of Lords select committee on Overseas Trade. Published at the half-way point of the decade, the Lords report immediately became the standard work of reference and quotation for all critics of the Government's attitude to manufacturing. Leaving aside the merits of its arguments, their force was such that the report made the rare transition from industrial study to representation of the strategic alternative to Thatcherism. Its themes were still being recalled at the end of the decade, as Britain reported a widening balance of payments deficit on trade in visible (manufactured) goods.

The Lords' point of departure was the need for a strong British manufacturing sector to take up the overseas earnings baton from North Sea oil as oil revenues declined. It concluded that 'urgent action' was required if this objective was to be attained. The crunch paragraph read: 'Unless the climate is changed so that steps can be taken to enlarge the manufacturing base, combat import penetration and stimulate the export of manufactured goods, as oil revenues diminish the country will experience adverse effects which include:

a contraction of manufacturing to the point where the successful continuation of much of manufacturing activity is put at risk;

an irreplaceable loss of GDP;

an adverse balance of payments of such proportions that severe deflationary measures will be needed;

lower tax revenue for public spending on welfare, defence and other areas;

higher unemployment, with little prospect of reducing it; and

the economy stagnating and inflation rising, driven up by a falling exchange rate.'

The Lords concluded: 'Taken together, these constitute a grave threat to the standard of living and to the economic and political stability of the nation.'

The committee accepted that 'the prime responsibility for industry lies with the industrial firms themselves'. It stated: 'Some of the aims of Government at present are laudable.' But then came the sting: 'The paramountcy of manufacturing has not been recognized in the formulation of policy with the result that policies, or, on occasion, the avowed lack of policies, have actually been inimical to manufacturing.' The Government, implied the report, had to adopt a national industrial policy, tailor its exchange rate and interest rate policies more closely to the needs of manufacturing, and increase its financial support for innovation and exports.

The report provoked a Government response which was not so much instant as positively pre-emptive. Even before official publication time of the report, Trade and Industry Secretary Leon Brittan rushed out a retort accusing the Lords of alarmism, warning that their study could give a 'totally biased and misleading view' of economic prospects, and rejecting every policy recommendation the Lords had made.

Brittan's over-reaction undermined what was and remains a good case against the conclusions of the report. One doubt concerned the qualifications of some of the peers themselves to pass judgment. Several of the committee members had held prominent positions in British industry during its pre-1979 decline. The committee's chairman was Lord Aldington, former chairman of the Westland helicopters company, which less than a year after publication of the report had to be controversially rescued from financial collapse. Two other committee members were Lord Ezra, who had chaired the National Coal Board in the days of Heath, Wilson and Callaghan, and Lord Kearton, the former head of Courtaulds, the textiles giant revived from the recession by Sir Christopher Hogg, who made a complete break with past strategy.

The report also saw only one side of the recession – its shrinkage of Britain's manufacturing base as companies failed and went out of business. In fact, this casualty list was a painful but inevitable side-effect of the cure that industry underwent in those years. The process could not, unfortunately, choose its targets and there can be little doubt that some companies which deserved to survive actually went to the wall, just as a number which should have gone under managed to hang on into the post-recession phase. 'Going to work everyday was a little like going to war,' John Small of the containers group United Glass told the Cambridge Manufacturing Forum in July 1984. 'We had to sacrifice some excellent factories from the point of view of labour relations. We had six months of very bitter strife with the trade unions.

'But once they were convinced of the need, our people would move a lot more radically than we had supposed. We fought hard to protect new investment throughout the period. As a result, we are a smaller, more cost-conscious and more cost-effective company.'

British industry did emerge from the recession leaner and fitter. That is a cliché, but no less true for being so. In contrast, the Lords report, for all its excellent analysis, took the view that industry had been emaciated to the point of anorexia.

Nor was Mrs Thatcher as antipathetic to industry as the Lords implied. She blamed weak managements for fuelling Britain's inflationary past – hence the deaf ear turned by the first Thatcher administration to industry's pleas for relief from recession. But she was quick to espouse new ideas, notably the whole movement which stressed the role of design in enhancing industrial competitiveness. It was a Downing Street symposium which provided the focus for the design campaign.

As the second Thatcher term wore on, after the 1983 election, the Prime Minister showed signs of a subtle moderation in her initially harsh conception of the manufacturing sector. She offered it some encouragement, instead of simply belabouring it for past errors. In September 1985, she attended the first Engineering Assembly, a congregation of engineers from every level of the profession, unprecedented in Britain's industrial history, which was organized by the Engineering Council – itself a product of the Thatcher years which was intended to raise the profile of the fragmented and rather hidebound engineering community.

Thatcher told the 114 representatives of Britain's 300,000 qualified engineers meeting in Birmingham that 'the success of the engineering profession and industry is the key to our future prosperity'. She accorded industry the rare compliment of recognizing its central importance in the national task of wealth creation: 'If you succeed, I do,' she told the assembly.

She also sought to lay the ghosts of suspicion about which side the Government was on in the debate about manufacturing's future. 'I want to have a go at the way pundits so glibly classify our growth industries as sunrise industries, service industries or the high-tech sector. Some of the biggest consumers of high-tech are established manufacturing industries. Service industries are major purchasers of manufactured goods. So manufacturing and the service industries are not in separate compartments. They go hand in hand.'

The speech, little noticed at the time, struck a keynote. Industry had been put through the hoop of recession. Now that the weight of economic depression had lifted, a new morning was breaking over the slump's survivors. They looked up to find encouragement from the Government for this new industrial order, but encourage-ment entirely on the Government's freshly-defined terms. No longer did the manufacturing sector hold sway atop the industrial hierarchy, attended by constant political interference. All that had been demolished. Henceforth, all industries, service or manufacturing, were equal under the same sun – neither rising, nor setting, but shining bright.

Moreover, the principle of disengagement from industry's affairs was now established. Fresh impetus was added to the drive to get State-owned manufacturing assets off Whitehall's hands. But right at the gateway to this new era, the Westland affair erupted. It was the biggest controversy of the Thatcher decade involving a British manufacturing company. Extreme interventionism turned Westland from an industrial problem into the colossal political controversy that saw the resignations of Defence Secretary Michael Heseltine and his foe, Trade and Industry Secretary Leon Brittan, and came closer than any other single event, including the Argentinian invasion of the Falkland Islands, to bringing down Mrs Thatcher. The supreme irony of the affair was that it originated in the Thatcherite doctrine of non-interventionist industrial strategy.

Sir John Cuckney, the veteran architect of numerous private and public sector rescues (including those of the Crown Agents, the Mersey Docks and Harbour Board, and John Brown) was installed as chairman of Westland in July 1985 in response to fears expressed by the Yeovil-based helicopter maker's main bankers, Barclays and National Westminster, that the company was fast falling towards oblivion. A 'black hole' in Westland's order book meant that, without the injection of significant additional funds and the reduction of its mounting liabilities, the company would soon lose the wherewithal to survive.

Cuckney says: 'When I first looked at Westland, there seemed to me to be a strong justification for the Government to assist Westland in some way. Most of the helicopters in the British armed forces were Westland-built, serviced and maintained. We were the only helicopter manufacturer in the country; we had some unique technologies in composite materials, blades for helicopters and rotor technology generally'. And the company had one specific order, for the Indian Oil and Natural Gas Corporation, to be financed by British Government overseas aid.

'So when one saw Westland drifting towards probable in-solvency at the year end, one's first reaction was to try and get the year-end excess of liabilities over assets bridged by a government standby facility, or by guarantee, or some other temporary method. There were all sorts of ways it could have been done. The Indian order could have been underwritten – it was government money paying for it anyway. There could have been adjustments to procurement pro-grammes which would have avoided a crisis.'

Neither the Ministry of Defence, which was Westland's main customer, nor the Department of Trade and Industry, its sponsor department and therefore the department theoretically responsible for it, would help. Cuckney says: 'One was told at the time that the MoD didn't mind if Westland went bust. And the DTI weren't prepared to fund Westland in any way.' So Cuckney went to Mrs Thatcher, and was bluntly informed that Westland 'was a private sector problem and it was on its own'.

This, Cuckney says, 'concentrated the mind wonderfully. Emotionally, one felt an inevitable degree of patriotism about Westland, because it was a defence company, and it was after the Falklands War. One felt jingoistic about it in a number of respects, and it was very sobering to be told these things.'

So Cuckney went ahead and found his private sector solution. 'Once you've been told it's totally a private sector problem, your concern is the shareholders, the banks, the employees, the customers. It didn't matter to me whether the [rescue] participants were Guatemalan, Korean or what. If you have 11,000 employees and you know that the moment you make the preliminary results announce-ment, you are bust, you want to get the best agreement, fully underwritten and legally binding that you can in the time available. In those days, you announced your results at 9.30 a.m. The final meeting with the support banks was concluded at 4.30 a.m.'

The turn-of-1985 battle between Cuckney's DTI-approved solution – the injection of product (Sikorsky's Black Hawk helicopter) and limited funds into Westland by Sikorsky's American owner United Technologies (UTC) and the Italian group Fiat – and a four-wheel drive business European consortium incited by Heseltine, was and remains primarily a political story. It is still sometimes mis-represented as a takeover battle, when in fact it was a contested capital reconstruction in which UTC and Fiat emerged with minority stakes in Westland. The spectre of foreign domination of Westland was finally buried in 1988 when GKN bought Fiat's stake and other shares to give it 22 per cent and a platform for a full takeover. A prime concern of GKN's in negotiating the deal was to secure Westland's alliance with UTC.

Cuckney believes that Westland had 'a very profound effect on the Government', in ensuring that alarm bells ring loud, clear and early on identification of a major problem – particularly one with the potential to cause an inter-departmental dispute. But its most fundamental effect was to reinforce the non-interventionist creed – the Government's determination that it would not be sucked into matters industrial. Cuckney maintains that this attitude was wrong in particular: 'I don't believe in the soft option or the right to subsidies, but I think it's utterly unrealistic to have a defence company where the MoD is the main customer, with millions of pounds of taxpayers' money in it as launch and development aid, then leave it totally on its own.'

An industrial reading of the Westland affair would point up the shortcomings that it highlighted in the Government's general privatization policy – and for Whitehall, marginalization of industries and industrial issues.

The redefinition and break-up of British Shipbuilders provided one persistent reminder of this disengagement theme. But its strongest illustration during the second half of the decade was the running saga of vehicles group BL cum Austin Rover cum, finally, Rover Group.

The Government's first attempt to dispose of this persistent headache failed comprehensively in the window of political vulnerability that followed Westland. The DTI had been in protracted talks during 1985 to sell the Leyland Vehicles side of the business, including trucks and Land-Rover, to the American giant General Motors. More recently, it had somewhat opportunistically decided to settle the BL problem once and for all, by divesting the Austin Rover cars side to Ford. News of the double sale plan broke just as the Westland furore was subsiding, and triggered an immediate Conservative backbench outcry, primarily against the Austin Rover sale, although Land-Rover also aroused considerable emotion.

The Government aborted the BL sale, but nevertheless held its underlying industrial course. Five months after the Prime Minister's Engineering Assembly address, new DTI Secretary Paul Channon explained to the CBI's 200-strong Council precisely where the Government stood on manufacturing.

'While we do need to counter the view that manufacturing matters above all, we need to be careful to avoid misunderstanding,' said Channon. Referring to the Lords report, he asserted: 'We do not share the starker analysis of the decline of manufacturing industry, nor the more interventionist solutions put forward to resolving the perceived problems.' Channon described the DTI as a 'business department', and declared: 'We are prepared to commit Government funds – your funds, collected from you as personal and corporate taxpayers – in areas where we judge that our doing so helps the economy. By working to improve the operation of markets, or to correct imperfections.'

But that was the limit. As company profitability increased after the recession, DTI aid for industry schemes had already moved from the specific – grants to microelectronics companies under the MISP programmes, or to small engineering firms in the SEFIS scheme – towards more general efforts to encourage collaborative research projects or provide advisory services on matters like design. Channon noted this evolution, and added: 'It has to be you, the practising businessmen, who play the major part. Neither of us would have it any other way.'

This was largely true, but it was not the whole story. What Channon meant was that the Government would not have it any other way. The 'hands-off' DTI doctrine outlined in his speech reached its apotheosis in January 1988 when Channon's successor, the former Employment Secretary and head of the Manpower Services Commission, Lord Young, announced the DTI's reincarnation as the 'Department for Enterprise' to the backing of a near-£5 million television and press advertising campaign.

The main plank of the initiative was a three-year, £250 million DTI commitment to subsidise management consultancy for companies with less than 500 employees. The consultancy covered every aspect of business, from marketing and design to manufacturing systems and educational links. Young had no doubts that this was the best way to improve industrial competitiveness. Asked if all he was doing was to give a giant boost to the consultancy companies, he riposted: 'This is the only means of spreading best practice throughout British industry. There is no better alternative.'

A significant change in DTI internal organization and objectives accompanied the new programme. Young ended the long-established system whereby the Department 'sponsored' different companies within different industries. Instead of the 'industry' divisions, Young created 'market' divisions – shifting the focus from the supplier to the user. He observed that there was 'a danger that "sponsorship" can give the impression of "responsibility" for specific industries. This is misleading and inhibits the DTI from its role of spreading best business practice.'

Although Young's changes were not quite as radical as they were said to be, and borrowed heavily from ideas already germinating in the department, announcement of the 'Department for Enterprise' was a landmark in the Thatcherite industrial revolution.

It signified the final and furthest departure from the interventionist concept of 'picking winners'. Not only did generalism now rule, but the department was to act more as a contractor of work to specialist agencies than a direct practitioner: the ultimate hands-off approach. The last nail was driven into the principle, which had never quite expired, that civil servants could play a direct role in corporate development.

The point was made completely when the DTI Enterprise launch was followed by the revelation that Young was about to dispose of the last two major State-owned manufacturing companies –

British Shipbuilders and Rover Group. The transfer of Rover's ownership to British Aerospace paid unconscious and ironic tribute to the power of interventionism: the Government barred any rival bid for the group, and intended virtually to pay BAe to take Rover off its hands. Even after the European Commission had forced Young to reduce his munifence, the deal remained a last witness to old-style industrial politics – intensely hands-on negotiation, but only so that the DTI could take its hands off the British car industry for good. The discredited tools of the past were used to clear out the nationalized cupboard.

The Rover deal finally dismissed lingering memories of the Government's Westland-inspired embarrassment over its previous failure to sell BL. It formed a piquant epitaph for the age of State corporatism that Thatcherism had buried. And it also showed how far the Thatcher Government had refined its own detachment from industry. Young's clinical and dispassionate handling of the Rover disposal seemed an age away from the night in early 1980 when Industry Secretary Sir Keith Joseph was guest of honour at a dinner in the oak-panelled room at Longbridge in Birmingham which Herbert Austin had once inhabited. Joseph had been to tour the new robotics lines that would produce the Metro, the first of the new models that BL hoped would turn the tide of its ebbing volume car sales. As the BL people talked about the efforts that had been made to stop the rot in the company, and what they now hoped to achieve, tears came to Joseph's eyes, as they are sometimes wont to do. After a while, the Industry Secretary said: 'This is a wonderful thing you've achieved here, for the workers, for their families, for the future of the country.'

CHAPTER TWO
A NEW ORDER

In June 1980, Owen Green called the managing directors of all his subsidiaries to the only world conference of executives that his company has ever held.

Green did not mince his words. He told the assembly at a hotel near Gatwick Airport that BTR, the company for which they worked and of which he was chief executive, could in 1990 be making pre-tax profits of between £600 million and £700 million on sales of £5 billion.

Green is not a man to be laughed at, but his words were received with a general air of disbelief. BTR had grown powerfully during the 1970s, from its base in rubber industry products such as conveyor belting and industrial hose into other basic engineering businesses like valves and actuators. Sales of £38 million and pre-tax profits of £2.9 million in 1970 had mushroomed by 1979 into pre-tax profits of £57 million and sales totalling £433 million. But to the 150 managers at the Gatwick Park Hotel, those 1990 numbers seemed light years, not a mere decade away.

Yet in 1989, BTR was going to exceed those projections, with pre-tax profits likely to top £1 billion and annual sales running at about £7 billion. The magnitude of its growth during the 1980s is matched only by that of Hanson, the conglomerate to which BTR is often – to Green and his colleagues' chagrin – compared but with which it, in some significant ways, contrasts.

More than Hanson, BTR stands at the heart of the manufacturing revolution of the 1980s. The two major takeovers on which its growth in the decade was founded epitomize the rise of a new industrial order. One, the acquisition of Thomas Tilling, was a watershed in British takeover history and signalled the eclipse of the 1960s-style diversified industrial holding company. The second, the purchase of Dunlop in 1985, expressed more vividly than any other single event the resurrection of British industry from the ruins of the historic, imperial manufacturing establishment.

For more than 40 years, from its foundation in 1924 as the British Goodrich Company in which the American B. F. Goodrich held a majority stake, BTR was nothing more than one of the numerous companies trying to make their way in the congested industry of rubber products. At the beginning, it was a tyre maker which also turned out foot pumps and golf balls. In 1934, the company broke away from Goodrich and was renamed the British Tyre and Rubber company, and the initials BTR appeared for the first time.

Owen Green, having spent the war in the Navy and then trained as a chartered accountant, joined BTR in 1958, when it took over the hydraulics company Oil Feed Engineering where he was finance director. In 1967, he was appointed managing director under the chairman, former ICI executive Sir Walter Worboys, and set about restoring the company's fortunes which had declined to a pre-tax loss of £317,000 at the end of 1966. Green already had around him the top management corps – finance director Norman Ireland, Don Tapley and John Cahill – which, under chairman Sir David Nicolson, masterminded BTR's rise through the 1970s.

As Green describes it: 'Our culture was quite home-grown – not homespun, that's too cosy a word. We looked inside ourselves. We were all well-read, but none of us had been to Harvard. Even the ICI influence in BTR had been good – it left a certain sophistication that might have been difficult to buy.'

The home-based group of Green, Tapley and Ireland (Cahill was in the United States) very soon established the precepts on which BTR has been run ever since: decentralization of responsibility to line managers whose operating companies are individual profit centres, with constant head office monitoring of results to ensure that targets are being met, and to provide for rapid identification and intervention when something is going awry. At its basic level, head office management by exception.

While Green, an accountant by training, and Tapley clearly influenced the mechanisms BTR developed to implement its manage-ment methods, the foremost role was played by Ireland. From the mid-1960s, he built up the concept of profit planning, reporting and

monitoring through key ratios – notably return on sales and performance against sales, profits and employment targets. Nicolson contributed experience from his management consultancy background.

The mechanism was consistently refined. For instance, BTR
went initially for five-year plans but then decided that these were
unrealistic, and dropped the timescale to three years. The most
important element, however, soon emerged as the 12-month profit
plan. According to Green: 'The three-year one enables us to decide
more or less where we are going. The 12-month plan is the one we can
really use for monitoring our business.'

By 1972, the system was 'pretty well honed'. By then, too, BTR
was on its way: 'The beginning of the renaissance of BTR was the need
for restructuring the British rubber industry,' says Green.

Green went to the Industrial Reorganization Corporation –
created by the Wilson Labour Government of 1964–70 – for
encouragement in rationalizing the industry, and was given IRC
support, but no money. The group expanded at home and laid the
foundations for an international business through the 1969 merger
with the Leyland & Birmingham Rubber company.

In the inflationary 1970s, BTR demonstrated one side of the
competitive advantage that it gained from the profit margin ethos – it
is much more than an emphasis – that permeates the entire
organization. Lionel Stammers, who became a non-executive director
in 1989 after a long period as joint chief executive of BTR's European
Region, asserts that a main secret of BTR's success has been its ability
to manage inflation.

In words which former British Lions rugby union captain
Willie John McBride would appreciate, the BTR system impels its
managers to get their price increases in first, and in full – always to
lead the customer, never to follow him. That speed off the mark
ensures that the companies never lag the inflationary pace. Once
the first price increase is in, a virtuous progression can ensue.

Green puts this principle in the context of the 1970s: 'We have
never been backward in passing on inflation straight through to the
market place. That is something British companies failed to do in the
1970s. They were producing very poor results because, although they
were passing on the cost of inflation to their customers, they were
losing the profit margin.'

BTR therefore emerged from the decade competitively strengthened. Then the recession struck, and the group showed another side of its success: the ability to react rapidly to changes in economic conditions.

In the City, investment fund managers still recall with admiration the speed with which BTR battened down the hatches against the economic storm of 1980. The timing of the Gatwick conference in itself testified to the confidence of the group. Here, in summer 1980, the very eye of the industrial hurricane, Green and his colleagues were looking forward to a decade of colossal growth.

Green told his managers that BTR was starting the decade 'with a strong line in technology of process, product and materials. We have a broad base of markets and an international coverage. Additional to all this and more than equally important, we have a management style.' He concluded that whatever changes occurred at the centre: 'Those considerations must never be allowed to mar the workings of decentralized profit-orientated operations – that holy grail which we have kept sacred these many years.'

Today, Green recalls: 'It was a useful time to bring together our top people and to talk philosophy and themes. It wasn't a profit-planning thing.' The 1990 sales and profits scenario – along with a projection that they would require between £1.5 and £2 billion of capital spending during the decade – were simply notional points on the horizon, Green says. 'They were just to show what would happen if we carried on growing as we had been. I was endeavouring to ensure that the sights of our people were raised, that they really understood what this rate of growth would mean to us over a period of years. I wanted to alert these people, to make sure that they weren't going to wake up one day and be frightened by size.'

Acquisitions were always a central element in the expansion plan. 'Organic growth, certainly in a country like Britain, wasn't going to give us anything like what we needed to satisfy our aspirations. Acquisitive growth was there to supplement, and even sometimes to lead, the growth programme.'

For a couple of years, BTR did relatively little by acquisition. But Green and co. were watching and waiting for a suitable opportunity to make their competitive advantage over other companies count. On the eve of Easter 1983, the London Stock Market –

whose recognition of BTR's superior performance added a crucial dimension to the group's industrial edge – was awash with rumours that it was about to bid for Burmah Oil, the Castrol company.

But BTR had something else in mind. It revealed the full extent of its ambitions to the business world for the first time on the following Tuesday – a day that Patrick Austen, among many, will never forget.

In 1989, Austen was chief executive of BTR's sports, leisure and hosiery division comprising the Pretty Polly, Dunlop and Slazenger brands. 5 April, 1983, was his first day in his new job as managing director designate of Thomas Tilling's Pretty Polly tights subsidiary. It was also the day that BTR's stockbroker Cazenove launched a Stock Market dawn raid on Tilling, which marked the start of the biggest takeover battle the City had ever seen.

The £573 million bid for Tilling that followed a week later broke new ground in another significant respect because, in industrial terms, BTR was so much smaller than its target. BTR's 1982 sales of £725 million were less than a third of Tilling's £2.24 billion. But it outgunned Tilling in two far more relevant areas: its pre-tax profits were much higher (£107 million in 1982 against Tilling's £43.7 million) and, most significant of all, it was valued by the Stock Market at £1.1 billion, three times Tilling's market worth.

Green says: 'We had followed Tilling for one or two years, and during that period its fortunes had declined somewhat. It hadn't collapsed, but it had plateaued. We had convinced ourselves – because we are not arrogant people, never have been – that the success that we had had in making a whole raft of acquisitions all over the world in the previous ten years or more must have been due to a particular ethos. We felt that much confidence that we could translate our way of doing business to a much broader canvas.'

Tilling had grown fast in the 1960s and much of the 1970s, but to maintain momentum, late in the decade it embarked on a $500 million expansion drive in the United States which resulted only in misconceived acquisitions that worsened the group's position when the economic slowdown began to bite.

While Tilling was vulnerable, BTR's bid nevertheless constituted a considerable departure for Green and his team, and not only because of its size. 'Up to then, we had stated that one of our criteria for acquiring businesses was contiguity to our own operations. The business concerned did not have to be identical in technology or market-place or geography, but any one of these things being present, or lying alongside one of our companies, would limit the downside. It was really a fail-safe philosophy. We have been cautious people – surprisingly, considering the rate of growth we have enjoyed.'

With Tilling, however, there was 'more of a managerial thrust to the whole thing. Tilling had good managers, but they were more like industrial investors than industrial managers, which is how we regard ourselves.'

With a Spartan single-mindedness which soon became recognized as a BTR hallmark, the group pushed through its bid – breaking its own record along the way by increasing the offer to £660 million. In the end, BTR's support in other quarters of the City was such that it overcame even the opposition of the big insurance companies, which owned 12.5 per cent of Tilling. All but two stayed with Tilling, prompting a verbal assault from BTR's merchant bank advisers, Morgan Grenfell, which accused them of abrogating their responsibilities and behaving like 'shop stewards in the City'.

BTR's success highlighted what had been forgotten since the merger boom of the early 1970s, and what became a feature of the decade. Once manufacturing industry had lost the engine of general economic growth in the recession, a company which was highly rated by the City gained an enormous advantage over its rivals. Many companies failed to learn this new fact of life until it was too late. On the other side, some relied for all their momentum on the relative advantage gained from their share rating: theirs was growth built on foundations of paper. When their ratings were savaged by the Stock Market crash of October 1987, their progress came to a grinding halt.

BTR was different. Apart from being first into the megabid field, what distinguished the group most clearly from the madding crowd of acquisitive predators was its immense organic cash generation. The Tilling takeover enabled BTR to make a quantum leap forward, because overnight it hugely increased the group's capital base, creating a much broader springboard for further advance.

Tilling's managers soon discovered one BTR technique of achieving profits growth. At Pretty Polly, one of Patrick Austen's first tasks had been to produce a 1983 profits forecast which would bolster Tilling's defence against the bid. Before the bid, Pretty Polly had planned for profits, before interest and tax, of £1.1 million, on sales of just under £40 million. Now the projected profits figure was hoisted to £4 million.

That August, a couple of months after the takeover, Green visited Pretty Polly. 'He wasn't keen to see the whole board and be introduced to hundreds of people,' Austen recalls (interview with the author 27 October, 1988). 'He just said, "I want to sit with you for the day". Basically, the message was that what we wrote as a component part of the Tilling defence document, we were now expected to deliver as a component part of BTR. He did it in the nicest possible way, but he certainly wasn't letting me off the hook.' That year, the company made almost £4 million on sales of just under £44 million.

BTR's next acquisition came in December 1984 on the other side of the world, when its 67 per cent-owned Australian subsidiary – BTR Hopkins – bought the Nylex Corporation for £64 million. Though small in relation to Tilling, the move acquired particular significance with hindsight, as BTR Nylex was built by Alan Jackson into the most dynamic force in BTR's growth late in the 1980s, with its sales soaring from less than six per cent of group turnover to almost 40 per cent in 1989.

It was 18 months after Tilling before BTR struck again in Britain. But when Green and Ireland did move, on 18 January, 1985, they brought off the deal of the decade.

Dunlop was the ultimate symbol of the decline and fall of Britain's industrial empire. One of the most world-famous of all brand names, with a range including Slazenger sports goods and Dunlopillo mattresses, as well as the tyre business that dominated the group, the company had been one of the six largest in Britain in the 1950s. Its chairman's car still displayed the prestigious A1 numberplate. By 1984, however, Dunlop's corporate health was anything but A1. The company was very nearly bankrupt.

The roots of Dunlop's decline lay deep in pre-1980s history. One former Dunlop executive identifies two central faults: 'A belief from the old Dunlop management, particularly in the immediate post-war period, that they were big, that they could never suffer – the great British colonial approach. Dunlop was very, very fat. You could see it at Fort Dunlop (its central tyre plant in Birmingham) where there were rows and rows of chauffeurs to pick up people like the plant manager – not even senior people.

'A number of the businesses were run by people who had got their experience in colonial markets, which are very different from modern European businesses. There was a self-opinionated view, combined with a lack of financial focus and acumen, and the general philosophy of "the bigger you could make the company, the better".'

According to the executive, it was this philosophy which fatally undermined Dunlop's 1971 union with the Italian company Pirelli, hailed at the time as a trendsetter in European collaboration, but whose failure became another milestone in Dunlop's downhill slide.

Dunlop had first considered a merger with Uniroyal, then the U.S. Rubber Company. But concerns that the alliance might fall foul of American Government anti-trust law caused the abandonment of a deal which would have taken Dunlop past Goodyear and Firestone and made it the biggest tyre company in the world.

The Dunlop board – not unanimously – then turned to Pirelli, and a cross-shareholding alliance was formed in which each partner took a 49 per cent stake in the other. Before the venture was up and running, the Dunlop board commissioned a consultants' report which predicted that unless full and proper integration of the businesses took place, cost economies would not be achieved and the whole enterprise would be doomed.

That warning was ignored. The grand alliance got off on the wrong foot when in mid-January 1971, less than a month after the joint venture had started, Pirelli told Dunlop that it was budgeting for a £7 million full-year loss. Dunlop had entered the agreement with a forecast from Pirelli that the Italian group would make profits of £3 million in 1971.

Pirelli's actual loss that year was £18.3 million, and soon Dunlop was having to write off £41.5 million against Pirelli's losses (ultimately, it was able to write back £12 million). Despite Pirelli's bad start, the former Dunlop executive is convinced that the real reasons for the alliance's failure were due to fundamental flaws in Dunlop: 'When Pirelli got into the union, they were horrified to find out how archaic Dunlop was in tyre production technology and general approach. Pirelli and Michelin [the French tyre giant] were clearly run by technically-orientated people. Dunlop wasn't. Their people lacked experience. At the time of the Pirelli venture, Campbell Fraser [later knighted and Dunlop's chairman] was the corporate planner whose only operational experience had been running Dunlop New Zealand. The Pirelli union was a corporate strategist's answer to the problem of how to get out of something that was going wrong – get even bigger. The union was a symptom of an attitude of mind.'

That attitude – a combination of technical backwardness, refusal to recognize the seriousness of a situation, and simplistic response – was what really put the skids under the company's tyre business. Dunlop's biggest mistake was its failure to react speedily to the arrival in the late 1960s of the radial tyre, which lasted roughly twice as long and performed better than the cross-ply tyre it superseded. Michelin grabbed the technological lead with the radial and established some patents on it. Allied with excellent marketing, the Michelin men seized pole position in the higher-value end of the tyre market and became the market price leader, selling on quality and performance rather than price.

In a contrast which epitomizes British manufacturing's neglect of such non-price factors, Dunlop remained wedded at least until the mid-1970s to the alleged lower cost 'advantage' of the cross-ply. But eventually it did react to the radial competition, with a technological breakthrough which could have quantum leapfrogged the opposition but the long-term success of which was sacrificed to the demand for instant returns.

Denovo was the 'run-flat' tyre – a tyre so designed that it would stay on the wheel rim even after a puncture at speeds of up to 50 mph, obviating the need for a spare wheel. It was developed in the 1970s at great expense, for several years consuming more than half of Dunlop's precious research and development budget. The pressure for returns on the project was understandable, but the Dunlop senior management made a fatal error when it insisted on launching the Denovo prototype in 1976 as a commercial product. Although it worked, the prototype was hopelessly complex: it contained 36 component parts. Dunlop then compounded the mistake by launching it on the Rover 3500 and the Mini Clubman – 'two of the worst cars you could have launched it on,' comments one former Dunlop manager. The perfect platform would have been a launch with Fiat – which was ruled out by the Pirelli union that denied Dunlop access to the Italian vehicle giant – or another major European manufacturer.

The premature launch of Denovo compromised the project so badly that when, in 1979, the Denovo Two was developed, it had to fight for acceptance against three years of dreadful publicity. So bad was the product's image that Dunlop's marketeers dropped the name and rechristened it Denloc, after the unique safety locking system that held the tyre on the wheel rim. Denloc was what Denovo One should have been and would have been, had it not been rushed into commercial production. It had been totally simplified: it was now a tyre, rim and valve, and could be fitted automatically.

With the Pirelli union unravelling, Denloc was launched on the Fiat Panda – as an option, since it was such a one-off that no car maker would fit it as standard. And as an option, it generated 12.5 per cent uptake in a market where Dunlop had no original equipment business. But this time it was caught in Dunlop's gathering financial crisis. To try to staunch some of the loss of tyre demand which was bleeding the group to death, the company put Denloc into production at Fort Dunlop, its most inefficient tyre operation. Then it was hit by the pound's strength against the lira, which meant that despite the Fiat orders, the product still lost money. For Dunlop, that was effectively the end, though the Denloc concept lived on to be taken up by both Jaguar and Porsche, among others.

Dunlop's slide was aggravated by the fact that the company had expanded capacity in its European tyre operations during the late 1960s – just before the radial bit into cross-ply demand and on the eve of the first oil shock. Not all the problems that contributed to Dunlop's extinction as a British tyre maker were the group's own fault. While the world tyre industry had to contend with the slump in demand caused by the two oil shocks in 1973 and 1979, Dunlop had the additional local difficulty caused by the decline of the native motor industry. In 1972, car production in Britain reached an all-time peak of 1.92 million vehicles. Output plummetted by a third over the next three years, and dropped below one million by the end of the decade.

The rise of trade union power and the British wildcat strike disease, which contributed enormously to this loss of production, impacted on Dunlop as on many other major British companies. Inflation-fuelled profits growth papered over the cracks here as elsewhere –in 1976, Dunlop's pre-tax profits hit an all-time peak of £72 million – but beneath the figures, the cracks were widening.

Despite the external influences, however, Dunlop's management failure was fundamental. The company seems either to have been incapable, or to have refused to recognize, the seriousness of its situation. The group's highly centralized structure built in this unresponsiveness, which could easily be transmuted into complacency. All daily tyre production figures – nominally the ultimate responsibility of the tyre operation managers – were reported to the Dunlop chairman. When one Dunlop manager was appointed to an executive position, he was immediately given a full-time personal assistant and two secretaries: 'The whole ethos was to keep the business away from the manager', he recalls.

As a result, Dunlop was an extremely slow-moving organization. Centralization, together with the group's misconceived image of itself, crippled its capacity to take the necessary corrective action when the financial rot really set in after 1976.

The group's first major tyre plant closure, at Speke on Merseyside, was discussed in management committees for about a year before it was actually implemented. 'They all knew it had to be done, but could the great Dunlop face the inevitable workforce reaction? That was what held them up,' comments the former Dunlop executive.

The pace of rationalization quickened after the appointment of Alan Lord, a senior civil servant, as managing director. Lord, who became chief executive in 1980, had arrived from the Treasury in the late 1970s, taking charge initially of the overseas companies. By several accounts, the quality of Lord's mind – 'he was brilliant,' says one former colleague – was not entirely matched by his man-management abilities, and this characteristic did nothing to reduce the enormous frictions and executive politics within the company. However, Dunlop's fundamental problems cannot be blamed on Lord: by the time he acquired overall control, the old Dunlop was about to pass the point of no return.

Precisely when that point came remains unclear. The former

executive maintains: 'I have no doubt that if action had been taken early enough, it would have been possible to avoid the crisis. Even as late as 1980, it would still have been possible if people had been draconian enough to have won the support of the banks. But they would have had to dilute their interests in the tyre business.'

That was the Dunlop board's psychological roadblock. It could not bring itself to pull out, even partially, of tyre making. The failure to make such a severe but essential move was not for want of trying by managers in non-tyre businesses. They feared that the whole company would be drained by the cash being poured into the bottomless pit of the tyre operations, which dominated the board's thinking. One non-tyres manager comments: 'Unless it was black and round and had a hole in it, they weren't interested.'

Another former manager recalls a presentation to Lord and other main board directors during a strategic management course for high fliers around the turn of 1981. One part of the presentation by the junior managers consisted of a turnround plan for the group. Its key element was a proposal that the European tyres interests be sold to Sumitomo of Japan. The suggestion was received by the directors with chilly silence. Later, the manager told a senior Dunlop corporate strategist what the group had proposed. The man replied that he had already suggested precisely the same thing, and met a similar response.

Possibly, Dunlop could have retained the West German tyre operation, which was the best of its European businesses, and sold the British end. Or even tried to retain its Washington, Tyne & Wear factory which had been the most modern in Europe when it was finished in 1969. But Fort Dunlop would have had to go. According to the former Dunlop executive: 'That was just too big a step for them to take.'

One of the former Dunlop managers believes the board's adherence to the British tyre operations betrayed Dunlop's critical flaw: 'Instead of the need to build the group internationally, it was the British tyre businesses which were seen at the time as being central. The philosophy was still one of a British company selling overseas. Everyone else in the UK saw Dunlop as one of the leaders internationally, but that was an illusion. It was not an international player. It did not take a global view. The directors might have said they did, but their actions did not reflect that.'

So the decline continued, relentlessly. On the same day, 24 April, 1981, Dunlop announced the dissolution of the Pirelli alliance and an attributable loss for 1980 of £15 million. Net debt, already high, had risen from about 80 per cent to 90 per cent of shareholders' funds. The next year, pre-tax profits were zero, the net loss rose to £41 million, but Dunlop held the capital gearing level at around 90 per cent.

A property revaluation kept gearing at just over 90 per cent at the end of 1982, but the writing was on the wall in the profit and loss account. Above the tax line, there was a £7 million loss; below it, the bottom line was an almost-doubled attributable loss of £80 million. And the group paid no final dividend.

At operating company level, the situation was dire. Dr David Speirs, managing director of Dunlop's steel wheels and suspension-making automotive division from 1983, says: 'There had been no investment for years. The business was disappearing through lack of investment, lack of attention, lack of knowing what the auto companies wanted in the future. To keep ourselves running, we needed capital investment. We couldn't get any capital, so we had to resort to other methods. We were borrowing, we were scraping, we were making capital somehow look like revenue. We had to have a new phosphating plant, and the board said 'get stuffed'. So we said to ourselves, 'what do we now?' We put it in and it went through as additional nuts and bolts.'

The sun set on the old Dunlop empire, by now the sickest man in the European tyre industry, in 1983. Michelin had made far bigger losses – £400 million in its worst year – but Dunlop was weaker. The group's disintegration was characterized by a series of events, each reflecting a feature familiar to historians of imperial declines more momentous than that of a mere limited company.

Decadence was all too apparent to shareholders who protested at the 21 per cent pay rise awarded the previous year to Dunlop's chairman Sir Campbell Fraser. It was subsequently explained that Fraser's real increase was only six per cent, the rest being pension-related payments made by the Dunlop board because of the chairman's loss of earnings from the ending of the Pirelli link. Whatever the reason, the salary row appeared at the time to demonstrate once more how out of touch the Dunlop board had become. And when it was remembered that Fraser was president of the CBI, and while preaching the gospel of wage restraint had recently described British workers as being 'bonkers about pay', the air of obloquy seemed to spread, to envelop a whole age of British management.

An age, however, that was bygone. In Dunlop, those whom the company had once colonized were turning corporate history upside down. A Malaysian investment group, Pegi Malaysia, had built up a 26.1 per cent stake in the company and was talked of as a potential bidder. In total, more than 35 per cent of Dunlop shares were in Far Eastern hands. In June, Dunlop bowed to Pegi pressure and appointed its chairman, Abdul Ghafar Baba, and Eng Chin Ah, chief executive of the company that controlled Pegi, as non-executive directors. Baba was the son of a rubber tree cutter who had worked for Dunlop Plantations.

The final chapter in the history of old Dunlop opened with an event redolent of the fall and rise of industrial empires. In September 1983, the group announced the sale of its British and West German tyre businesses to Sumitomo of Japan for £82 million.

Although the decision came so late in Dunlop's day that what could have been a strategic retreat looked closer to outright surrender, the deal – negotiated by Alan Lord – made the very best of a bad job.

By late 1982, the Dunlop board had at last faced the inescapable fact that if the company was to be saved at all, the European tyre business, at least, had to go. Moreover, since Dunlop could not afford the enormous costs that closure would entail, it had to find a buyer for the operations. The only identifiable potential purchaser was Sumitomo.

Sumitomo had been associated with Dunlop for 70 years, and Dunlop owned 40 per cent of the group's subsidiary, Sumitomo Rubber Industries. Sumitomo was a Dunlop licensee, producing tyres in Japan under the Dunlop name. It took technology from Dunlop under a 20-year agreement due to expire in 1983. There was only one drawback: although Sumitomo was keen to acquire the Dunlop name, it did not want the physical assets of the tyre operations in Europe.

When it was told that it could only have the name if it also took the factories, Sumitomo's response was to offer to take Washington, but nothing else, and then only if Dunlop would pay Sumitomo to have it. Lord persevered, and eventually struck a deal in which, apart from buying the Washington and German operations for £82 million, Sumitomo agreed to look again at Fort Dunlop. Dunlop then began an exercise in persuasion designed to convince the Japanese that they needed the Birmingham plant. Eventually, Sumitomo agreed that it would take Fort Dunlop too – subject to the exacting conditions that the 2,400 workforce be cut and about 30 per cent of its capacity removed before the sale, and that this rationalization be carried through by a certain date and without industrial disruption. If any of these stipulations were not met, the agreement would be cancelled.

The streamlining – involving the loss of about 900 jobs – was executed without a hitch and on time. Sumitomo took the Fort Dunlop working capital and 1,500 workers who would otherwise have gone in plant shutdown. The deal saved Dunlop redundancy costs which would have broken the company. In return, Sumitomo got the factory for next-to-nothing.

After the problems of the 1970s, the smoothness with which this British withdrawal from volume tyre-making was effected might have carried a bitter irony, except that it was vital for the salvaging of the rest of Dunlop that the Sumitomo deal went through. 'The whole thing was on the verge of bankruptcy. If we hadn't got that sale, Dunlop would have gone under,' remarks the former Dunlop executive.

While the agreement was being negotiated, Sir Campbell Fraser's era at the top ended somewhat abruptly. After seven years in the chair, he departed at the end of 1983. It was said at the time that he had intended to resign the previous May, on reaching the age of 60. But this official version was soon punctured by news that he had received a £137,400 golden handshake, compensation for having his contract 'terminated'. It appeared that he had been ousted by the Malaysians. Much to some shareholders' disgust, Fraser was also given several fringe benefits including the honorary office of Dunlop president.

Fraser's successor, British Home Stores and former ICI chairman Sir Maurice Hodgson, had much more to worry about. Dunlop reported a £17 million pre-tax profit for 1983, but that figure was an irrelevance beside the attributable loss of £166 million that was due mainly to a £115 million write-off on the sale of the European tyre business. Net debt of £320 million towered over shareholders' funds which had been slashed to £110 million, raising capital gearing to the forbidding heights of almost 241 per cent.

It was now clear that only a huge capital reconstruction could save Dunlop. Other famous manufacturing names – Stone-Platt, Acrow and Alfred Herbert among them – had gone under because of the recession; more companies had been rescued as their banks rallied round a balance sheet reorganization, frequently encouraged by the Bank of England's Industrial Finance Division (otherwise known as the intensive care unit) headed by executive director David Walker.

But Dunlop, which after all the disposals still had sales of more than £1 billion, was of an altogether different magnitude. About 20 months passed from the moment in April 1983 when the clearing banks, led by Barclays and National Westminster, started informal discussions of Dunlop's problems, to announcement of the reconstruction on 15 January, 1985. At the Bank of England, Walker was closely involved in the epic process which concerned 53 banks worldwide.

Both Hodgson and Alan Lord, chief executive since 1980, left before the rescue package was completed. Lord went first, because the banks insisted on the appointment of a new chief executive as a condition of supporting the rescue. Hodgson resigned in November 1984 because he disagreed with the banks' choice of chief executive: Sir Michael Edwardes, renowned as the saviour of British Leyland and in the market for a job because computer group ICL, where he took the chair after leaving BL, had just been acquired by Standard Telephone and Cables.

The Dunlop board favoured Gene Anderson, the American vice-president of Celanese Corporation. But the banks held the power and Edwardes took over. Anderson remained to answer the Bank of England's call to salvage an almost equally celebrated near-collapse: that of the metals group Johnson Matthey.

Edwardes arrived as chief executive on 8 November, 1984, having executed the previous night what was immediately and erroneously christened the 'Breakfast Massacre'. It was a strange affair, bloodlessly carried out by proxy. Quite simply, Edwardes rented an office near the Dunlop headquarters and refused to enter the Dunlop building until the group's directors had left. This message was conveyed to the Dunlop board through the intermediary channel provided by the company's main banks. Hodgson resigned and with him went ten of Dunlop's other 12 directors.

Only two executive directors remained as members of a new management board, while the two Pegi non-executives stayed on the full board, for the moment. Edwardes became chairman as well, and installed two of his former ICL colleagues, Robin Biggam and Roger Holmes, as finance director and head of strategic planning and communications respectively. Biggam, who did much of the donkey work in establishing a new organization, quickly won respect both for the job he was doing and the understanding way in which he did it.

Edwardes promptly axed the Dunlop personnel department. He believed that personnel departments were dangerous because they were always producing reasons why things couldn't be done. He was also convinced that Dunlop had a major industrial relations problem, which with the tyres operation out of the way was not the case. When he immediately made his presence felt at the grassroots, there was a ready response to his initiatives. He ordered information boards to be put up in each factory. The old Dunlop had never used any. 'Communications just didn't exist under the old Dunlop,' says Barry Sharratt, now general manager of Dunlop Automotive in Coventry. Now, recalls David Speirs: 'There was a cascade of communications and videos.' Edwardes hired a firm to telephone all the Dunlop operations to see how prompt they were in answering calls and responding to sales inquiries. A white 'H' painted on the car park at Coventry remains as evidence of an Edwardes flying visit by helicopter soon after his appointment.

His top priority, as it had been at BL, was to assess the managers below board level on whom Dunlop's recovery would really depend. 'He entered into a period when, at great speed, he was trying to get to know as many as possible of the next two managerial layers,' Speirs says. 'We were all summoned down to London in groups of six or seven to meet those piercing eyes.' Bringing Dunlop back from the brink also entailed sending its managers back to the shrink. Edwardes used the psychological assessments he had employed at BL to establish the strengths and weaknesses of Dunlop executives, and to determine whether they were in the right job within the company, or belonged in the company at all. Extensive reshuffling, departures and some fresh arrivals ensued.

The way was now being cleared to build a devolutionary structure on Dunlop's new foundations. The old regional organization of the group precluded a coordinated global strategy for international businesses like sporting goods. A week after taking over, Edwardes split the group into four main product groups and three overseas tyre-making units, specifically to help the non-tyre businesses 'grow profitably worldwide' while allowing the remaining overseas tyre companies – of which North America was the most notable – to operate on an individual basis. Within the new divisions, more than 60 profit centres were created.

Out went Ernst & Whinney, the group's auditors for the past half a century, in favour of Price Waterhouse, which had been called in by the banks months before to produce a reconstruction plan. Speirs comments: 'We had had Price Waterhouse running us for 12 months. In American parlance, Dunlop was under Chapter 11 (the protection from bankruptcy proceedings that companies obtain under American law).'

Dunlop now entered a final period of purgatory. On 5 December, 1984, its shares were suspended pending announcement of the financial reconstruction which had been worked out by an inner core of six principal banks. It was still not plain sailing. 19 December was pencilled in as the date for publishing the reconstruction, but the time taken to win over Pegi and the company's other 47 banks meant that announcement was delayed, perhaps appropriately, until the New Year, and on 15 January, Edwardes at last revealed a £142 million refinancing programme to bury the tragedy of old Dunlop.

The package combined conversion of £70 million of bank debt into ordinary and preference shares, a £43 million rights issue, and a £29 million placing of new shares with institutional investors. It would reduce Dunlop's capital gearing from the astronomical 1984 year-end level of more than 400 per cent, although gearing would still be no less than 100 per cent. Meanwhile, the British banks also agreed to lend the group up to £260 million.

The new price of Dunlop shares established by the reconstruction was 14p. It was the most profound reminder of how far and how long Dunlop had fallen from its days of prosperity. In the late 1960s, years which now seemed to belong to another, illusory business world, Dunlop shares had traded at up to 235p.

The ordinary shares jumped to 31.5p when dealings resumed the day after the reconstruction was announced, but the most portentous move was a near-50 per cent rise in the value of the preference shares, caused by stockbroker Hoare Govett's purchase of a fraction over 25 per cent of the shares on behalf of a mystery client.

When the identity of the client became public the next day, a clear end to the Dunlop saga was at last visible. After tracking Dunlop for years, BTR pounced with a £33.5 million bid.

The timing of the BTR move was ruthless, catching the vulnerable reborn infant Dunlop at the very first light of its first day in its new world. By buying just enough preference shares to prevent Edwardes obtaining the 75 per cent majority he needed to clear the financial reconstruction, Green, Ireland and their team had effectively staked an unshakeable claim. That shareholding spoke eloquently for BTR's objective. What it said was: 'Dunlop is mine.'

BTR's bid, rich in resonance, was a milestone in British manufacturing history. For the country's rubber products industry, it marked the culmination of a 20-year rationalization process. For the two companies, it concluded almost 15 years of discussions on possible acquisition, joint venturing and collaboration. And when BTR won, its victory signified the triumph of the new British manufacturing order over the old industrial elite.

In the 1960s, when talks started, they concerned the possibility of Dunlop buying BTR. Then Green took over and continued the discussions, on and off, into the 1970s with BTR first seeking to buy, then to joint venture, the Dunlop hose and belting interests. Dunlop did not like the idea. 'I don't think Dunlop could bring themselves to think they could be a partner in a UK situation,' Green says. 'I suspect that they had to be the Dunlop company, and I can understand that. They had had a lot of years of being the leader in the industry; when you talked about rubber, you talked about Dunlop. So I don't think they felt humble about anything.'

As the humbling of Dunlop occurred in the early 1980s, BTR waited 'until things got bad enough to make them listen to us'. By selling the European tyre business, Dunlop did some of BTR's work for them, because 'the thing that had really made us not inclined to go for an aggressive bid for Dunlop over the previous five years was the fact that they were heavily into tyres.'

Although Edwardes inadvertently continued to clear the way for BTR by agreeing the American tyres sale, his sudden arrival did catch BTR somewhat unawares. 'We were a bit surprised at the change, and there wasn't much we could do at first when Edwardes came in.' But if Edwardes to an extent dictated BTR's timing, that was the limit of his influence. 'He really wasn't going to be able to do much because he didn't have a lot of money. We were a much more natural owner for the Dunlop company once the tyre business had been sold off,' says Green.

Edwardes fought a typically determined rearguard action, considering the initiative had been seized entirely by BTR. First, he, Biggam and Holmes dropped the share options they had received under the refinancing which would have given them five per cent of Dunlop's equity, worth a paper profit of £1 million to Edwardes alone for every 5p rise in the share price over the 14p base.

Then Dunlop set to work to revise the reconstruction package and circumvent BTR's preference shareholding stranglehold on the proposals. It negotiated a $120 million management buy-out of its United States subsidiary, making the last great break with the tyre business. But for all this action, and the sound and fury generated by the bid battle, BTR's grip on Dunlop never slackened. Indeed, that hold was tightened when BTR reached agreement with the banks that they would continue to support Dunlop if BTR took the company over. The end came suddenly on 8 March, 1985 when the companies announced that Dunlop had accepted a higher (£101 million) BTR offer, and mutual cordiality flowed where before acrimony had reigned.

Edwardes told Dunlop shareholders: 'In considering BTR's offers, we were conscious that we were only two months into the year and the bulk of our rationalization and divestment programmes had still to be successfully implemented. We were about to have to ask our shareholders to put up a very large sum of new money to recapitalize the company and after this we did not expect there to be significant earnings for shareholders in 1985.

'Against this background, we concluded we could not recommend the continued independence of Dunlop in the light of the more-than-trebled cash offer from BTR.'

John Cahill, now BTR's chief executive, believes that the Thomas Tilling takeover was more vital to BTR. Certainly, Tilling made the group big enough to contemplate the Dunlop deal. But in both financial and industrial terms, Dunlop was as perfect as any acquisition can be. And BTR bought it for a bargain price.

BTR's winning bid may have been triple its original offer, but that was only for the equity. The final terms actually represented a minimal increase in gearing compared with the sighting shot. Because the level of Dunlop debt was common to both offers, the effective increase in BTR's terms amounted to no more than 17 per cent.

For that, Green and company obtained a unique growth opportunity. Dunlop was making next-to-no profits on sales of more than £1 billion – a fantastic situation for BTR, which more than any other group accentuated the positive value of return on sales and could now apply all its power to lift those margins. The difference between this and Tilling is visible in BTR's margins: in 1983, the year of Tilling, they dropped from 18 per cent to 12 per cent, and to 11 per cent in 1984. In 1985, margins rose to 12 per cent. The following year, the first full year of Dunlop, they climbed to 14 per cent.

The consensus among Dunlop executives is that BTR did not depart dramatically from the strategy lines laid down by Edwardes. The difference, of course, was that BTR's infinitely greater resources enabled it to accelerate Dunlop's recovery process enormously.

BTR proceeded with the sale of the American tyre operation. It also picked up on two key investments approved by Edwardes, subject to Government grant aid, during the bid. One was a £16 million project to make Armaline, a high-pressure flexible pipe for the oil industry invented by Dunlop years earlier but never developed commercially because of the group's chronic lack of cash. The same problem had prevented much-needed spending on new equipment for the Automotive subsidiary's steel wheels operation, as a result of which starvation Britain's last independent volume supplier of such wheels was in danger of going out of business. Edwardes and Biggam okayed a £6 million investment programme in the Coventry plant.

BTR continued with the projects, but at least on the wheels front its approach was subtly different and distinctively pragmatic. It hedged the risk, by phasing in the investment. The end result was spending of £10 million in three years, including the installation of highly flexible manufacturing systems to allow rapid changes in the product mix. A further £10 million is likely to be invested within the next three years.

Companies gasping uniformly for investment – that was the legacy of Dunlop's long years of decline. While the money had been poured into tyres, the only other recipient had been Dunlop Aviation, the aircraft brake and wheel business whose leading-edge carbon composite technology made it be regarded as the jewel in Dunlop's non-tyre crown. And even Aviation had wanted for cash in the last terrible year of old Dunlop, when the banks took control.

Former Tilling man Patrick Austen, now at Dunlop Slazenger under Alan Finden-Crofts, found that mattress-to-car seating company Dunlopillo was 'running in its final days under Dunlop on a cash management programme. Every week, it was literally waiting to know whether it could draw the cheques to pay the wages.'

Dunlopillo had no new latex and polyurethane moulding equipment, while its transport fleet vehicles were so old that they had 280,000 or 300,000 miles on the clock. 'In the last year or so under Dunlop, even if something had a very short payback period like six to 12 months, it was just not possible to fund it,' says Austen.

He found a similar state of affairs in the Dunlop Slazenger businesses: 'A lot of the tennis and golf ball manufacturing, despite personal efforts by the management, had very ancient capital equipment. Much of it was 20 years old.' In some areas, that did not matter: 'Rubber moulding technology, for instance, hadn't changed so provided the basic equipment remained serviceable there was nothing wrong with it. But in areas of technological change like golf ball moulding, where modern plastics had come in, Dunlop was just not up to date.'

At least as serious for Dunlop Slazenger was the impact of old Dunlop's penury on its marketing effort, absolutely vital in the intensely competitive and publicity-driven sports goods industry. The orders of advertising magnitude required to grow a sports business are much greater even than those in other sectors of consumer products. 'At Pretty Polly, we got tremendous mileage from spending three per cent of sales on advertising and promotion,' Austen recounts. 'But in sporting goods, you are looking at three times that amount, around ten per cent.

'Dunlop didn't do that. By the end, they were spending only 1.5 per cent or 2.5 per cent of sales; they had come out of sponsoring golf tournaments or new players. Public awareness and perception of the product range had been allowed to deterioriate.'

As a result, the symbiosis between product development and marketing image was undermined on both sides: by the lack of innovation and the failure to spend on promotion. Out in the market place, itself changing more rapidly than ever with the growth of fashion sportswear, Dunlop did not lose the recognition factor of its brand name. But that name was tarnished by association with all the wrong features: unexciting products, obsolescent style.

The only positive new influence to buoy up the business in the early 1980s was John McEnroe, using the Dunlop Max200G tennis racket, and Austen believes even the McEnroe influence was double-edged: 'It was extremely beneficial to them in selling the 200G, but that benefit was limited to one product. The range was not balanced. It needed money to diversify, to make that product more fashionable so that a lady would use it, and to develop the range.' Moreover, within its limited resources, the Dunlop Slazenger marketing strategy was contradictory and ill-defined. In rackets and balls, the two brands competed against each other.

Fundamental problems of management organization, which had accumulated under the old Dunlop, had to be tackled. One former Dunlop executive notes that, even where investment had taken place, the board had a very low level of expectation of the returns on that spending. Consequently, very little pressure was put on management to improve the returns beyond a once-a-year 'we've got to do better' exhortation. Moreover, Dunlop's reporting systems were very difficult to understand, making it hard to see what was really happening in the businesses.

Sectional politics had run wild in the years of neglect. 'One department couldn't get on with another; it set up a department to watch the other department; and the whole thing had reached an appalling state,' says the former executive. 'There was no logic in the organization. It was purely developed to tackle a problem at a time. And instead of solving the problem, they just made an organizational change.'

In one case, 'There was the engineering side, including design and testing functions, under a technical director, and then we had the manufacturing director and a lot of staff. They were two armed camps lobbying mortar shells backwards and forwards, each side coming to the boss to complain about the other one.'

As a result, the business exemplified a variation on the British failure to integrate product design, manufacturing and marketing. 'The engineering people were designing the product to meet the customer's needs without knowing whether we could make it. The first time the manufacturing people saw something, it was the finished prototype. Then they had to work out how to make it. The whole thing was costing an absolute fortune.'

Not surprisingly, the Dunlop businesses suffered from poor morale – no doubt aggravated by the fact that salaries in the company were very low. In one sizeable subsidiary, senior manufacturing and sales and marketing executives were being paid around £16,500. Under BTR, which is not renowned for extravagance, salaries like that were doubled within a few years.

Edwardes had made an impact, started the new ball rolling, but now BTR carried Dunlop's transformation right through. BTR brought immediately to the Dunlop companies two massive new elements: money, and a culture geared to realizing maximum operating efficiency. The people were largely unchanged. As Green observes: 'Basically, we did it with the managers that were in position in the old Dunlop.'

Within Dunlop, there was widespread ignorance of BTR. 'I'd never heard of them', says one Dunlop worker. Lou Fitzgerald, now managing director of Dunlop Aerospace, remembers that 'when BTR first came into the picture, everybody said 'Who?'. Dunlop was a household name.'

Managers soon learned that this relative anonymity was both a feature and an effect of BTR's decentralization ethos. David Speirs describes the application of BTR's methods as 'a culture shock'. The way that managers were judged was far different from Edwardes' psychological tests. 'Their measure of whether you can operate under pressure is by talking to you and looking at your results, not by sitting you down in a classroom,' says Speirs.

The morale problem was particularly acute at Dunlop Automotive, whose sense of chronic neglect under the old Dunlop, one it shared with most of the non-tyre group, was aggravated by its adjacency to the favoured Aviation business. 'The feeling here was, nobody ever visits us, and when they do come on site they only go to see Aviation. We knew we weren't glamorous, but the whole thing plumbed ludicrous depths of morale,' says Speirs.

BTR's attitude, by contrast, was egalitarian and utilitarian – though never altruistic, as it rapidly proved by scrapping Dunlop's generous redundancy terms. For Speirs, and many others once they had made the necessary operating adjustment, BTR's ownership yielded instant benefits inside the companies and externally, in supplier and customer relations. 'Now we had a company which was well thought of in the business world,' declares Speirs. 'Instead of slinking in through the back door and saying, "can we sell you something – by the way, we aren't going bust this week", we were able to show strong financial backing. That was very important.'

Internally, BTR's muscle gave the managers of the Dunlop subsidiaries, cornered for so long by the penury of their parent, room to manoeuvre. Instead of blanket redundancy programmes governed by the blunt instrument of 'first-in, last-out', managers could cut jobs selectively. In at least one case, this allowed the company radically to improve its ratio of direct to indirect employees by slicing back on canteen, security and cleaning staff and contracting out those services.

The Dunlop turnround was virtually instant. Profits of Dunlop Slazenger, for instance, jumped from £0.7 million in 1984 to £8.6 million in 1985 and almost doubled to £16.7 million the next year. That increase represented an enormous jump in return on sales, from 0.4 per cent in 1984 to five per cent in 1985. At Dunlop Automotive, returns on sales more than doubled in three years. Much the same improvement was achieved at Dunlop Aviation (now Dunlop Aerospace).

Many Dunlop managers knew what the priorities were. They had been waiting for a chance to act on them. At Dunlop Slazenger:

'The first thing you had to do was to get your technology in good shape, and get your designs right,' says Patrick Austen. 'Then you had to start to advertise and re-advertise to the consumer.'

The process 'started with capital, which unlocked various things which the management had wanted to do for years. In several important cases, we started with relocation to better premises. Dunlop had large sites which were appropriate for a much greater scale of production.' Rackets were a case in point. Production was moved from a 'large, wasteful' old Victorian mill near Wakefield to a custom-built factory in the same area, but close to the M1.

Then there was the technology. Years earlier, Dunlop had invented a unique injection-moulding process for racket manufacture. 'The biggest hang-up the Dunlop people had at the time of the takeover was that they weren't able to buy new injection moulding machinery, because they didn't have the cash. The first thing that Alan Finden-Crofts asked BTR for was some capital to do this. The payback was six months. We had a squash racket and a tennis racket. We wanted to broaden the range into slightly different compositions and mould shapes. The new investment enabled us to scale up production and to add some new moulders to develop the range further into squash. Without that, Dunlop would have missed all the rise in the squash market, whereas we have put in a little bit of money and built a successful volume business,' says Austen.

Product improvement was widespread. Footwear, notably the classic Green Flash brand, had developed a 'good value' image. 'The shoes were worn by the mature guy in the civil service,' remarks Austen. Dunlop set out to change all that by developing new designs for more 'aspirational' products. In late 1988, one of the new shoes made it on to the front cover of a major American sports magazine.

A similar drive to higher-price, higher-margin products was made elsewhere. Dunlop tennis rackets had historically tended to be stuck in the £60 or £70 bracket. A new Max Impact Plus was developed which sold for well over £100, at last taking the business into the top price segment occupied by Head, Prince and Yamaha. In golf, Dunlop moved into high-cost materials at the top of the range when it launched its first-ever set of graphite shaft clubs in 1988/9. And there was a new ball, with a different dimple pattern which improved the aerodynamics and carried a shot further.

'Because of the improved products, we are building a much better image,' says Austen. The widened product stream cleared the way for sharper market differentiation, notably between the Dunlop and Slazenger brands, and more profitable market coverage.

'In golf, Slazenger had been left over many years to be a second brand, put into discount chains and so on,' Austen notes. Across the product ranges, the Dunlop and Slazenger brand images were refocused, so that Dunlop was firmly established as the aggressive product range aimed principally at men and the professional sports-person. Slazenger's market was defined as younger, more fashionable, more laidback.

The marketing techniques applied to Slazenger exemplify one key way in which BTR secures underlying profit growth. Dunlop Slazenger set out to 'bottom slice' the golf club market – to take the whole business away from down-market outlets where margins were tightest. But instead of surrendering its share of the low level market, it introduced a new product range under a different brand name to cater for the segment.

Rebuilding the brands' pre-eminence in their different market segments has been a long haul which BTR is still some way from completing. Patrick Austen learned this lesson literally at home, after taking over as chief executive of Dunlop Slazenger International in April 1987 following the departure of Finden-Crofts to run the Raleigh cycles business for Derby International.

'I brought back the product brochure to show my four children, and told them that this was what I was now looking after, and if they wanted something I could get it at trade price. I didn't have one taker. Even my daughter, then aged nine, said she wouldn't be seen dead in the shoes. One of the teenagers exclaimed: "Dunlop – even if you brought them back and we didn't have to pay for them, we wouldn't wear them. They are the pits!"'

Austen accepted that back-handed tribute to the abiding influence of John McEnroe, and continued to plug away at the Dunlop image. Late in 1988, when he brought home the catalogues for Dunlop's 1989 collection, he encountered a happier reaction: 'This time, they were queuing up to look. It is the same story in the trade. There has been a total change of emphasis and attitude.'

Austen readily confesses that: 'I am not suggesting that we have got it right yet. For instance, we have a very serviceable golf shoe, but it is not as good as that of our main American competitor.' Nor has the rebuilding programme been entirely smooth – a major capacity expansion of the South Carolina golf ball plant hit snags which affected profit in 1988, and triggered top management change – while the business's European strategy has to live with one legacy of old Dunlop: the fact that Sumitomo owns the rights to the Dunlop trademark in France. Aside from effectively frustrating Dunlop

Slazenger's desire to develop total European coverage, Sumitomo's position in France is a constant reminder that the Japanese group believes it should own the Dunlop sports business worldwide.

Outside France, the lines are clearly drawn. Sumitomo has the rights to the name in Japan, South Korea and Taiwan, Dunlop Slazenger everywhere else. The demarcation line is no barrier to manufacturing by Dunlop in the low labour-cost Far East, as all other sports shoe producers do. Indeed, Dunlop has gone further still. In late 1988, it began the process of moving its footwear design staff – whose numbers have been doubled since the BTR takeover – from their office in Crosby, Lancashire to Thailand, where much of the footwear is actually sourced.

For other Dunlop businesses, joint ventures have played an important role in their development under BTR. Dunlop Automotive put its steel wheels operation, which accounts for about 60 per cent of its sales, into a new company in which the Japanese wheels manufacturer Topy held a 20 per cent stake. The move was conceived specifically to extend Dunlop's prospects in the European market by providing an entry route into the Japanese car makers, led by Nissan, to whom Topy is a major supplier.

The partner was carefully chosen. In the vertically-structured Japanese motor industry, most component companies have a semi-in-house position where instead of supplying the vehicle producers in general, they are designated Tier One or Tier Two suppliers to a particular company which holds a sizeable equity stake in the supplier. Topy, by contrast, is an independent company and its largest single shareholder is Nippon Steel, with less than ten per cent. The joint venture has proved successful and as a result, towards the end of 1988, Topy was keen to increase its stake in the venture. BTR, however, was reluctant to see its own holding fall. Topy's 20 per cent involvement, and no more, suits the British group's purpose.

At least as significant a link was forged by Dunlop Aerospace with the American aircraft brakes manufacturer Bendix, part of Allied-Signal. The companies joined forces to bid for the brake orders on the new European Airbus A330 and A340 long-haul passenger aircraft, the last major European civil aircraft programme of the century. The idea of the joint venture encountered early opposition from some long-established Dunlop Aerospace managers, but it was a percipient move which also put the companies in line for the brake contracts on the European Fighter Aircraft project. It provided total world market coverage, with Bendix in North America and Dunlop in the rest of the world, and limited Dunlop's exposure to exchange rate changes (the dollar being the world currency for aircraft and related equipment orders).

More, it gave Dunlop an intimate yardstick against which to measure its performance. The company may still have ground to make up on Bendix in product support and sales per employee, but Dunlop has an enormous technical reputation and full brake and wheel manufacturing capability.

Such joint ventures would not stand – would probably not have been feasible at all – without the absolute corner-stone of Dunlop's transformation under BTR: the instilling of BTR's disciplines into the core of the Dunlop companies.

For some Dunlop managers, the advent of BTR was – as one says – 'a godsend, because it enabled me to put that driving force behind a lot of things which had to be done anyway'. Some, but not many, could not adjust or simply found that the BTR way of resurrecting Dunlop was not the way they wanted to do it. For most, behavioural change was followed by psychological evolution.

While development of BTR's key operating ratio criteria was the achievement of an executive group, the personal imprint on the BTR system in which only the fit managers survive is that of Sir Owen Green.

'BTR is very much Owen Green's company,' says one former BTR manager. 'He knew exactly what he wanted from each division. With Norman Ireland, who was a very strong influence, he would set the strategy and the parameters. Lionel Stammers, Hugh Laughland (joint chief executives of the European region) and John Cahill were the hitmen who went out and made sure the targets were reached.'

As chief executive, Green would sit in at the monthly board meetings of the divisional groups, which considered the individual company reports detailing latest performance. Green would scrutinize the reports. It was not unknown for him then to declare what immediate action should be taken, including how many jobs had to be cut in a particular company by the end of that month.

As soon as Dunlop's acquisition was completed, Green was closely involved in setting the Dunlop companies their first set of targets for return on sales, sales per employee, number of employees and the like. One Dunlop manager recalls: 'He popped off into his office and came back with a piece of paper. He had written all the criteria down there – things like "personnel costs should be no more than 30 per cent of sales".'

Green took an equally personal hand in BTR's advertising and corporate communications. Throughout the decade, the group bought national newspaper space for small, rectangular, homily-like notices dispensing such abstract nounal notions as 'Worldwide'; 'Excitement!'; 'Simplicity'; 'Magic'; all ending with the declaration: 'That's BTR'. These were Green's own creation.

The ads say something about the continuity and intimacy of Green's identification with a company which has grown out of all recognition since the first such publicity appeared.

Although they reveal no more than the tip of an iceberg, they are the closest that Green comes to regular populist advertisement. His disregard for personal publicity – he is retiring to the point of shyness, according to some close observers – is well documented and most obviously evidenced in the way he for a long time eschewed an entry in Who's Who.

Behind the mask stands a tremendous individualist, the diametrical opposite of late Twentieth Century corporate man. In October 1985, when Green received the British Institute of Management's gold award for outstanding performance, guests at the presentation dinner caught a flavour of this idiosyncrasy. Green revealed a life-long admiration for the comedian W. C. Fields, whom he proceeded to mimic in quite professional style. Sir Peter Parker, then head of the BIM, told the Fieldslike story of a Mr Edwards, the assistant divisional general manager of a British company who in a 1963 study of European management problems described the company's head office executives as 'either a bunch of experienced amateurs or a bunch of amateur specialists. I don't know which.' To make his point, and show his contempt for group accountants, Mr Edwards then grabbed 30 feet of head office computer analysis and threw it in the rubbish bin. He said that it would take days to work out what the stream of numbers really meant. Mr Edwards, Parker revealed, was really the future Sir Owen Green, in pseudonymous person.

Behind the scenes, there had been considerable disagreement in the BIM about whether Green should be given the gold medal. Some BIM members involved in the debate took the view that BTR was less a management achievement than an acquisition machine. In his acceptance speech, Green produced some particularly provocative thoughts of his own. On technology, he observed: 'We have never seen the ethical need or the material reward for placing research and development at the forefront of our activities. Research does not seem to fit easily into the cut-and-thrust environment of industry and commerce. Development *per se* – divorced from the production and commerce of a business – is also vulnerable to the debilitating influence of timelessness and the weakness of the lack of focus.'

Thirteen months later, such issues exploded into blazing controversy when BTR launched a near-£1.2 billion bid for the St Helens, Lancashire-based glass manufacturer Pilkington Brothers.

The Pilkington battle began on 20 November, 1986 and ended two months later, when BTR dropped its bid in the face of a massive political furore. The significance of BTR's defeat was rather less overpowering than seemed the case at the time (see Chapter Five), when many people jumped to the conclusion that it signalled a seismic shift against hostile takeover bids and the acquisitive companies which made them. The lasting ramifications of the contest were more specific: both during the bid and afterwards, BTR's culture was subjected to more rigorous external scrutiny than had long been the case; while Pilkington's escape – more narrow than it appeared – gave the company a jolt which spurred it to clarify its objectives and accelerate their realization.

For Green, BTR's failure to win Pilkington still rankles. Recantation, however, is out. Green stands by the analysis that motivated the bid, the timing of the offer, and the arguments that BTR employed during the fight. BTR had not been tracking Pilkington for years, *à la* Tilling and Dunlop. Instead, says Green: 'We came across it because we were looking at an American company in the automotive glass business which had a joint company with Pilkington.' (Probably

Libbey-Owens-Ford, where Pilkington held a 29.5 per cent stake which in March 1986 it exchanged for LOF's glass division and the LOF name).

Green notes: 'This was about nine months to a year before we actually bid. I thought it would be a rewarding buy based on the price, which when we first looked at it was 250p. I personally began to do some work on it, and it was worth, I thought, up to 700p. I made a number of tests to establish this, in terms of the people, the location, the marketplace, its overseas situation.' Green viewed, and continues to view, Pilkington's dominant position in the British glass market as making it a 'registered monopoly'.

Whatever judgment one made, Pilkington as a target clearly fell into the Tilling category of a management situation rather than that of Dunlop-like product and market contiguity/identity. Pilkington, maintains Green, 'was clearly overmanned by any test. Our view was that it was under-managed. Presumably (this with tongue moving towards cheek) the technology was great, because they had had the Queen's Awards and so on. It was very much a family-orientated company. It ran on a family basis.'

BTR, as Green had explained to the British Institute of Management, strove for a family ethos, but it was a different kind of family: 'Small is beautiful, simplicity is preferable to complexity, a corporate culture embraces a family feeling and the individual matters. The whole is always more than the sum of the parts.'

Green went much further in January 1987, when the furore roused by the Pilkington bid was at its height and embracing every conceivable divide, real or imagined, between North and South, Industry and the City, short-term profit-making and long-term development.

Driven to enlarge on BTR's culture, Green wrote to Pilkington shareholders on 10 January. In a section headed 'The BTR business philosophy and the R & D factor', came a passage whose like has rarely, if ever, appeared during takeover bids or in any other context of investor communication.

'There has been considerable comment to the effect that BTR has no commitment to research and developments, reflecting a short-term approach to business,' ran the introduction. 'These criticisms are based on the outmoded mechanistic philosophy which has dominated much of Western thought and holds that complex phenomena can be reduced to their constituent parts. We at BTR have over many years subscribed to and lived by the general system theory – holistic thinking – which recognizes the importance of basic organizational principles rather than elementary building blocks.

'The clearest manifestation of this philosophy is the extent to which, along with other successful companies of broad or narrow base, we ensure that the identity and the wholeness of each of our many operations is preserved by conducting it as a 'business-in-the-round.' Only by a long-term commitment to this philosophy can each of our businesses generate the wealth required to sustain and nourish long-term growth in changing markets and in all economic conditions.'

The letter had been subjected to considerable revision by merchant bank and public relations consultancy advice, but beneath this veneer Green's mission to explain his personal philosophy came driving through. After the initial section, the letter made easier reading: '. . . R & D is a part, and only a part, of any business and it is deliberate and intentional that our central R & D activities are on a limited scale. Each business, however, maintains and supports a development thrust capable of satisfying current and projected needs of the marketplace.

'Such requirements will vary. For example, in the Aerospace field R & D costs represent some ten per cent of revenues – in Health care some six per cent. In the distribution of products of other manufacturers this ratio may be zero. Overall the cost of R & D has been and will be that amount required to maintain the successful growth of BTR in like fashion to that of the past 20 years. References to short-term horizons are fanciful phrases introduced to embellish the alibis of long-term and heavy spenders, the dinosaurs from the mechanistic age.'

Green concluded: 'The most successful economy of the last 30 years, Japan, has found that, as opposed to investing in expensive high-risk research, the development and use of imported technology has been instrumental in accelerating its economic growth and building export prowess. The Japanese case is well made for a nation of limited available development resources to direct those resources into the education and further training of its people for the assimilation and exploitation of imported technology to expand its industrial base.

BTR does not put any component part of its business to the forefront in meeting its *raison d'etre* – service to the marketplace. R & D is no exception. Its funding will be as large as the market s perceived to require from each business as an entity.'

In the historical context of the Pilkington bid, this letter appears now as one of BTR's last throws. Ten days later, Green abandoned the struggle after the price that would have been needed to win it had been driven to levels that BTR was not prepared to pay. A combination of a profits forecast by Pilkington which was much higher than expected, and, more significantly, the tidal wave of popular antipathy against hostile bids unleashed by the Guinness scandal, meant that Pilkington's institutional shareholders were putting a price on their acceptance containing not just the normal financial premium for ownership, but a political premium as well. Green states: 'The message to me from the marketplace was that it was at least £9, and possibly even more than that. It could be that BTR was being taken to the cleaners. It could be that somebody had decided that this was a deal that BTR wouldn't walk away from. Well, if that was the reason, people made a mistake.'

That letter to Pilkington's shareholders remains much more than a footnote to a failed bid. Impenetrable as parts of it were to its recipients, incongruous in its mundane form, it is at once the most concise and revealing exposition of BTR's approach to manufacturing industry. Cut to the quick by the furious public reaction against the bid, Green let go with both barrels. The more difficult sections are refinements – admittedly to a rarefied degree – of the crude precepts that Green had outlined at the BIM award dinner: the whole is greater than the sum of the parts; coming a good second is better than being a bad first.

Clearly, the letter cannot be divorced from its context. Much had been made in some areas of the Press and the City of Pilkington's scientific, 'business school' approach both to its products and its strategy. Ever-disdainful of this style of management, this was Green's counterblast. It may have gone over the top and the heads of its readers, but that fact does not dispel the authenticity of what Green was doing: anatomizing the complex phenomenon that makes BTR, in the words of his own advert, simplicity itself.

Looking back, Green says: 'I was really trying to raise the tone of the debate, of the war that Pilkington and we were engaged in, above all this short-termism stuff. We haven't talked about this often, because I don't believe it has been my job to do that.'

This reticence has only intensified the quest for the BTR philosopher's stone. The nearest popular equivalent is probably the eternal ruminations of sports commentators on the secrets of Liverpool Football Club's unparalleled run of success. Revelation there has proved equally elusive.

Like Liverpool, Green stresses the virtue of simplification. 'We do things in simple ways. We are simplistic. When we say that, people describe us as cunning, or Machiavellian. Look at war games. If someone is doing something simple, you think he might be doing something else. But in this world, those of us who are very clever are required to think in simple terms. Simplicity, common sense embraces the whole thing.'

But if common sense is the compound, the mix is more profound. 'We are convinced of the need for profit being the nourishment of the organization. If people want to call us short-term, they can call us what they like. You can't be in the aviation industry without being long-term. But we insist that we are doing it for profitable reasons; not just for profit one year, but profit ever year. Profit is the lynchpin; we also want growth, but we mean growth in profit.

'We are low risk-takers. We would look for fast paybacks. Therefore, we either buy things that other people would call short-term, or we buy situations that have to be managed better. That gives you the quick pay-off. People say that it's short-term, but it isn't really. You are correcting long-term mistakes.'

Then there is the question of structure, where the one-time Mr Edwards has remained consistent in his view. 'A few years ago, and even today in big companies, the conventional large company management was a combination of line and function. Shadowing the line managers, sometimes disrupting them and always completely buggering up the operation was the staff function. That is something we couldn't tolerate, because it's too clever for me. There was no way of finding out where the lines were drawn. The ordinary man is confused having more than one master. I found that out in the Navy.

'Similarly, we haven't gone for complex Treasury situations.

We've been very simple about currencies. We have accepted that currencies go up and down, but they aren't our business and so we have never been great ones at speculation.

'We have never deliberately gone for highly educated people. It has never been a requirement that when someone joined us, he had to be a degree person. We were much more concerned with the ability of the man to do the job.

'Status really doesn't come into it. Competence is the thing we are after. I once went to Belgium for a two-day European Management Association course, and a guy was giving a lecture on authority. He talked about three or four types of authority, and the fourth was the authority of competence. That was the only authority that was worthwhile. If your boss wasn't competent, you didn't respect him anyway. It might be that one of your colleagues was really the competent one. That fits with the idea that rank is not that important.'

Competence in BTR is proven by a manager's performance against the targets set in the annual plan, and subjected to the monthly test of the key ratios report. 'I would regard the ratios as one of the basic features of our success,' Green observes. 'Because we've been able to persuade managers of all backgrounds and disciplines to accept that these things are informative, useful and almost necessary – that they can't really do without them.'

One former BTR managing director goes even further: 'What has driven the company is the annual planning review. I know a number of people who have seen it, introduced it, and they agree that there isn't a finer document. It gets to the guts of the business, puts it in standard form and allows anybody to see where the weaknesses of the business are.'

BTR's annual planning process is fundamentally a massive negotiating session between the managing director of a subsidiary and his bosses. The smaller companies are reviewed by their group chief executive – there were seven such groups, ranging from aerospace to mechanical engineering, under Lionel Stammers when he was joint chief executive of the European region. Larger companies are seen by the regional chief executive as well as the group head; and the largest by John Cahill, BTR's chief executive.

After preliminary work, which starts in mid-August with forecasts being submitted by the individual managing directors, the process builds up to a crunch in November. On one side of the table sit the chief executives and their finance men; on the other, a managing director and his finance director. Every component of the business is discussed, from the profits forecast to the margins to the material, labour and salary costs as a percentage of each pound of sales.

'It's a challenge,' says the former BTR managing director. 'Because of the process, it's very easy for the chief executives to challenge the guy, and he then has either to justify his point or concede that he's probably got too many people or he ought to have his prices up or cut more overhead.'

The chief executive concerned then does his calculations and produces the next year's plan. Not only does this set the profits target, it also dissects the business to show what each component of the operation must contribute to attain that target. The starting point is a restatement of the previous year's sales at new year prices, which immediately raises the target threshold. The managing director is then confronted with the question of how he will get to the profits target from where he stands now, taking on board anticipated changes in volume and pricing. This isolates the true price increases that are being sought.

Then the same procedure is followed for next year: sales are stated at the end-of-year prices anticipated by the plan, always taking into account changes in the volume mix. In many cases, the effect is to show that managing directors are not raising their prices enough.

Sales are broken down into product groups, showing the percentage of sales taken by materials, the internal return on sales, and which products are contributing to the overheads. This isolates the product types that are being carried by the rest. Psychology rules. 'The guy says: "it's not worth being in this business unless I put my prices up ten or 15 per cent". So he puts his prices up, and he never loses as much business as he expected, because he has probably been underpricing,' says the former BTR managing director.

The same process is followed on labour costs, taking into account the effect of wage and salary increases progressively through the year. The anticipated change in volume mix is also covered. Thus the size of productivity increase – and the extent of any job cuts – required to meet the target is isolated.

The whole picture is united by a sheet, the PB6, which details all the overhead cost elements: price increases; volume mix changes; development work; and productivity. 'That tells you if you are covering the cost increases and crystallizes the issue about competitive pricing.'

Says the ex-MD: 'It's a negotiated plan. It may be negotiated under pressure, but it is negotiated. So the guy can never say that it is imposed.' If one key element in business is the price-determining balance of power between supplier and customer, then the negotiating process for the annual plan must be both the ultimate duel between supplier (the managing director) and customer (his boss) and a proving ground where a managing director's bargaining skills are honed for the price negotiations to come in the course of business.

The managing director works through the following year with those agreed annual targets forever at his side through weekly and monthly reports to Silvertown House. By the end of every Monday, each division has to have sent in its sales and orders figures for the week. Into the computer they go, and out the next day comes a schedule listing the total for the month to date, the year to date and compared with the annual plan and the previous year's position at the corresponding stage. 'By Tuesday afternoon, if one division was having trouble, the regional chief executive would be on the phone,' says the former BTR managing director. 'If someone was showing a pattern, they were quickly on to that.'

Immediately after the end of the month, a BTR managing director flashes his operation's results to head office. The flash result is quickly followed, by the third or fourth working day after the month's end, by a standard seven pages on which the individual MD records his key ratios – operating profit, sales, return on sales, orders, employment levels – in three categories: actual; against plan; and against the previous year's corresponding level. 'The documents are superb. They concentrate everyone's mind. They mean that the controls for an MD are great,' says the former BTR man.

David Speirs testifies to the psychological conditioning effect of the process: 'BTR doesn't like to be surprised. You must communicate. There are three words I found I shouldn't use: 'If' and 'I think'. When you promise BTR something, you deliver. When you aren't sure, then you are cautious.

'BTR exerts a subtle type of pressure. In the end, some of it is

self-inflicted. It becomes a measure of personal pride and achievement. You want to perform. You know what you've got to perform
against, which you never did under the old Dunlop. Soon I was saying
to my managers, I don't like any shocks, so we ran some financial ratio
reports weekly. I got like BTR.'

If BTR did a lot for Dunlop, the benefits were mutual. At the
macro, corporate level, the acquisition of Dunlop's mountainous
accumulated tax losses provided a great boost for BTR's earnings.
The tax losses maximized BTR's gains from the virtually universal
above-the-line surge in earnings from the Dunlop operating companies. The profit and margin figures from Dunlop Slazenger provide
graphic evidence of the impact that BTR's systems had on Dunlop –
and of the consequent benefits that Dunlop yielded for BTR. After the
initial surge, 1987 profits still jumped by almost 50 per cent from £16.7
million to almost £24 million. Sales by then had increased by 48 per
cent since 1984, to about £240 million. The proportionate profits rise
during that four-year-period – more than 1,000 per cent – is eloquent
testimony to the impact of BTR's margin-orientated doctrine.

Now that the Dunlop businesses have been dispersed among
BTR's various divisions, it is impossible to state the overall impact of
the acquisition in hard statistics beyond the first nine months under
BTR, when Dunlop made an underlying profit of £60 million,
compared with the £27 million pre-tax profit of 1984.

However, there exists abundant observable and anecdotal evidence that Dunlop has changed the nature of BTR in a way that
Tilling did not. Tilling made BTR much bigger. Dunlop made it
different. Green himself acknowledges a Dunlop effect, albeit a
limited one: 'In certain areas, Dunlop took us up-market. Their
production and product technology was probably better than
ours – they had good production technology. We had better
equipment than they had, because theirs had run down through
lack of investment.' But Green also maintains: 'I don't think there
has been a lot of cross-fertilization. The fertilization has been of
the Dunlop people by ours in the BTR ethos.'

According to the former Dunlop manager: 'In Dunlop, BTR
discovered a level of engineering and technical development which

was unfamiliar to them, and product development cycles which were much longer than they were used to.' Dunlop's Aerospace business, where the product cycle can be ten years, is the most obvious such instance. Lou Fitzgerald, an employee there for more than 30 years and now its managing director, says: 'We felt some apprehension that BTR would not understand the aerospace business because it had much longer gestation periods than their existing business.' But under BTR, Aerospace has continued to spend ten per cent of its revenues on research and development. 'They have been both realistic in their expectations, supportive with their capital – and tough. The money is there for investment, but you had better get your sums right.'

The former Dunlop manager believes, *pace* Green, that Dunlop has had a more profound effect on BTR: 'The formula hasn't changed, but Dunlop coming in has mellowed them. The original BTR line was "generate the cash to fund the next acquisition". With Dunlop, that has changed somewhat.'

If that is true, such a change may be due as much to force of circumstances – the Pilkington defeat – as to any creative Dunlop effect. After Pilkington, the acquisitional running in BTR that had previously been made by Europe was taken up by Alan Jackson's Nylex. Through a series of takeovers, notably the March 1988 purchase of the whole of ACI in Australia, Nylex boosted the proportion of sales generated by BTR's Orwellian-titled 'East' region from less than six per cent in 1984 to almost 40 per cent in 1989 – nearly as much as Europe – giving BTR a position in the Pacific Rim, the world's fastest-growing region, which many other Western Hemisphere companies can only envy. Early in 1989, there were signs that Green and Cahill's focus was switching to build up North America ('West'), which at that stage produced about a fifth of group sales. BTR would like to replicate the Nylex approach there, by taking a majority stake in a public company which could then use its stock market quote to become the vehicle for American expansion.

Even with North America slightly out of balance, BTR has established a global manufacturing base of rare scale for a British group. Its multinationalism contrasts completely with the British industry's former colonialism, epitomized by the old Dunlop. As Green points out, it is the source of enormous strength, a colossal insurance against business risk. 'We are quite broadly spread in national economies and in our markets: some are seasonal; some are cyclical, but they are so different one from the other that they give us built-in security.

'We hope we never fire on all cylinders, because it would be something we could never repeat. We always have something that's not performing quite to schedule, but we rarely have more than one or two of our nearly 300 profit centres which are actual loss makers. And it is amazing how fast you can turn a company round. You can do it within three months.'

Hand in hand with this global span goes a truly formidable continuity. Green naturally enthuses: 'It's the same last year as before. The company goes from strength to strength and it does have an ethos, a separate identity from the people inside it. And that lasts as long as the people inside it can be persuaded to adapt and accept and practise that ethos.

'Of all the companies that I know, except perhaps ICI, we import very few people. We acquire through the acquisition process a whole lot of new managers. As long as the top executive in our company can come from within the ranks, can be a man who is really nourished in the BTR ethos because it makes sense, that way the company will just carry on. There won't be an end to it because it will be a corporate body, a separate corporate entity with its own life. There will be personalities in our company, not just grey figures, but it will be the BTR system that will go on.'

Patrick Austen testifies to the deep implantation of BTR's operational devolution and financial centripetalism: 'Ask the managers about BTR, and they will all mention the financial targets and controls. But everyone below that level in the company won't even acknowledge the existence of BTR. For a managing director, though, you aren't respectable, you aren't in the family until you produce a ten per cent return on sales, and you don't get smiled at until you are at 15 per cent.'

Green's forthright opposition to the common industrial practice of appointing non-executive directors from outside the company is another face of the system. BTR's non-executives are few, and the group grows its own. When Norman Ireland relinquished his finance director post in 1987, he became a non-executive. When Lionel Stammers and Hugh Laughland stepped down as executives in

1989, they remained on the board as non-executives.

Nonetheless, BTR is approaching the critical phase when continuity of the industrial empire built by and under Sir Owen Green will be tested by the transference of power to a new top management generation. This did not happen in 1987, when Green handed over the chief executive reins to John Cahill. Cahill, only four years younger than Green, was part of the original group that built BTR. In a sense, the only transition test so far was set by Ireland's departure, and the system only passed that second time around and thanks to an outsider – Chris Bull, who came from British Telecom after Barry Romeril, the original Ireland successor as finance director, had left BTR for British Telecom.

BTR chief executives retire at 60 under a rule introduced by Green in the late 1960s, although the stipulation can be varied and was when Green stayed on slightly beyond that age before Cahill took over. With the appointments of Mike Smith and Bob Faircloth to succeed Laughland and Stammers in 1989, two of the most likely successors to John Cahill are now in position near the top. The third is Alan Jackson at Nylex in Australia. Green, who celebrated his 64th birthday in May 1989, will probably be there to manage the chief executive succession.

If BTR can avoid the kind of internal division which has plagued successions and corroded empires from time immemorial, it should hold the place among Britain's top corporations that it claimed during the 1980s. Of the largest groups in manufacturing industry, only Hanson has established itself on such a scale in a similar timespan alongside the older guard headed by ICI and GEC, and Hanson is a unique Anglo-American animal, dominated by the personal flair of Lord Hanson and Sir Gordon White, motivated by financial rather than industrial management, and anchored on either side of the Atlantic with no aspirations to globalization.

In contrast, BTR's achievement of its basic strategy – its companies' drive for 'niches in their marketplace which offer high margins and where we can be the leader' as Cahill put it in 1988 – makes it in many respects the definitive British company of the 1980s. Company after company emerged from the recession with a mission statement – albeit frequently implicit – to be a manufacturer of higher value-added components occupying a top position in niche but global markets. Very few have yet achieved this on any scale.

BTR is different because it is the biggest of them and the most mature. Its strong consumer brands of Pretty Polly and Dunlop Slazenger add to its exceptionality in British manufacturing, which has abandoned such business. But the margin imperative that drives the consumer businesses is the same article of faith that inhabits every other company in the group, and its universality obviates one potential weakness of the niche market, component culture: the supplier's reliance on its end-customer.

BTR turns this potential area of vulnerability to its advantage. It is not volume driven, and as Patrick Austen notes, it spends little time discussing market share. Indeed, from the earliest days of the Green regime, it has always been ready to sacrifice business where it judged the margins to be too low. Similarly, it is quite prepared for trials of strength with customers to establish the right to supply on its price terms.

At Dunlop Automotive, this principle was established shortly after the BTR takeover when with Government approval, the then-loss making and State-owned British Steel hiked its prices 16 per cent. Dunlop Automotive immediately insisted on passing that rise on in the steel wheels it supplied to Britain's Austin Rover group, even though at that time 75 per cent of Automotive's wheel sales were dependent on Rover. Harold Musgrove, then head of Austin Rover, was furious, and refused to pay the price. BTR stood fast. No wheels were supplied and very soon the Rover assembly line ground to a halt. Having threatened to remove all the business from Dunlop, Rover took away half and paid the price increase on the rest.

The case also highlights the strengthening of the Dunlop companies under BTR. In January 1989, Automotive regained 100 per cent of the Rover business. But instead of dominating the company, sales to Rover at that point accounted for just under 30 per cent of steel wheels sales. In less than four years, the company had diversified its customer base both at home and overseas to include Ford, Nissan and General Motors. The well-spread customer base, a BTR characteristic, minimizes component supplier vulnerability in its own right and reinforces the ability to pass on external costs.

Dunlop has not been a total success story for BTR, but that is primarily because of the opportunities foregone during the cash crisis of the early Eighties. The Armaline sub-sea hose project into which

BTR has pumped sizeable investment has yet to show a return. The investment famine meant that the product was not developed for the North Sea oil boom at the turn of the Seventies. BTR's project approval was then hit by the slump in the North Sea industry when the oil price fell later in the 1980s. Similarly, Dunlop Slazenger completely missed the 1970s fashion running shoes boom which saw the likes of Nike and Reebok seize a lead in a new market which, although Dunlop had never had a running shoe, should have been made for the British group. Under Austen in 1989, Dunlop took some cautious steps in the running and jogging shoe market.

The real question about how suitable BTR is as a role model for aspiring British industry concerns the extent of its limitations. Green himself admits that: 'I think our planning system would find something which took longer than a three-year view would tax us. We could run something with a first-year development loss, and with a second-year loss maybe. But in the third year it would have to break even.'

As he pointed out in that letter to Pilkington shareholders, a high absolute level of research and development expense is not for BTR. It smacks too much of research for its own sake, not the market's. But that was a judgment made in the context of BTR's – and, as he saw it, Pilkington's – business. The high technology industries which have strong growth prospects demand high R and D levels for genuine market reasons. Green affirms:

'There you are very much in the hands of the scientist. I don't think I would feel comfortable in the hands of a scientist or an inventor or the developer. I feel very vulnerable myself. Any BTR man would, if he wasn't able to bring a simplistic assessment to bear. So the very high technology stuff we probably wouldn't manage well, because it would be too dependent on the intellectual hunch.'

Hence his admiration for the Japanese. 'They make simple solutions, and things that work, from some of these inventions. And they produce answers to complex problems of production which make you say, "I could have thought of that". When you buy a piece of Japanese equipment, you know that a lot of thought is going into it.'

Criticism of BTR's 'keep it simple' approach focuses not so

much on the system as on the use to which it is put. Possibly the odd business with well-above average returns is not driven to produce the even-better performance of which it might be capable. Such discerning objectivity can be a casualty in a giant corporation with the size and spread of BTR. Likewise, according to one former manager, 'Major investments could be made as much on the reputation of the management as on the quality of the project'.

But this manager's fundamental complaint is different: 'There is a lack of preparedness to look at things from a strategic point of view. There is also very little sense of belonging to one company, yet the mechanisms to achieve that were superb.

'BTR often said "no" to projects almost as a matter of principle, but if a managing director really believed something had to be done, then often they started to listen. And if he then came back and had the balls to insist on something, then they said yes. That is all very well, but it tends to breed a particular kind of manager. It can discourage the more creative, conceptual, strategic type of manager. It is not constructive. Investment is about improving productivity or putting in capacity that's immediately required, but not about investing in R and D or putting in the seedcorn for the future.'

The charge that BTR resents most strongly is that its insistence on short-term paybacks amounts merely to asset-stripping in a sophisticated form, with the asset that is stripped being intellectual property. That accusation must be tempered by the irony, appreciated by the former BTR manager, that 'a lot of the businesses have been driven to produce better quality because that is cheaper in the long run. It's all about doing what is now better and better, rather than building for the future. A lot of businesses can go on that way for ever and ever.'

With the influx of Dunlop's technology, BTR has had the opportunity to substitute organic knowhow for the technology that it previously imported. Dunlop's recovery potential was so huge, and has been tapped so fruitfully by BTR for so long, that some businesses did not face the challenge of building a platform to generate long-term growth until several years after the takeover.

In 1988, Dunlop Slazenger's rate of profits advance slowed markedly, partly because of the hiccup in the United States which was rooted in the pre-BTR dearth of investment.

But the results reflected the inevitable plateau reached by Dunlop Slazenger after its revitalization under BTR. At that point, BTR had the option of reaping further instant profits growth from the business, or reinvesting more than half the immediate additional profits potential in marketing support to put firm long-term foundations under some of the relaunched products.

This kind of choice, writ large across the group, is what BTR's new generation of top management may have to face in the 1990s. For if the Japanese can jump the industrial chasm which divides brilliant derivation from real innovation, the Green philosophy which permeates the group will stand in need of adjustment. As things are, BTR's chairman can maintain his doctrine of the 'good second' industrial nation which channels its 'limited available development resources' into 'the education and further training of its people for the assimilation and exploitation of imported technology to expand its industrial base.'

Being a good second may be preferable to coming a poor first, but it does not approach the ultimate combination of rank and quality, the good first. Green asks, with the authority that troops with enormous experience and achievement: 'How practical is that? How probable is that? How many good firsts are there?' It is an ideal, which can only be realized by the cultural fusion of BTR's lucid management disciplines with a higher-risk, more strategic, more creative ethos. Few companies may attain this ideal balance in the 1990s, but some are trying. They may be asking the impossible, but at least the question is being put. Perhaps, in the post-Green era, BTR will have to pose it too.

CHAPTER THREE
UNDER NEW MANAGEMENT

Shortly after Sir Michael Edwardes arrived at Dunlop in November 1984, the magazine *Chief Executive* published a remarkable interview with the new chairman of British industry's capsized flagship. In it, Edwardes launched an outspoken attack on the quality of British management. He accused industry's captains of 'wallowing in consensus' and declared: 'There's more cowardice around today than I've known in the 18 years I've been in Britain. The amount of compromise is frightening.'

Edwardes expressed 'great sympathy' for trade union leaders. 'They see a company getting into deep trouble and they apparently oppose any action to put things right. But all the time they're hoping like hell that management will be strong enough to grasp the nettle. But it doesn't happen.' Warming to his recurrent theme that many British managers were in the wrong jobs, Edwardes commented: 'If you fill leadership posts with people who lack inborn courage – something which can't be taught at business schools – what else do you expect?'

Edwardes' strictures did nothing to endear him to that – sizeable – section of the British executive population which had already built up a strong resentment of the former BL boss. Indeed, his comments probably enlarged the anti-Edwardes faction. But while he provoked outright hostility in some quarters, other, more balanced eyes read them with ambivalence. On one side, Edwardes' view was a timely warning against a return to complacency now that the recession was over and business conditions had improved. However, Edwardes also appeared strangely out of tune with the keynote that was being struck even as he spoke in numerous companies where a new generation of managers was taking command.

This new breed of executives was most prominent in those companies which had come closest to oblivion during the slump. They were characterized by a tough, no-nonsense professionalism and a determination, in the cliché of the time, that their 'leaner and fitter' companies which had been streamlined during the recession should gain further muscle rather than relapse into flabbiness.

These executives constituted the sinews of a revolution in British industrial leadership. Ironically, in view of Edwardes' position, few companies surpassed the scope of the management revolution undergone by Avon Rubber, which survived Dunlop to develop in the late 1980s as Britain's only independent tyre manufacturer. Avon, most of whose operations are clustered in small towns close to Roman Bath amid rural Wiltshire, appears an unlikely vehicle for corporate revolution. And Avon's chief executive Tony Mitchard, a lifelong Avon man and father of five, scarcely fits the conventional profile of a revolutionary.

But Avon under Mitchard has been and remains the cockpit for an industrial metamorphosis which embraces most elements of British manufacturing industry's past errors, present achievements, and future aspirations.

Avon today has set its face firmly towards the horizon of the 21st century. It is very different from the company that entered the decade in gathering gloom under lowering industrial skies. Most obviously, the balance of its business has shifted mightily away from the commodity tyre market in which it was anchored ten years ago. At that time, 80 per cent of Avon's sales came from tyres, and around three-quarters of that total from the commodity end, where it was a minnow among the whales like Pirelli, Michelin and the Americans Goodyear, Goodrich and Firestone.

In the year that ended on 1 October, 1988, tyre profits rose by about 15 per cent on sales which accounted for slightly over 25 per cent of the group's £227 million turnover. Out of tyre sales of £60 million, higher margin 'premium' speciality tyres – supplied to the likes of Rolls-Royce and Rover and as 'own label' models to Dutch and Swedish tyre makers – together with racing tyres, accounted for half the total. The balance came from original equipment supplied to a wide range of specialists like J. C. Bamford construction vehicles, and replacement tyres for the car market. In 1989, Avon sold its Motorway tyre replacement business to Sumitomo, which also took a 20 per cent stake in Avon's tyre-making business. Avon is now well on the way to raising the proportion of premium tyre sales to 80 per cent. And at that point, it will be poised to concentrate exclusively on the premium market.

Aside from demonstrating this successful movement up-market to higher added value, the 1988 results marked two major milestones in Avon's development. For the first time in its history, its tyres-related interests – both manufacturing and the tyres and accessories service centre business Motorway – contributed less than half group operating profits. Avon's other businesses, notably Industrial Polymers, whose products range from automotive hose to hovercraft skirts and Army respirators (gas masks), but also its Inflatables dinghies-to-combat craft subsidiary, raised profits by almost two-thirds to a combined £10.4 million out of the group pre-interest and tax total of £18.9 million. The figures showed the benefits of successful geographical as well as product diversification, because the French base newly-established by Industrial Polymers contributed significantly to the profits rise.

The second landmark was even more fundamental. The increase in pre-tax profits from £11.4 million in 1987 to £16.3 million in 1988 constituted Avon's sixth successive year of profits growth – by far the most sustained upward trend in the group's 102-year history. Avon has advanced from the depths of near-disaster in 1981/2 when the company stared financial collapse and loss of independence in the face.

Before its 1980s revolution, Avon had been the epitome of the stop-go British company. From the 1950s onwards, it had acquired or formed a string of operations, many of which were subsequently closed, liquidated or sold. The ultimate instance was Avon's radial tyre factory in Washington, Tyne and Wear, which the company began to build in 1968 as the most modern tyre plant in Europe. Avon was only months into the project and had invested almost £6 million, when the tyre industry hit one of its habitual cyclical slumps. In 1969, one year after launching the project, Avon sold Washington – to Dunlop.

For half of the 1970s, Avon's results fluctuated wildly. A near-£2 million profit in 1974 subsided to a £500,000 loss in 1975 and recovered to a £2.45 million profit the next year. By then, there had been a palace revolt which brought to the fore a new management group. In 1975 three main board directors – Peter Fisher, Avon's present finance director John Bradbeer and Tony Mitchard – rebelled against the regime of then-managing director John Swanborough. According to Bradbeer, Swanborough and his financial advisers had gone overboard on decentralization to the point where each subsidiary was given the autonomy to negotiate its own bank lines of credit. 'They were totally let off the leash, and that's when the trouble started,' Bradbeer maintains.

The trouble, which almost sank Avon in the early 1980s, was its level of debt. At first, however, with Fisher installed as managing director and Lord Farnham of the group's merchant bank Brown Shipley on board as chairman, all went well above the line. In 1977, pre-tax profits hit what was then an all-time high of £5.4 million, but that marked Avon's pre-recession apogee. As with Dunlop, tyre industry world over-capacity began to take its toll. Capital gearing rose to 70 per cent of shareholders' funds in 1980, while profits declined remorselessly until, in 1981, the group slipped into the red. The following year, Avon faced the crunch. It decided that it must make the break from commodity tyres by cutting that side of the business by around 30 per cent, but its balance sheet would not bear the redundancy and restructuring cost burden required to finance this fundamental strategic shift.

'We had no money, and went cap-in-hand to the banks,' Bradbeer recalls. 'We had 15 banks in tow, and they agreed to lend us £6 million. We gave an undertaking that we would repay the money in a year. They tied us up in little knots. They already had floating charges over everything. Now they took fixed charges over every bit of asset we had. And they cost us £250,000 in legal fees. It was very much touch and go. If the banks had not been prepared to put the money in, the company would either have been wound up or somebody would have bought us at a giveaway price.'

The banks put accountants Price Waterhouse in to verify what was going on. That caused an upheaval – 'Deloitte Haskins and Sells had been auditors here for 100 years'. Apart from this foreshadowing of the Dunlop crisis, the irony of Dunlop's contemporaneous troubles was not lost on Bradbeer. 'Dunlop was Avon's white knight. Dunlop had always said, "if anyone has a go at you, we will always be here",' says Bradbeer.

Avon considered other sources of financial support, including an infusion of external venture capital. In the end, it didn't need anyone. In October 1982, capacity at the Melksham tyre factory was slashed by a third and 850 jobs, mostly in tyres, were cut. There was no final dividend, capital gearing jumped to 140 per cent and the shares tumbled to 69p. The extraordinary costs left a bottom-line net loss of £5.77 million.

That was Avon's nadir. It had to survive the attentions of a prospective predator, James O'Hara, who at one stage built up a 22 per cent shareholding; but profits increased steadily to £4.5 million at the end of 1985. Then the real revolution began.

In October 1985, development work started on Avon's great experiment: an audacious drive to increase efficiency at its Trowbridge industrial hose plant by sweeping away the working habits of the factory's lifetime. The initiative was Mitchard's. Then aged 51, he had been the driving force behind Avon's recovery under Fisher whom he was now on the point of succeeding.

Mitchard had no illusions about Avon's ostensible return to health. He believed that the profits bounce-back had merely papered over the cracks in the company, and that the next time market conditions turned rough Avon would be back in, perhaps terminal, trouble. 'We were hanging on just to survive,' he said.

So Mitchard set about making fundamental changes. His attitude was the antithesis of the complacency that had riddled British industry in the pre-recession good times. Like Avon's near-calamity, that complacency was history. It was banished to the past. For Avon, there was no going back; only forward. 'Of course people didn't like it, but I think people recognized that something had to be done. I have heard nobody say yet that there wasn't the requirement for radical change,' says Mitchard.

Mitchard called in consultants because, although 'I've been traditionally anti-consultants, I'm absolutely convinced that they are needed particularly by a medium-size company like Avon which doesn't have a large staff organization to bring people in on a selective basis.' However, he ensured that at every site a cadre of local management was formed to work alongside the consultants, both to emphasize that the efficiency drive was an Avon management decision which the consultants were simply helping to implement, and to ensure that Avon had managers in place to take over completely once the consultants had moved on.

Mitchard's objective was to achieve a huge increase in Avon's efficiency, proceeding from the premise that the 1982 cuts had 'reduced output and labour, but didn't achieve efficiency'. The efficiency drive required a significant cut in manning levels, removal of shopfloor workers' demarcation lines to provide increased flexibility, and reorganization of the factories. Above all, it demanded a radical change in approach by all tiers of management, but most crucially at shift manager/foreman level. Essentially, Avon's managers had to be turned from 'reactive' to 'provocative' beings – anticipating problems rather than responding to them.

The efficiency reforms substantiated the principle of restoring management's authority to manage. Successfully and successively implemented at Avon's Wiltshire plants, their total cost of just under £10.49 million was completely paid back in little over three years, with each individual project repaying the investment in two.

At the start, Avon trod carefully but firmly. Trowbridge was chosen as the guinea-pig project, the test bed, both because it was a relatively isolated, stand-alone, small (204 manual workers) operation and, as Avon tyres's manufacturing and personnel director Rod Pottow explains, because it was 'probably the most efficient part of our organization, and certainly one of the most profitable at the time. We thought, "let's take that, and if we can make it more efficient, we have got to be able to do the same elsewhere". What we found was that the most efficient part of the group was very able to improve by a substantial amount'.

Appropriately, implementation of the efficiency programme at Trowbridge – following the preparation work – began in February 1986, the same month that Mitchard was appointed Avon chief executive. Pottow's 'substantial' is an understatement of the programme's benefits. Labour productivity soared by 70 per cent. Overtime, previously running at between six and seven hours a week per worker on average, was almost eliminated. Materials waste was cut by 30 per cent. The productivity transformation created a 30 per cent increase in the plant's physical capacity. Return on sales – always Mitchard's key performance yardstick – doubled from five to ten per cent. The manual workforce was initially cut by just over a third, but promptly climbed back to 170 shopfloor employees because of increased orders. Avon did not expect to get something for nothing. The newly-flexible workers received wage rises amounting to an annual rate of 15 per cent.

Equally dramatic improvements in performance were achieved in autumn 1986 when Avon, convinced by the Trowbridge experiment, took the major step of enacting the programme at its Melksham tyre and industrial polymers plant, the largest in the group with almost 2,300 workers. The Melskham project was so large that it had to be split into seven phases implemented over eight months, and at £6 million, it accounted for more than half the programme's total group-wide cost. But the results were spectacular.

On the tyre manufacturing side, which occupied roughly two-thirds of the Melksham operation, labour productivity increased by 25 per cent in the two years between autumn 1986 and late 1988. At the efficiency programme's inception, the plant was producing 128,000 Equivalent Tyres (the unit of productivity measurement) a week and using 33,800 man hours to do it. By late 1988, Equivalent Tyre output was up to 160,000 a week, while the number of man hours needed to produce that total had fallen to 30,000. The workforce profile had also changed. Just over 1,600 had been employed in the tyres operation when the programme was launched, of whom 982 were rubber workers, 210 engineering personnel, and 424 staff. In late 1988, the number of rubber workers was 860 – 12.5 per cent down – there were 180 engineers – a fall of just over 14 per cent – and 432 staff – a slight increase reflecting a management development initiative to hire specialists to build up new businesses. As at Trowbridge, the initial job cuts were more severe – approaching 25 per cent of manual workers – but employment recovered as new business was won.

The bottom line was the extent to which the efficiency programme cut Avon's unit costs. In tyres at Melksham, unit costs were reduced by no less than 41 per cent.

The programme was based on two key elements. First,

intensive training to change the way that management behaved. The training, much of it on the job, involved all management levels – about 100 managers at Melksham, for instance – but particularly concerned shift and supervisory managers. Second, the installation of an operating and control system, following detailed analysis of the manufacturing process, to support the new 'active' management approach.

What this meant in practice was a system of regular checking by supervisors (foremen by another name) of the different jobs throughout a shift. The new methodology was encapsulated in Melksham's 'core building' department, where the tyres were physically made by the labour-intensive process of putting pieces of rubber together in a machine. Under the new system, the shift manager was required to ensure that the tyre building machines were set up properly at the start of a shift, that the machine operator had all the materials he needed, and that he knew how many tyres he was to build of each type before he moved on to another job. The shift manager was given certain predetermined points out on the shopfloor to check at specific times, 'rather than sitting in his office filling out bits of paper,' as Richard Steele of Knox d'Arcy, the consultants which advised on the Melksham and Bradford-on-Avon efficiency programmes, described the new practice. Similarly, the programme improved logistics in the Melksham mixing department, where the materials for tyre making were mixed in giant machines on four floors of the factory. The key to the operation's cost-effectiveness was the continuous running of the highly expensive machines, and the only way to guarantee that was to have sufficient materials ready at all times on the appropriate floor of the mixing process.

Problem-elimination was another ingredient of the new approach. Steele said: 'What we find in every company we go into is that people tend to adopt a fairly passive management style, and tend to wait until problems become urgent rather than preventing them from happening. It's also a question of getting people to take action once they have identified a problem.' Again, the onus was placed on the shift manager to communicate regularly with an operator to pre-empt problems, or if something unforeseen occurred, to act immediately to resolve it.

To increase the 'focussing' process of which the new problem-avoiding approach was one part, shopfloor operators were reorganized into small teams, at Melksham comprising between two and six people. An increase in flexibility compensated for the smaller workforce: jobs were redefined, and demarcation lines eliminated to provide for multi-skilled operators. From top to bottom, Avon's was to become a performance-led culture.

The principles and practice of the efficiency programme appear simple to the point of banality. But they were absolutely fundamental. And they shook Avon to its roots, because however blatantly obvious they appeared, if they had ever existed they had been long forgotten.

Rod Pottow says of the Melksham tyres operation: 'We knew that we had a large labour inefficiency in the place. We knew that we didn't have control of the man-hours that we were paying for, that we were not getting a fair day's work for a fair day's pay.'

That malaise inhabited not just Melksham, but Avon as a group; and, as Pottow believes, not just Avon, but the commonweal of British manufacturing industry. This was 'British disease'. 'People were deciding for themselves what equalled a day's work. It was a "stint" mentality: you came in and did your stint for the shift and when you'd completed that, the rest of the time was yours.'

'As for the management, we were all thinking decline. The whole strategic planning of management was just to try and defend yourself. It was a reactive style. The shift manager had become a progress-chaser and problem-solver for the employees. If an employee had a personal problem, the shift manager would go off and chase it.

'We were operating in a culture that was very typical of what was going on in British industry. Everything was negotiable, and that was the way of the Sixties and Seventies. Even government was, by consensus, with the unions. We were really a product of the time. Every time we wanted to do something, the first thing we did was to talk with the unions to see if they would go along with it. We were in the Sixties and Seventies loop, and had built in the slack that went with it.'

Avon was one of the silent majority of medium-sized British

companies, operating quietly, out of the strikebound spotlight that transfixed national giants like BL. The company had no great history of labour strife. Its last major strike had been in 1930. But its quiet life was in just as urgent need of galvanization as that of any strike-ridden headline maker.

Aware of this, Mitchard ensured that Avon's break with the past was decisive. There was no negotiation with the unions about introducing the efficiency programme. 'There were quite considerable risks involved in this; we were taking very strong measures to improve Avon's performance,' Mitchard says.

'You can negotiate the wages, but there is no way you can negotiate with anybody the fact that you intend to run the business with "x" hundred fewer people. You've got to say: this is what we are going to do, now let's make the best of it.'

The first time this new, decisive management line was pursued – at Trowbridge – it nearly exploded Avon's tradition of harmonious labour relations. 'We almost had a lockout. We told the workforce that if they walked out, we would lock the gates.' The line held, and the workforce went with it. There was no strike.

With the initiative firmly recaptured, Mitchard and co. advanced on Melksham – but not with flags waving in a show of management machismo. As personnel director of the tyres business, Pottow played a pivotal role in preparing the ground: 'I spent a great deal of time with the unions, preparing them for what was about to happen. The most significant thing was to convince them of the need to do it.

'With the level of performance that it was turning in at that time, the tyre company did not have a future. It was not profitable enough; because of the cash crisis in 1982/3, it was not allowed to grow. Quality and price competition were becoming greater all the time. There was no point in us producing a better quality product and not making any money doing it.

'I prepared the unions for a major cultural change and shock, but we did have the benefit of looking at Trowbridge. We were very fortunate in having thinking unions. The leadership of all three unions [the main two were the TGWU Transport and General Workers and what is now the AEU Engineering workers, along with the EETPU electricians] accepted the need.'

Pottow made a significant pledge to the union representatives. Despite the overriding management commitment to effecting changes involving shopfloor fundamentals like substantive agreements and piece work rates, the established consultative processes were retained. 'The machinery had stood us in good stead for many years. We would make the changes through the courts; we wouldn't just set up a hanging judge.'

That said, management's determination to enact the reforms was absolute. 'What we did was to demonstrate that we were right and in any fair and reasonable society, you have to do that. But we didn't sit down and barter a day's work. We said what equals a day's work. Fundamentally, the unions accepted that principle. We sold them the idea, because anything less than that wouldn't have worked. The whole validity of what we were trying to do could have been brought into question if we were going to negotiate change.'

To underpin the conviction with which Avon was making its case, Mitchard and Pottow had to avoid the obvious danger attendant on the use of consultants: that the executives were seen as abdicating authority to the outside advisors. If that view had become established, the cornerstone of the efficiency drive would have been undermined.

Avon took several steps to ensure that in the eyes of its employees, the initiative was identified in the first instance with the company's management, not with the consultants. 'We tried to keep the consultants away from them as much as possible, because it had to be seen as management-led,' declares Pottow. His preparation work, which was started in Spring 1986 and completed by the time the consultants arrived on the Melksham site in July, played an important part in creating this impression. 'The consultants were leading us into situations, and putting us through them, but it had to be Rod Pottow who stood before the unions and told them what we had to do and how we were going to do it. The whole credibility of the thing would have been destroyed if there had been a bloke sitting alongside me whispering in my ear.'

Once the consultants began work, Avon took care not to leave anything entirely to them. Mitchard seconded a task force of 13 Avon managers to operate alongside the 10 consultants from Knox d'Arcy. His move was prompted by a design far more substantial than the mere maintenance of appearances. It established a management 'spearhead' to carry the precepts of the efficiency thrust into the heart of the factory, with the result that when the consultants moved on, there remained behind a cadre of Avon people closely associated with the programme and equipped to sustain its momentum. In the process, of course, they also became greatly improved managers.

Mitchard had done the same at Trowbridge. There, despite the results achieved, Avon's experience of consultants (the then-American owned Metro Proudfoot) was less than ideal. Avon executives found Knox d'Arcy – a subsequent breakaway from Proudfoot – more user-friendly, but it had learned the importance of caution in employment of consultants.

But while not ceding overall control to the consultants, Avon's top team had at the same time to invest them with sufficient authority to make sure that their messages went home. Pottow introduced the daily training sessions conducted by Knox d'Arcy. 'My main role was to get up there and say, "listen to these guys: they will help us achieve these things. I am totally committed to the programme; unless you all are, it won't work."'

Even after Trowbridge, the consultants' first lesson came as a shock: 'I don't think we had realized how many people could go,' Pottow notes. 'They said we could lose 700.'

Mitchard recalls: 'Melksham was the big one. When we announced the redundancies, a great gloom descended not only on the Melksham plant but on the entire community.' Fortune, however, favoured the brave. Having prepared the workforce and their families for the worst, Avon was able to reduce the actual number of job cuts to 550 because of buoyancy in the tyre and polymer products markets. Aside from easing the pain of the efficiency transformation, this turn of events highlighted the new British industrial management dynamism. A change for the better in market circumstances was seen not as a cushion on which Avon could recline complacently after its exertions during the recession, but as a springboard adding momentum to the process of implementing the operating reforms; as an opportunity for action, not an excuse for recumbency.

Avon's determination to sustain the management lead it had taken was perhaps even more instructive than its seizure of the initiative at the outset. 'A productivity exercise is like a diet,' says Pottow. 'It's not that difficult to lose weight, but it's extremely hard to keep it off. Yet keeping it off is more important. It's easy to wave flags and then bend a bit here and there the first time you meet any resistance. Not negotiating afterwards is just as important as refusing to negotiate change in the first place. It would have been easy to negotiate back in all the crap we had got rid of. It's relatively simple to identify what you want to do, but to have the total commitment to keep it there and run the organization through thick and thin as a tight ship is the real challenge.'

Pottow had the delicate task of constructing a redundancy package which would encourage sufficient voluntary departures to obviate any need for compulsory job cuts – something which could have poisoned the inevitably disturbed industrial relations atmosphere at Melksham – but avoid the perennial hazard of voluntary schemes whereby the company would lose the wrong people and undermine the whole purpose of the efficiency exercise. 'That was another major watershed. We wanted to extract the people who would gladly want to go, but at the same time to leave ourselves with a balanced workforce to live beyond the holocaust. It was absolutely essential to us that we were left with a fighting fit army at the end of the day,' says Pottow.

As at Trowbridge, a large part of the answer was a substantial increase in wages for the workers who remained. Pay rises at each Avon plant in the year that the efficiency programme was implemented there averaged between ten and 15 per cent. If the Holy Grail for British industry was a high-wage, high-performance economy, then through its efficiency drive, Avon moved some way towards locating that elusive object.

The efficiency programme laid the foundations for subsequent moves to improve productivity still further. In 1987, confronted with intensifying pressure from the market for greater cost-effective output, the Melksham tyres operation embarked on an innovatory scheme to achieve seven-day working. After careful consideration, Avon rejected the conventional method: the so-called 'continental' pattern in which the five-day working week simply rotated through a full seven-day cycle, with employees having some Saturdays and/or Sundays on, and others off.

Avon knew that one or two of its larger tyre manufacturing brethren had encountered problems in attempting to adopt the continental pattern, and it decided that such a shift system would do more harm than good. Pottow notes: 'It became apparent fairly quickly that our workforce would not be delighted with continental working. They were five-day people. To tell them all of a sudden that they were going on a seven-day pattern would not have been impossible, but it wouldn't have been popular.'

So Avon kept its existing workforce on their Monday to Friday week, and hired a group of workers – eventually totalling more than 100 – specifically for the weekend. To make up a sufficient working week, these employees did one eight-hour weekday shift, but their main duty was two 12-hour shifts on Saturday and Sunday.

Unemployment in the area had fallen, so to attract applicants Avon had to offer a good pay package. At the same time, the company was determined to ensure that weekend working did not cause spiralling costs. Saturday working was not paid at time and a half, nor Sunday at double time. The weekenders received a flat day rate for the job, with the difference that for their 32 hours' actual working they were paid a wage equivalent to 36 hours' work. That left two related dangers: first, that the weekenders would try to run other jobs through the week, and second, that their absenteeism rate would consequently be intolerably high. Avon eliminated much of the former risk by ensuring that a weekender did not have a regular weekday for his eight-hour shift. Instead, his weekday on changed every week. Then, to minimize the absenteeism risk, Avon made the '36 hours' pay for 32 hours' work' arrangement an attendance premium which was only triggered when the employee came in for all his three days.

The scheme took some time to implement. 'We had a problem of recruiting and training. It was almost six months before we had the whole thing ready to go,' Pottow says. Nevertheless, Avon continued to refine its working procedures in the cause of greater efficiency. Some years earlier, the company had changed one of its four holiday weeks from a 'floating' week, which allowed each employee to choose when to take the time off, into a fixed holiday timed to coincide with the autumn school half-term. In 1989, Avon reinstated the floating week. The move shed one more sidelight on the transformation in managerial authority and efficiency at Avon. Its switch to a fixed week was the child of the old ethos, reactive and defensive, forever plugging gaps and covering mistakes.

'We went to a fixed week so that we could cover absenteeism better. When you are running a slack ship, coverage is not as tight,' Pottow comments. 'But provided you have a controlled absence, you are fine.' A maximum five per cent of the workforce are allowed to take the same week off. In the days of the old floating week, up to 15 per cent were away at any one time. To some extent, the change was an enforced consequence of the efficiency programme: 'After the changes in productivity, we had far fewer people using a much wider range of skills. So we had to retain them, and the floating holiday is more attractive than a fixed week.' The bottom line, however, is Avon's new confidence in its managerial abilities. Pottow says: 'We've learned to run the place more slickly now.'

The Avon experience of successive productivity-enhancing measures is symptomatic of a whole variety of flexible working moves by companies in the post-recession period. Other common instances concerned companies with a heavy seasonal demand bias, which introduced differential working weeks – a longer week during the months of peak demand being balanced by fewer working hours during the quieter period.

As in Avon's case, this shift in working patterns reflected two factors: a determination by companies to sustain the advances in productivity and unit labour cost restraint sparked by the elimination during the recession of historical over-manning levels; and, underlying this persistence, a recognition that progressively-higher efficiency and lower cost manufacturing were essential responses to the ever-more exacting demands of the market. Thus, too, the Avon-like insistence that such operational change was non-negotiable. Recent British industrial history was littered with cases where moves to increase efficiency had been thwarted by union refusal to accept different working methods or new machinery at less than a price – a pay increase – which made the innovation prohibitively expensive and therefore self-defeating. The manufacturing landscape was scarred by 'Who does what' demarcation disputes in which two or more unions squabbled over whose members should operate a new piece of equipment. Such disputes epitomized the loss of management authority that plagued British companies.

At first, the new management drive for constant improvement was often taken as being mere union-bashing. No doubt it was, in some cases. But as the Avon example showed, there were many managements which, having recovered their lost 'right to manage', set about building on that foundation a company-wide commitment to continuing efficiency improvements.

The labour relations issue was duplicated by, and related to, the productivity debate. As output per person in manufacturing industry soared during the three years after 1981, climbing by more than 20 per cent between the start of 1982 and the end of 1984, the rise was accompanied by analyses which attributed it almost entirely to the once-for-all de-manning process. This version predicted that the productivity advances would stall once the rationalization pace slackened.

The rate of productivity growth did slow in 1985 and 1986, but it did not die. In 1987, productivity rises more than kept pace with booming demand. Output per manufacturing industry worker increased by almost seven per cent that year and at the end of 1988 stood almost 43 per cent higher than in 1979. Productivity growth offset the continuing high level of earnings increases in manufacturing, which throughout most of the decade remained well ahead of the annual rate at which earnings grew in competitor countries.

Thus, unit labour costs, which had jumped by more than five per cent in 1985 and 1986 when output growth had slowed to a trickle, rose by only 1.2 per cent in 1987, the second-lowest annual increase of the decade. The recrudescence in 1989 of wage demands commensurate with eight per cent-plus inflation, together with Chancellor Lawson's interest rate increases to damp down the spending boom, severely tested the ability of companies to sustain that record of improvement in competitiveness. But there could be no doubt that the 1980s management changes had put in place an executive corps at least capable of confronting the challenge.

A key role in what constituted a literal regeneration of British management was played, mostly behind the scenes, by the Bank of England. From 1979 – when it took an influential hand in the takeovers of the troubled flour-millers Spillers by Ranks Hovis McDougall and foods business Lyons by drinks group Allied

Breweries – through to 1984, the Bank was involved in efforts to rescue about 200 companies, most of them Stock Market-listed. Architect of the Bank's intervention was its Industrial Finance Division, colloquially known as the 'intensive care unit', which was headed first by Lord Benson and then by David Walker. By no means all its patients were manufacturers – Sir Freddie Laker's Laker Airways was the subject of a notable Bank-led rescue attempt – but just as the recession bit deepest into the manufacturing sector, so that was where the Bank's involvement was greatest.

In numerous instances, the Bank's was a supporting role with a company's major clearing bank, or banks, taking the lead. But in many cases, of which Dunlop was a notable example, the Bank stood at the absolute heart of the situation, marshalling the clearing banks and institutions involved, talking straight to the company concerned. In these cases, the whole future of the company depended on the initiative taken by the Bank.

Benson, Walker and their team were not always successful, in the sense that a number of companies went down despite their efforts. Acrow, the crane builder, and the engineer, Capper Neill were two cases in point. Perhaps the most celebrated was Stone-Platt, an engineering conglomerate whose interests included textile machinery and air-conditioning equipment for trains, which was rescued in 1981 but then collapsed the following year when its main banker abandoned the Bank-constructed lifeboat and called in a receiver amid a welter of mutual recrimination among the institutions concerned.

Nevertheless, Stone-Platt was something of a turning point. The Bank of England, the banks and the other institutions involved all learned lessons from the experience, and while Stone-Platt disappeared as a corporate entity, most of its businesses survived in different hands.

Only a handful of companies actually went into receivership despite the Bank's endeavours. And even in those cases where it occupied the central, coordinating role, the Bank was careful not to exceed its self-established brief. One insider says: 'It wasn't the job of the Bank of England to get authoritatively to the bottom of the problem, and how the company had got there. Nor was it to provide solutions. The job was to provide a breathing space in which sensible men of goodwill with common cause – because they all stood to lose – could take time to make a careful, detached study while clearing bank facilities were made available on an extended basis.'

When the Bank came to talk to the companies themselves, it was told frequently that the root of the firm's troubles was a problem with its bank or banks. In most cases, the Bank concluded, that complaint was an alibi for industrial relations, marketing and financial problems which originated from a common source: management failure.

In about a dozen instances, this analysis led the Bank directly to the ultimate sanction: the removal of the chairman or chief executive on whose desk the buck stopped. This difficult task appears to have been accomplished not with all guns blazing in a High Noon shootout, but in a spirit of delicate but determined insistence on the Bank's side, which commanded the appropriate, deferential response. Typically British as this technique seems, it recalls the manner in which defeated Roman generals and politicians were invited to make an honourable exit from worldly cares.

Occasionally, the Bank's biggest difficulty was locating the chairman or chief executive concerned. In one case, the chairman received the fatal message by telephone while, with the company tottering, he was holidaying on the Isle of Wight. The Bank's basic line was that the chairman, or chief executive, had lost the confidence of those on whom the company's future depended, including either one or a combination of its institutional shareholders. It was therefore suggested that, in the best interests of the company, the individual concerned give place to somebody else. In no instance was this lethal advice resisted.

Having ejected the top man, or somehow changed the management, the Bank had to find a successor who could turn the ailing company round. In the most notable cases, this executive was pulled from a select group of crisis managers, often called company doctors, despite the fact that several of those so described regard the expression as inadequate.

'These people are worth their weight in gold,' says one of the men who had to recruit them. 'They must actually like crisis situations; they have to be very tough, because there is not much room for sentiment. They need to have some track record so that the banks and institutions have confidence in them. They need to be very self-confident. They do start with the one big advantage that they have no responsibility for what went before.'

The select group of crisis managers included Sir Francis Tombs, who was called in by the Bank of England, first to the Glasgow-based pump manufacturer Weir Group and then to industrial materials company Turner & Newall; Sir John Cuckney, who went into process plant contractor John Brown and helicopter group Westland; and Lewis Robertson, who led the turnround in a string of companies including F. H. Lloyd, Triplex Holdings and F. J. C. Lilley.

While Cuckney's Westland operation was by far the most politically contentious of all the resurrections engineered during the decade, the seminal event was the 1981 rescue of Weir Group. Aside from its chronological significance – it was the first major reconstruction of the recession – it brought Sir Francis Tombs to prominence in private sector industrial management. Tombs' various chairmanships of Weir, Turner & Newall, the aero-engine maker Rolls-Royce, the audit committee of merchant bank N. M. Rothschild where he is a director, the Research and Development advisory body to Mrs Thatcher, and the Engineering Council make him a one-man leitmotiv for the experience of manufacturing industry in the 1980s. Whether this stocky, immensely pragmatic West Midlander would describe himself as such – he went to the second-best school near his Staffordshire birthplace because his parents could not afford to send him to the top establishment – is highly doubtful. Flights of fancy are something in which he does not indulge.

What Tombs has brought to each of his jobs is a no-nonsense drive which cuts through to the essence of a business, and makes its nature and objectives clearly and universally visible. By identifying suitable executives and applying financial controls and targets, Tombs breeds clarity of purpose and accountability in the organization, which becomes as logical as the man who has reformed it.

Tombs was 56 when he answered the Bank's emergency call to rescue Weir. Trained as an engineer, all his working life had been concerned with the electricity industry, mainly in the General Electric Company and the South of Scotland Electricity Board, where he was chairman from 1974 to 1977. He then went to head the Electricity

Council, on a promise from then Energy Secretary Tony Benn that the English and Welsh supply industry, including the Central Electricity Generating Board, would be united under the control of the Council. Benn never carried through his pledge, and Tombs resigned from the Council in 1980 when the new Thatcher Government refused to enact the change.

His resignation, which caused a great stir at the time, was characteristic of an individual who has always been his own man and never blanched from publicly upholding causes in which he believes, however out of line his views may be with the prevailing political or industrial orthodoxy. In this vein, he championed the cause of the Advanced Gas-Cooled nuclear reactor (AGR) against the CEGB-supported American Pressurized Water Reactor. Long after the battle was lost and the Government ordained that the PWR should form the core of Britain's nuclear power station programme, Tombs continued to argue the AGR case. He commented later: 'I'm old-fashioned enough, or naive enough, to think that if you have strong views on a topic of which you have some experience, and they are counter to what is happening, you should at least say so. I don't do it in a self-seeking way. But that PWR decision was so wrong that I had to say so. My view wasn't very popular in political circles, but so what.'

or all Mrs Thatcher's now well-known respect for strong-minded, dependent characters fundamentally in sympathy with her free-market principles, it is a reasonable supposition that in 1980, ombs did not figure high among industrialists whose advice the rime Minister valued. He earned his place at the interface etween industry and Government by what he did at Weir and &N.

'They were both companies with good products that had run out of credibility with the City and the banks, that had run out of cash and management control. In both cases, the task was to restore some individual discipline and win some confidence back through results,' Tombs says.

The moment of truth for Weir, Scotland's largest engineering company, came on 31 March, 1981. It was then, in a foretaste of rescues to come, that 80 people, including representatives of more than ten banks, clustered in the Royal Bank of Scotland's London office to hammer out a recapitalization package which would save the company. Their deadline was midnight because, on the following day, Weir had to publish its results for the 1980 financial year. Its capital gearing was so high, having reached 168 per cent of shareholders' funds, that unless it agreed a financial reconstruction before announcing those results, it would have to go into receivership.

To be precise, there were several moments of truth. One Weir executive recalls: 'It took the last minute of the last hour to get agreement in place – and then they had to stop the clock at midnight, because final agreement was not reached until 2 a.m.'

In the document published later that day detailing the complex recapitalization, Weir directors told shareholders that, without the reconstruction, 'the company's future would be in jeopardy' because of the damage done to 'the confidence of customers which is vital to the group's ability to continue trading'. It was as direct an explanation as there could be for an event which shook Weir to its very foundations.

As part of the agreement, Tombs took over as chairman from Lord Weir, who stepped down to vice-chairman after nine years combining the chairman's role with that of chief executive, the fourth generation of Weirs to work in what had been the family firm. Those years had not been unsuccessful, with group profits climbing to a record of almost £10 million in 1977 and diversification into the North Sea market more than compensating for the decline in British shipbuilding, which had been a major purchaser of Weir's pumps.

Accounting for nearly half the 1980 group sales of almost £166 million, pumps were the heart of the group, and the group was one of the world's biggest makers of pumps outside the giant American market. The pumps division employed 4,400 people in Scotland, the vast majority at its headquarters plant in Cathcart, Glasgow. Although a slump in orders for desalination equipment – a relatively new field for Weir – played a part in the group's near-collapse, the major problem was the pumps division, Weir's very hearth and home.

On one analysis, it was a reorganization of pump factory layout in 1977 which started Weir down the slippery slope. The changes, carried out in tandem with the introduction of new sophisticated machine tools, encountered numerous obstacles which hit productivity and piled up costs, making contracts unprofitable even before the recession cut into Weir's customer base.

However, these difficulties only exacerbated Weir Pumps' real problem, a failure of financial controls which dated back years. Ron Garrick, now Weir's managing director but in 1980 production director of the pumps company in Glasgow, says: 'The financial systems, which had been used for many years and should have been telling us what was happening, were slow to point out where the trouble was. The business was organized into all-embracing divisions, so that the energy division could take a job for a power station and do all the contracting. Each division was the only one that knew what was going on in a particular contract, so if the costs started going the wrong way, that division did not have to own up. The whole flow of information from contract costing to pricing, which determined our quote for the job, was flawed. What we thought it was costing was actually the wrong figure. By the time the systems did tell us what was happening, there were a lot of provisions to be made and bills to be paid.'

Even so, Weir had started to act in 1979, closing some loss-making subsidiaries with consequent write-offs below the line which weakened the balance sheet. The group continued to cut back as recession set in, choking the cash flow that Weir needed to replenish its shrunken reserves. Nevertheless, net borrowings rose only slightly in 1980.

Garrick, a man of laconic wit and dispassionate analysis who is widely respected in industry and the City, clearly believes that the whole reconstruction and streamlining of Weir may have resulted in financial overkill. He still shows hurt at the memory of the banks' effective takeover of the company in the months preceding 1 April. 'At one time, we had 80 consultants from Peat Marwick Mitchell crawling all over the Weir group, because the banks wanted them in before they would lend us any more money. Their report cost £400,000. We were on our uppers, and we had to pay for it.'

But Garrick, who was managing director of Weir Pumps by the end of 1980, also recognizes that the bankers' perception of the group had by then become more important than any, perhaps different, underlying reality: 'The banks didn't quite understand what the company was all about. But when the whole financial community doesn't have any faith in you, you have to have that faith re-established.'

He also acknowledges that the trauma generated a huge force for change from top to bottom and side to side of the group. In describing the extent of that change, Garrick effectively provides a grassroots account of the 1980s manufacturing revolution and the old manufacturing world that it overthrew.

'I joined Weir in the Sixties, at a time when there was a huge power station building programme and a lot of shipbuilding still going on. Probably less than 30 per cent of the business was exported. In the Fifties, there had been a massive shipbuilding programme and people used to come along to Weir and say, "I want this piece of equipment or that system". We were order-takers: the guy who used to book the orders had the job of telling the customer that he was on the waiting list.

'While we were doing that, the Germans and the Japanese were going through a different experience. They got their trade union systems in order; the Japanese acquired lots of technology through licences from the United States. Nobody bothered too much about them, but they were hungry for work. Things changed, but we were sheltered in the Sixties by the power station programme.

'So we got to the Seventies, and there were no more power stations; there was no more marine business because shipbuilding was oversupplied, and after the oil crisis tanker demand came to a grinding halt. Inflation was horrific; our competitiveness was non-existent. And the trade unions were ridiculous. In Place of Strife [the abortive 1969 attempt by Harold Wilson and Barbara Castle to reform the unions] would have made things better, but Wilson ducked it.

'In the Seventies, we communicated with the workforce until we were blue in the face. A lot of people did have an ongoing vision of the company, and I used to collar them and say, "If you carry on like this, this place will shut". Their attitude was, "This place will never shut; the Government will come in and save us. We employ 3,000 people in Glasgow, that's too many to let us go down."'

After breaking into the North Sea market, Weir won its biggest-ever order in 1978 from the oil major Aramco. 'We told the unions how important it was, that we were trying to diversify from the power business and so on. The job was blacked 14 times in ten months over any little issue. In one case, a guy claimed a bereavement allowance; we knew damn fine that he hadn't had a bereavement – he was away somewhere. The union said the job was blacked until he got paid. We knew we were overmanned; we knew that our productivity was half that of our overseas rivals, but we couldn't do much about it. We tried to cut the workforce by natural wastage, but the union used to say that if someone left, we had to have a replacement. The first numerically-controlled machine tools came in around 1977/8: it took us 18 months to get them started, because the union demanded flexibility payments for operating them. So we just hoped we could muddle through somehow and get things better. If you had asked me then what was the future of engineering in Scotland, I would have said "no future, it just can't go on".

'The whole attitude changed in 1980 because unemployment changed it. There was no way anyone from outside was going to save everybody. In our case, the banks had to decide whether they put us into receivership. It was a time when there was a lot of fear in the company. We managed to get a lot of changes in place quickly.'

Tombs immediately set about paring Weir down to a core of efficient businesses which could build on the reconstructed financial base. He had pledged to step down as chairman when the group had paid three consecutive dividends, was lending money to the banks, and had changed its executive management. Those three milestones were reached in only two years. 'I thought it would take five,' Tombs says – and he left at the end of April 1983.

Lord Weir returned, as a non-executive chairman, while the new management team headed by Garrick – managing director from October 1982 – maintained the streamlining momentum. Weir had setbacks: profits fell in 1983 and the dividend was cut, and the group was thwarted in a 1986 attempt to take over its Glasgow neighbour, engineering services and electronic systems manufacturer Yarrow. But the underlying drive to achieve world-class efficiency in a limited number of businesses did not flag.

The new regime's reversal of its post-war, pre-1980 strategic trend to diversification culminated in the 1986 disposal of its steel foundry interests – foundries having been its first resort when shipbuilding business started to decline in the late 1950s.

While Garrick and his team retained the desalination side which had been entered in the 1960s, and worked to establish a sizeable engineering services operation, their main focus for most of the decade was the pumps division which continued to be the group's mainstay and which encapsulated the reformation of British engineering.

By 1987, the workforce in pumps stood at 2,200 – half the 4,400 employed at the start of the 1980s. But the organizational changes went much wider than manning levels. Other lessons were also learned and acted upon. 'We have put in an organization which means that information can't be hidden,' Garrick notes. 'Responsibility is separated, not concentrated as it was before, so that when a contract is received the sales side passes the cost estimate to contracts, who take it over and are responsible for running it and checking against the estimate. That gives us total visibility: on every contract, we can see what the costs are to date, what it will cost to complete and who has made any mistakes: not to get after the people concerned, but to increase the knowledge of the people who are estimating, buying and so on. As a result, more and more people have an understanding of the dynamics of the business.'

Another child of the reborn Weir was related to this new transparency in financial organization. 'We tried hard to tell people what the important things were for the business in terms of initial survival, and where we saw constraints in performance. People respond to that well,' says Garrick.

Today, down to shopfloor level, there is open discussion of problem areas: 'Why we lost the last order; why we are facing a big loss on a particular job. We make that information available and ensure that it flows through the place so that people can understand what they must do. A lot of companies keep such information secret, but if you do what we do, then a lot of people can come up with solutions. It's not the board who comes up with answers, it's the guys down the line. After a while, this openness starts to feed on itself and once it does that, it becomes established in the system. We have got the company into a shape where I'd like to think people understood its problems better,' says Garrick.

The fundamental motive of this 'hearts and minds' drive for employee awareness is to 'allow innovation to flourish'. This, says Garrick, invokes Weir's traditional strength in technical engineering capability: 'Weir was always a quality outfit, the Rolls-Royce of pump-makers. Probably it was over-designed: it was a quality product but the organization was a bit sloppy. There are some strengths within every company.'

But in the new Weir, this technical ability has been fused with open communication into something different: a system dedicated to respond to market demands. 'We came through the Seventies being an organization which didn't really think very much about the customer, and in the Eighties we nearly came to grief. We thought, what must we do – we must provide for the customer. Now product development is led by sales and marketing, not by engineers.'

This precept has led to a succession of new products, including the turbodrill for the oil industry which gave Weir a world lead, and the downhole pump which improved the efficiency of oil extraction, but, equally naturally, to an emphasis on quality, reliability and service, underpinned by design. Weir has moved to modular pump design, so that if a unit fails, that piece of equipment can be immediately replaced without having to remove the whole product. Having secured its home market dominance by acquisitions which have mopped up other British pump manufacturers for the power oil industries, by emphasizing these non-price factors, Weir has set out to establish an international competitive advantage which does not depend on price. 'We are really a market-driven organization which has taken a bigger market share at better margins,' says Garrick, who is now hearing what he regards as the supreme compliment: 'Our Japanese and German competitors are talking about fierce international competition.'

Although Weir's rapid recovery from the trauma of 1981 prompted suggestions that it could have done without some of the agony, Tombs is convinced that it was necessary: 'I don't think the bullets would have been bitten without that sort of change.' Both at Weir and T&N, he was well incentivized for his work, though through share options rather than basic salary – which has always been modest compared with many other company leaders. 'I'm a great believer in payment by results. If you are being asked to pump water out of a sinking ship, there should be some reward for doing so,' Tombs remarks.

At T&N, he received a fee of £540,000 from National Westminster Bank and share options worth £600,000 from Prudential Insurance and M&G, for increasing the company's share price to a certain level by a certain date. Tombs points out that the options were taxed at 60 per cent: 'The Chancellor did rather better than I did out of it.'

One banker involved in several major 1980s corporate rescues has no doubt that Tombs and the other crisis managers were, and remain, worth their weight in gold simply for their liberating influence on company managements. 'Very often the new management is there: you've just got to appoint the deputies. There are demotivated guys in all these organizations who can perform wonders given the opportunity.' In Weir, three of the principal members of the new team – Garrick, finance director Ian Boyd and company secretary Bill Harkness – were already working for the group.

Where the banker does voice a doubt is over the suitability of some of the survival experts for management in the post-recovery phase. 'Some of these people who are terrifically good surgeons are not necessarily people who are good at developing the business, and the latter is much harder.'

If that is a rule, then Tombs is a notable exception to it. After more than seven years at T&N (which he left in late 1989) he maintains: 'If you go after the first stage, you miss the most interesting part of the job. You need two pairs of spectacles, one to look at the problems of today, this year and next year, and another to look way beyond the problems of survival to where you would like to be.

'You can't disconnect the two. If you just look at the long term, you don't survive; if you don't survive, you can't plan for the future. So you need harmonized views. British management's great mistal : for a long period of years has been failing to look at survival, which is the precondition of the future.'

Massive, once-for-all job-cutting and favourable exchange rates were the motors which fired ɔritish industry out of recession, fuelling cash inflows which replenished exiguous reserves. Strengthened balance sheets guaranteed survival, for the time being. But industry now entered a new phase, where basic survival was not enough. The imperative was to obtain and sustain growth. In this second phase of recovery, a battle was fought within manufacturing industry over the different means employed by companies to achieve that elusive short term-long term harmony.

CHAPTER FOUR
TAKING OVER

It was well past 5pm on Friday, 6 December, 1985. After hours trading in the Stock Market had closed. Most workers in the City of London were heading home, some no doubt still digesting the tumultuous events of the previous five days when takeover bids worth more than £4 billion had been made or proposed.

What happened next turned an already remarkable week into one of the most extraordinary in Britain's industrial and financial history. Hanson Trust, the conglomerate built by Lord Hanson and Sir Gordon White over the previous 21 years into the fifteenth biggest British company, launched a £1.89 billion hostile bid for the John Player cigarettes company Imperial Group.

By a mere £30 million, Hanson's offer was the largest takeover bid ever tabled in Britain. The record it broke had been set only four days earlier, when James Gulliver's Argyll stores group made a long-anticipated bid for the Scottish whisky giant Distillers. That same Monday, an equally widely-predicted £1.2 billion merger had been announced between United Biscuits, the McVitie's and KP Nuts group – and Imperial. In between then and Friday, the giant GEC had announced its intention to bid £1.1 billion for the smaller electrical and electronics company Plessey.

But it was the breathtaking move by Hanson that established 2–6 December as five days which shook the takeover world. The earthquake detonated by Hanson's intervention was both a culmination of tremors felt since the start of 1984, and a seismic disturbance of such Richterian scale that its reverberations were still to be heard as the decade drew to a close.

While Hanson's bid was the epicentre, the GEC-Plessey plan provided a unifying link with Britain's takeover past. The 1968 battle between GEC and Plessey for English Electric, which GEC won, helped to make that year of student revolution also the biggest year for deals in post-war British industrial history. At constant 1986 prices, the value of acquisitions and mergers in 1968 totalled £11.5 billion – marginally higher than the £11.4 billion total in 1972, the second biggest year by far (*DTI Business Monitor*).

Until 1986, that is. Although the GEC bid for Plessey fell by the wayside, being blocked by the Monopolies Commission, the concurrent battles between Hanson and United Biscuits for Imperial, and between Argyll and its rival Guinness for Distillers, ran on to the point where the Imperial bids reached £2.7 billion apiece – just ahead of the £2.6 billion offered by both suitors for Distillers. The two takeovers together accounted for more than a third of the total value of acquisitions that year – a record-setting £14.9 billion (1986 prices, *DTI Business Monitor*).

They may have taken place side by side, but the contests for Imperial and Distillers were fought on different planes. Distillers was a street fight littered with dirty tricks and suspect practices – ending, two years later, in the legal proceedings against several in the Guinness camp and some who had supported it. The alleged extremes to which Guinness chairman Ernest Saunders, his close associate Thomas Ward, and adviser Roger Seelig of merchant bank Morgan Grenfell went to secure victory appear to have reached a unique scale. The other, quite distinct point, is that the level at which battle was conducted at the start was to some extent influenced by the depths of decline and inertia to which Distillers had sunk.

Imperial, on the other hand, was on the way up – albeit from a low base, having just extricated itself, at considerable cost, from its disastrous American diversification into the Howard Johnson motels group. But although Imperial made the first move, and although its foods division chief Gerry Sharman had initiated the idea of a deal with UB, Imps was really only the anvil on which Hanson and UB's chairman Sir Hector Laing hammered out their diametrically opposed corporate philosophies.

No anvil was more valuable. The importance of Imperial to both parties was not so much what it did as what it was. It was stuffed full of strong brand names – HP Sauce and Golden Wonder crisps, Courage Bitter and Harp lager. But above all, it had tobacco. It was not in itself the brands – Castella, Embassy, John Player – that so attracted UB and its non-smoking chairman. Indeed, a streak of Scottish puritanism in the Edinburgh-registered group's corporate culture did not incline it favourably towards the weed. But what overrode any moral reservations UB might have entertained was the enormous cash flow generated by the terminally, but slowly, declining tobacco business.

Imperial Tobacco produced the massive total of £100 million a year in cash. It may not have been Benson and Hedges, but for both UB and Hanson that was pure gold. UB made biscuits and Terry's chocolate oranges, served up hamburgers in Wimpy restaurants and pizzas in Pizzaland – and ate cash. Between 1975 and 1985, the group made four cash calls on shareholders to fund acquisitions and investment, notably in its American biscuit business Keebler, which faced tough competition from Nabisco and Procter & Gamble. Only 2½ months before the Imperial deal was announced, UB issued yet more shares to part-fund its $73 million purchase of Early California Olives.

Because of all this new paper, UB's earnings per share growth had lagged way behind its considerable sales and pre-tax profits expansion. Between 1983 and 1985 alone, while sales climbed from £1.4 billion to £1.9 billion and pre-tax profits from £83.3 million to £102.2 million, fully diluted earnings edged up from 17.9p to 18.7p and back slightly to 18.5p. As a result, UB shares had underperformed the Stock Market for much of the decade. No-one doubted UB's industrial management ability to squeeze margin improvements out of its mature British biscuit business, but the fact remained that this business had been like a treadmill, demanding incessant capital investment (and incurring ongoing rationalization costs) for relatively little increased return.

Keebler, acquired in 1974 and the largest single unit in the group, was recognized as a good business, but it too was cash demanding – particularly when the so-called 'soft cookie war' hit part of its market in the mid-1980s. Terry's had been bought in 1982, one further step in a strategy of diversification away from biscuits which had begun with the purchase of Wimpy in 1976. Terrys looked a good buy. The quality of other deals, like the Speciality Brands business (bought in 1979) to which Early California Olives was added, was less certain. The upshot was that Laing and the company he chaired were not universally loved by either the City's food manufacturing analysts or the investing institutions. Ultimately, this fact told decisively against Laing's case for the Imperial deal, and added potency to the philosophical conflict sparked by the bid battle and still unresolved as 1990 approached.

However, neither could Hanson be entirely sure of its ground after a year which had already been the most eventful in the group's extraordinary history. Once the darling of the City, its share-price performance had deteriorated of late as investors sensed that the group had grown to a size where earnings advances would be exceedingly difficult to sustain. All UB's rights issues together came to nowhere near the blockbusting £519 million cash call made by Hanson six months before the Imperial bid. That call – the second-largest rights issue ever made in Britain – was not answered by investors with great enthusiasm: only half the ordinary shares offered were taken up, although the rest were subsequently placed. Nevertheless, Hanson did now have £1.2 billion in its war-chest.

What it did not have was an unblemished recent record of takeover success. Its last completed bid, for the lacklustre industrial holding company Powell Duffryn, had ended 11 months earlier with a whimper, as Hanson refused to increase its offer.

But there was method in Hanson's apparent meanness. With the hindsight inspired by the Imperial battle, it seems clear that the main aim of the Powel Duffryn move – at £180 million, a sideshow for Hanson – was to give the City an object lesson to the effect that Hanson would not overpay for anything. It appeared designed to erase the impression left by Hanson's preceding British bid for London Brick, which the group had raised three times – an unprecedented decision, and one into which Lord Hanson felt he had to some extent been forced (*Takeovers* by Ivan Fallon and James Srodes, Hamish Hamilton).

If the Powell Duffryn exercise achieved its psychological aim and restored Hanson's full credibility as the most astute takeover exponent in the country, then the Imperial bid promptly threw up a fresh challenge. It meant that for the first time, Hanson was fighting massive takeover battles on both sides of the Atlantic.

In August 1985, Hanson's fellow Yorkshireman and long-time

partner Sir Gordon White had launched a $750 million bid for SCM, best known for its Smith Corona typewriters. It was by far the biggest move made by White in the 12 years since he had established Hanson's American arm. Moreover, it had proved a bitter battle, fought as much in the courts as out in Wall Street, mainly against the financial services titan Merrill Lynch which was attempting a defensive leveraged buy-out of key SCM businesses.

The SCM battle was still running, now entering its fifth month, when Hanson descended on Imperial. The speed of the move took the UB-Imperial camp aback. The day before Hanson's stunning intervention, Laing declared that he was 'as sure as I can be – although that is obviously not very sure – that there won't be a takeover bid for Imperial or us.' He added: 'I don't know who would do it. US companies on the whole do not make opposed takeovers, and in this country I don't see anybody.'

Imperial chairman Geoffrey Kent may have had an inkling of Lord Hanson's interest – the two men were non-executive directors of Lloyds Bank and Kent had asked Lord Hanson that summer to join the Imps board as a non-executive, but Hanson had politely declined the invitation (*Takeovers*, Fallon and Srodes). In fact, Hanson had been stalking Imperial for two years. As Imperial's Howard Johnson-inflicted problems had mounted, so had bid speculation, with Hanson frequently tipped in Stock Market despatches as the predator.

The Imperial-UB deal was received with some scepticism in the City, where it was branded a defensive move by both take-over-threatened sides, with questions asked about the willingness of Imps' shareholders to accept a deal which would have left the smaller UB with a disproportionate share in the enlarged group. Hanson was immediately the name on many lips as a likely counterbidder.

Nonetheless, Hanson's willingness to countenance a bid for Imperial before it could know the outcome of its SCM offer demonstrated a breathtaking confidence in its takeover abilities. It also marked an apotheosis for the group whose origins lay back in 1964 when James Hanson and Gordon White bought into Wiles Group, a Yorkshire coal sack hirer and fertilizer business.

In the ensuing years, Hanson and White had built up the expertise and the structure of the company (renamed Hanson Trust in 1969) to the point where it was ready to handle two simultaneous bid battles. The group was, and remains – despite its many imitators – a unique corporate entity. Geographically, Hanson is concentrated almost entirely in the two domestic markets of Britain and the United States (exports and overseas involvement elsewhere have been minimal except in the Ever Ready battery subsidiary with its strong South African business). White runs the United States side while Hanson looks after Britain, with the simple concept of balancing the business roughly 50–50 between the two.

In product terms, Hanson has looked for the most basic businesses – shoes, bricks, frankfurters and duty free stores (these last two sold before the end of 1989), vending machines and car heaters. And no excess baggage like the desire for long-term industrial logic has encumbered its progress. If a business – any business – can command a premium price, it may be sold. One former Hanson manager observes that the only operation that ever receives the chairman's special, personal attention is the original Wiles sacks business.

For more than one reason, therefore, Imperial was the ultimate Hanson business. Products did not come much more basic than beer, tobacco and food. With each of those three principal divisions a prize in itself, Imps was made to be broken up. And in the meantime, it offered enormous short-term scope for improving returns: it was making pre-tax profits of £220 million on sales of £4.66 billion. Hanson had pre-tax profits of £250 million on sales of £2.7 billion. Not surprisingly, Hanson was valued at about £2.5 billion against Imperial's £1.6 billion.

But for United Biscuits (with a Stock Market worth of £1.2 billion, the smallest of the trio), Imperial was the business opportunity of a lifetime. Laing explained the merger's logic: 'We have a unique opportunity for the British food industry to operate in the world class. Rather than just be minnows in a world pool, we will be able to swim along with the whales. If we can't form major food groups in this country, the consequences will be that American companies ultimately buy up our British companies.'

As support for the idea of tobacco-food marriages, he could cite recent industrial precedents from across the Atlantic. In two giant moves within the previous year, UB's long-standing rival Nabisco had been bought by R. J. Reynolds, creating a group with £13 billion annual sales, while tobacco major Philip Morris had taken over General Foods to produce a combine with annual turnover of £15 billion. Laing sounded an apocalyptic warning. Backed by their tobacco cash flows, the new American groups would have massive resources to deploy in new markets like China and South America, he declared. The Americans 'are going to use that strength to hammer food companies round the world. It's no use us sitting down here thinking things haven't changed.'

From the moment that Hanson entered the lists, the contest became a battle for Imperial shareholders' hearts and minds between Laing's long-term industrial vision and Hanson's emphasis on secure, guaranteed financial returns. Less than an hour after Hanson launched its bid, director Martin Taylor attacked the UB-Imps proposal. 'We can see the value of the proposal from the United Biscuits management's point of view. But I'm not sure that we perceive the value for Imperial shareholders of seeing their cashflow invested in biscuits for the Chinese,' said Taylor.

Hanson sustained this line of attack throughout the battle. At one point, Sir Gordon White flew in to dismiss UB's pretensions to compete with RJR Nabisco (as the merged group was renamed) and Philip Morris-General Foods. 'Living and working in America,' White opined, 'I feel great sympathy for anyone who attempts to take on these great American food giants. I would not want to put two cents into a war against them. We are just not big enough in this country.'

The issues were defined still more sharply when, under the pressure exerted by Hanson, UB stripped away the original merger facade and made an outright (and agreed) bid for Imperial. UB's bid expired before Hanson's, and it was in the last week of UB's offer – effectively the end of the contest – that the clash between Laing's vision and Lord Hanson's version of it reached a climax.

All along, Laing had plugged away with his view that the UB-Imps deal was in tune with the times because the food industry was going global. Hanson dismissed the notion. A global food business was 'nonsense, because such a thing doesn't exist. To talk of global products sounds the most grand and patriotic thing to say, but I heard

Harold Wilson say the same thing about British Leyland. It's a pattern for disaster. The only global food and drink products are Coca-Cola and Pepsi-Cola . . . The only really truly international people are the oil companies. All Imperial would do for United is to give them the resources for something which won't succeed.'

UB's Keebler biscuit business in the United States was 'a minnow' beside Nabisco and General Foods, Hanson said: 'If you take on the American food giants, then you've got to have a good deal more knowledge than just a dream. "I have a dream" is what Hector is saying, but he has indicated no plans as to how he's going to break into those (overseas) markets.' Instead, declared Hanson: 'He'll get his brains beaten out in the US.'

Laing responded to this comment, reported in *The Scotsman*, by sending Hanson a leaflet showing that Keebler had been out-performing all its American cookie and cracker competitors. He attached a note, which read: 'Keeping my sense of humour high, the enclosed demonstrates how I am getting my brains beaten out! And I'm enjoying it!'

Despite Laing's joviality, Hanson had the last laugh. When UB's £2.8 billion bid ended on Friday, 18 April, 1986, it had received acceptances from shareholders with only 19.2 per cent of Imperial. UB already owned 14.9 per cent, leaving it with a total 34.1 per cent – well short of victory.

UB's defeat was a strange affair, partly occasioned by the fact that Hanson's offer did not expire at the same time. As a result, many financial institutions with Imperial shares did absolutely nothing on that decisive Friday, voting for neither UB nor Hanson. This element – accounting for up to 15 per cent of the Imperial register, on one estimate – highlighted the dismissive manner with which most of the institutions turned their backs on Laing's grand design to create United Imperial, as the group was to be called. Nothing became their attitude so much as the way they left the UB-Imps plan to wither and die on the vine.

Perhaps the most bizarre case of all, however, concerned the Norwich Union insurance group, a major Imperial shareholder, which cast its vote against UB almost a month before the end of the bid for the simple reason that the board meeting at which the decision was taken was the last scheduled before UB's offer expired. Despite subsequent representations from the UB-Imps side, and some reconsideration of the issues, Norwich Union stuck by its original decision.

It was joined in its support for Hanson by the Prudential and Legal & General insurance groups. This trio together held about 12 per cent of Imperial. Major institutions which backed UB and Imps included the M&G fund management group and two of the biggest pension funds, PosTel and the National Coal Board (now CIN).

There were several reasons why UB failed so conclusively to bring off the deal that would have taken it into another dimension. Clearly the biggest factor was the nature of the opposition. The major institutions had a huge commitment to Hanson through investment in the group. And as the battle drew to a close, they were left in no doubt how vital it was for Hanson's future that this, of all bids, be won. But the need to justify their investment in Hanson was not the only element. There was also the utter certainty, the predictability, of what would happen if Hanson won. One investment manager declared: 'The deciding point is where do you go in two years' time? There are certain benefits to be gained immediately, whether it's Hanson or UB. Hanson has a proven record of developing companies by acquisition and expansion. That was the clincher.' He omitted the word 'disposal', but the point was made.

The familiarity with Hanson's approach was counterpointed by the uncertainty about United Imperial, as the new group would have been called. One institutional fund manager commented: 'I don't believe that the benefits which they [UB and Imps] claim will result from the merger could necessarily be carried out in practice.' Another observed: 'I have some sympathy with the idea of a global foods company, but I'm not totally confident that they'll achieve it.' A third fund manager was harsher, dismissing Laing's case for an international British-owned consumer products group as rhetoric which 'didn't match the position that United and Imperial would have been in. He [Laing] was not talking about an international group, but one which would have enlarged his business in the United States and, with tobacco, given him a cash flow to finance this US cookie war.' After all Laing's efforts to communicate his ambitions for United Imperial, this interpretation of his intentions represented the ultimate City rejection.

The complete misunderstanding of UB's objectives could not

be blamed entirely on the fund manager concerned. It stemmed partly from United Biscuits' record of communication with the financial community, which was not particularly good.

UB's attitude to the City, and the financial community's feelings about UB, epitomized the gulf between the two spheres. Out in what Laing might have called the real world, UB was a model company: socially conscious, if in a rather paternalistic fashion; an early participant in the Business in the Community movement for fostering local enterprises; founder of the Per Cent Club, whose member companies contribute 0.5 per cent of their profits to social causes in the community. UB under Laing had devoted rather less time and attention to its relationship with the financial institutions. During the bid, Laing came to appreciate this omission. But his efforts to repair it appeared ambivalent.

In the last fortnight of the bid, as Hanson's offer of cash and convertible loan stock held the lead it had maintained almost throughout over UB's shares plus cash offer, Laing exhorted Imperial shareholders to support UB: 'Let's not just sit down and get more earnings per share. Let's actually create something. If things as big as this are going to be decided on the share price over a very short term, then I suspect we won't have too much industry left. When the unions wanted to take the highest thing that was on offer, they then complained about unemployment. If the City wants to take the highest things on offer, which is with somebody [ie Hanson] who doesn't invest, then we in industry will be criticized for not investing.'

Laing might have started out with the intention of accommodating the City view, but all his instincts and gut feelings that City priorities were inimical to those of a successful manufacturing business soon took over. He emerged from the bid declaring that UB 'really must be more in touch with the institutions'. Therefore, he said: 'We have to put more emphasis on earnings per share, even if it means that we have to watch our investment policy more carefully.' But UB's brands did not include humble pie, and Laing continued to browbeat the City. 'In looking at earnings per share, the underlying reasons for it should be examined: is the company investing enough? Is it keeping our industry the most efficient in the world, the lowest-cost producer?' he asked.

Then he delivered another treatise on good industrial practice and institutional responsibility: 'United Biscuits' procurement decisions used to be taken by managers down the line. Then we set a strategic objective to buy more British materials. Since then, we have saved £15 million a year in imports. I hope there is a link between that, and the directors of the great institutions saying, "we leave the decisions to the fund managers". A lot of decisions about whether to accept the Imperial bid were taken down the line, because the institutions couldn't suddenly change the way they work. I'm sure that, as a result of the bid, institutions have been concerned as to whether they are taking a long-term view. I think we've at least put that question mark in the minds of many.'

Laing was correct in identifying the fact that the Imperial battle had highlighted the great issue of City-industry relations. But the truth of the matter was cloudier than his own view of it. Apart from UB's own comparative neglect of the City, there were the group's evident shortcomings as an investment. For all its manifest, low-cost efficiency (returns on capital employed of around 20 per cent through most of the 1980s) the group was not a particularly attractive entity. Yes, it was Britain's national champion in biscuits, successful in the home market and in America, but biscuits was essentially a mature business in these markets. Snacks were dominant in the United Kingdom. Confectionery was small beside the British giants Mars, Cadbury and Rowntree. Restaurants looked a slightly uncertain proposition, an impression confirmed in June 1989 when UB decided to sell the business. And UB's other diversifications – notably Speciality Brands – were more dubious still.

UB was boxed in, dependent for growth on geographical expansion in biscuits and further product diversification. Both these routes would be expensive. A decisive majority of Imperial share-holders did not trust Laing to make best use of their company's money.

It was Catch-22: UB's only chance of breaking the funda-mentally vicious circle of growth by attrition or equally costly acquisition was to get its hands on Imperial, but because of its earnings record – caused by this growth impasse – the institutions would not sell Imperial to UB. And by denying Laing that oppor-tunity of a lifetime – access to resources that were quite unique – the institutions condemned UB and its shareholders (including many of themselves) to a future more like the past.

A FIGHTING CHANCE

The full ramifications of the Imperial battle were still working themselves out as the decade neared its end. But it opened plenty of windows immediately, and despite the flaws revealed in UB, many faults lay on the other side. The charge that could most obviously be levelled against the institutions for backing Hanson was one of short-sighted lack of imagination, a defect emphasized by the sheer predictability of the bid's outcome. As one fund manager kindly disposed to UB commented two days before the deadline: 'Hanson will win, and that will be a pity.'

All along, Laing's grandest card was his appeal for Imperial shareholders to embrace his vision of a new British consumer products group able to hold its own worldwide. Against it, Hanson had astutely ranged its emphasis on the returns that it could guarantee to wring from Imperial. Hanson argued on international industrial grounds only to disparage UB's claims for the Imperial alliance. The company had no pretensions to the world of global industry. It ran basic businesses in two domestic markets – America and Britain. Exports were negligible. So was continental European and Pacific Basin involvement.

The concept of business 'synergy' – the combination of two supposedly complementary businesses to make a whole greater than the sum of the individual pieces – was wittily derided by Lord Hanson as being 'like the Yeti: it is believed to exist, but few can claim to have seen it'. The only part of Imperial that Hanson appeared certain to retain was the tobacco business. The foods and brewing and leisure sides looked destined for sale, and the only eventual surprise was that Courage went first, while Hanson retained Imperial Foods for two years. What happened to Imperial Tobacco was entirely predictable. Its British market share, already falling at the time of the bid, slid downhill under Hanson as marketing spend took second place to cashflow maximization.

No greater contrast could have existed than that between the Hanson internalized 'break up and enjoy' approach and United's expansion thrust. In geographical terms, UB stood almost exactly where Hanson did: 96 per cent of its sales were made in Britain and the United States. The difference was Laing's claim that Britain needed United Imperial to help secure the food manufacturing sector's prosperity. The national interest argument did not wash with the institutions. 'I'm not really sure that we should actually determine our future policy on arguments like that alone,' said one insurance group. 'If it doesn't interest the Government, why should it interest us? Our interests have to be the long-term benefits to our policyholders. The other things all ought to lead to that.'

The group did not ignore the issue of what influence the institutions wielded over the shape and competitiveness of British industry. 'It's a question we address ourselves to from time to time.' And the answer was that the same limitations applied to the institutions as to the Government: 'Mrs Thatcher has often said she can't affect the unemployment of the country. She can merely change the conditions in which unemployment exists.'

This was patently not the case with United Imperial, a vote for which would have overthrown the status quo that was instead reinforced by Hanson's victory. But a more pointed explanation for the institutions' refusal to acknowledge their significance came from one pension fund manager. Suggestions that the institutions had a key part to play in determining British industry's future, he said, were 'the sort of view that investment managers shy away from. They'd rather not believe that they have the power to make those sorts of decisions. They'd rather not be given that responsibility.'

As the volume of takeover activity built up even before that watershed first week of December 1985, so did controversy over the pressures to which companies were subjected by their shareholders. The debate soon became characterized, in shorthand polemic, as a battle between long- and short-termism. Long-termism meant that companies should be given time to achieve returns on the investments they required to secure sustained competitiveness; short-termism was the pressure applied by financial institutions demanding instant results to justify their own, very different investment.

This was a crude, though not entirely inaccurate, simplification of a debate which was properly initiated on 24 October, 1985 in a speech to the Glasgow Finance and Investment Seminar by David Walker, the Bank of England director responsible for industry, who had been at the centre of many corporate rescue operations during the recession.

With hindsight, the location acquired an additional significance given the subsequent major bids involving Scottish-based
companies – UB, Distillers, the textiles groups Coats Patons and
Dawson International, and oil company Britoil. More crucially, the
debate that Walker started was still running, having naturally evolved
and grown in sophistication, as the decade drew to a close – with little
sign that it was nearing a resolution satisfactory to British manufacturing industry.

It was the time the speech was made, rather than the place
where it was delivered, that most concerned Walker. British industry
had put the recession behind it. The takeover wave that was swelling
up was a sure sign of returning confidence. But, as Walker saw, it was
also a threat which could divert companies from making the changes
necessary to secure their future in the new world of international
competition.

Walker's view was that many companies still occupied
'standard product areas where, despite the large efficiency gains
achieved over the last few years, the actual or prospective comparative
cost production of British producers is often weak'. The companies
needed to move up-market, where cost and price mattered less. 'But
such products tend to involve long lead times, which means substantial foresight and the ability to make a significant advance
commitment. In other words, there is a problem of how to reconcile
short-term horizons of portfolio investors with the need for boards to
make long-term commitments to particular lines of Research and
Development, product development and capital spending.'

Walker noted that, buoyed by the still-rising bull market, fund
managers were dealing more frequently: in 1979, unit trusts had
turned over 35 per cent of their portfolios and insurance companies
had turned over 11 per cent. Five years later, the proportions had risen
to 54 per cent and 18 per cent. The reason, he said, was clear: 'the
increased attention to performance on the part of portfolio managers
which, since it is measured only on a short-term basis, means that they
are unavoidably driven to concentrate on the short-term rather than
the long haul.'

He acknowledged that such increased activity could sharpen
up complacent managements, but the burden of his speech was that

this benefit was likely to be outweighed by the damage institutional short-termism was doing to corporate psychology. The central factor identified by Walker was the takeover threat. It underscored 'an attitude that attention to the longer run is a luxury and risk that can be indulged only within tight limits, especially by companies that see themselves as potential takeover targets'.

Walker made the point that in many cases the possibility of takeover was more imagined than real. Nevertheless, as the year turned into 1986 and the wave of bids increased, a feverish mood developed in which it seemed that almost any company could be a target. The concern extended to companies such as Smiths Industries, which had been among the first to follow the up-market route subsequently recommended by Walker. At the end of January 1986, Dr John Constable, then director-general of the British Institute of Management, told a conference on diversification strategy held by the Society for Long-Range Planning: 'Many senior executives feel that the acquisition process is out of control and producing inordinate emphasis on the short term. Much that is done in the name of diversification strategy is today driven by quite other forces. Those forces are not, in my view, serving the long-term interest of the UK economy.'

Constable went to the heart of the matter when he remarked that the takeover boom on both sides of the Atlantic had made management decision-making in Britain and the United States 'very short-term'. He declared: 'This might not be such a problem if everyone else in the world would play the same game. Unfortunately, most of the existing and emerging industrially-powerful countries are taking very long-term views of product and market development. Our focus on the short term can only help ensure their long-term market success.'

The contrast in expansion strategies and takeover practice between the Anglo-Saxon nations and others, notably the two most successful manufacturing economies on earth in Japan and West Germany, where hostile takeover bids are virtually unknown, was and remains the essence of the debate sparked by the mid-1980s bid boom. What was really being explored was a hitherto neglected field of industrial relations: not the relationship between management and workforce, important as that remained, but that between managements and their shareholders, between those who ran companies and the financial institutions which majority-owned them.

Of course, as percipient participants in this relationship were quick to point out, the division was to some extent artificial. A large chunk of most companies was owned by other companies, through corporate pension funds managed by external organizations but controlled by company trustees. When companies complained about City short-termism, in the shape of financial institutions which accepted hostile takeover bids and, as the emotive phrase went, 'sold companies down the river', the financial community therefore had a ready answer: 'Physician, heal thyself'. The solution lay in the companies' own hands; it was for their own pension fund trustees to set the standards to which the fund managers must conform. As one fund manager, sympathetic to United Biscuits, commented after Hanson had won the Imperial Group battle: 'If City horizons are narrow, the only people who are at fault are the people who set the targets.' Antony Pilkington took him at his word during the BTR bid for Pilkington in 1986/7. The Pilkington chairman wrote to his counterparts in all companies whose pension funds held shares in Pilkington asking for their support.

But Pilkington was exceptional. There were few companies which had given much thought to the pension fund strategy issue when the takeover tidal wave built up in the mid-1980s. The only companies which had a demonstrably close connection with their own funds were probably those in which the fund actually had a large stake. The automotive, aerospace and industrial component maker Lucas Industries was one: its pension fund held about 16 per cent of the group at one stage. Perhaps the most celebrated example of fund influence in such a situation occurred when the housebuilder Bryant defeated a hostile takeover bid with the aid of its own pension fund, which voted a crucial stake in Bryant's favour.

Following the Bryant case, and partly as a result of it, the practice of pension funds holding shares in their own companies fell into bad odour and was the subject of certain strictures by the National Association of Pension Funds. Questionable as such situations might have been (and might be) they dispersed an element of rough justice in a world where the scales seemed to be weighted in the bidder's favour. During the takeover boom, the onus often appeared to fall on the target to prove it deserved to retain its independence, not on the predator to justify its attack. In other words, if the defender could find something, anything, to support its cause then good luck to it.

This reductio ad absurdum contained the potential for causing damage – in the shape of perpetuated inefficiency – just as great as that inflicted by merger mania.

There was considerable truth in the argument that the great divide between industry and the City was as much the companies' fault as the financiers. Many companies did not work hard enough on their investor relations, or think deeply enough about the influence they could have on their pension fund investment strategy. But this was by no means the whole truth. The rise of the independent, external pension fund manager during the 1980s bull market created a momentum and competition of its own which required an enormous special effort to counteract. As every merchant bank developed its own fund management arm – Warburg Investment Management, which became Mercury Asset Management, was the biggest – this trend was followed by the rise of a small industry which monitored the fund managers' performance. The pioneer monitoring outfit started life inside stockbrocker Wood Mackenzie, but eventually set up independently as the WM organization, producing quarterly league tables of fund management performance. The next step was monthly performance measurement.

This development created its own pressure within the world of fund management. The driving force was to get into the upper quartile – the top 25 per cent. Below that, and insecurity set in. Trustees might see that their fund management group was not performing, and jettison it for an outfit which was. The edgy, uncertain, keeping-up-with-the-Joneses atmosphere this generated was probably the City equivalent of industry's paranoia about bids: companies whose earnings growth did not match the best saw themselves under threat of takeover; fund managers who underperformed in the league tables believed themselves under threat of the sack. In both cases, part of the threat was more perceived than real. But, as David Walker remarked in Glasgow, this did not lesson its impact on corporate behaviour.

The rise of pension funds' influence was immensely assisted by the tax system, which made contributions to pension schemes tax-free. Vast money pots developed during the bull market, and as one observer noted: 'I think they grew faster than their capacity to manage themselves. These managers had enormous responsibility, often without the maturity to match.'

But the character of these times, the mid-1980s, was extremist. There was no happy medium in which the companies that were bid for fully deserved to be on the receiving end, and those doing the attacking unquestionably had right on their side. Instead, the predators had might: the mighty advantage of shares rated highly, relative to those of their prey, on a booming Stock Market. A bidder with shares rated at, say, 15 times earnings could offer its paper for that of a company valued at ten times earnings. Its shares were more attractive than those of the target, and victory in the bid brought undiluted earnings growth, thereby accentuating the share rating. Growth was aided and abetted by the somewhat lax merger accounting laws which allowed bidders to make write-offs on completion of the acquisition which could subsequently be added back to boost profits. Such sharp, but legal, practice was not unknown. The growth spiral twisted ever-upwards. This period was, as a merchant banker remarked several years later, one great paper chase.

The tenor of the times recalled less the merger boom 20 years earlier than the height of the Swinging Sixties with which that boom coincided. Earnest the Eighties may have been, but the takeover wave that swelled up from 1984/5 was redolent of much that characterized the Sixties. Along with the wonderful liberation from the stultifying labour problems of the Seventies, and the harshness of the recession, came an inevitable excess. Companies discovered the power of their paper in a booming market, and some of that power was abused. Equally, merchant bank advisers strove to find the edge over their rivals that would mean victory for their clients and lucrative fees for themselves. And out there among the institutional shareholders of target companies was the new breed of fund management group well disposed to take the chance of a quick profit on their investment.

This symbiosis highlighted the real truth about the mid-1980s takeover boom. Contrary to the propaganda of the 'City bad, Industry good' school, it was not manufactured by a parasitic financial sector determined to dismember honest, hard-working companies for the sake of a quick buck. That description was partially true of the takeover spree in the United States, but it did not translate to Britain, where *companies*, not financial groups, made the bids.

The British boom was the product of collusion between aggressive and ambitious companies, the merchant banks that advised them, and the elements in the Stock Market that responded to them by rating their shares highly and accepting their offers. The Market was the key. As Walker commented in early 1989: 'The bull run was well in train. There were quite big differences among the performances of different companies, facilitated by accounting conventions, which meant that the institutional investment manager could get for his £1 million investment very different performance within the same sector.' (The basis of most fund managers' equity investment strategy was and remains the different sectors of the Financial Times Share Index.)

The essential misgiving, which prompted Walker's original and prophetic Glasgow speech in October 1985 was that the takeover boom was unbalancing British industry at the very moment when it needed to be building a secure springboard for long-term international competitiveness. Takeover conditions were so favourable that acquisition was rapidly becoming the preponderant route to growth, eclipsing the organic method of capital investment. Conversely, companies' perceived need to keep shareholders sweet was encouraging dividend distribution to investors at the expense of retentions for investment.

To some extent, the acquisition orientation was perfectly justifiable. British companies, having lagged the growth of rival groups in other countries, needed to catch up in size as well as efficiency. But one problem with takeovers, demonstrated by contemporary studies in Britain and the United States, was that while they could certainly provide the former, they were no guarantee of the latter. Indeed, whether takeovers, overall, did produce greater effectiveness was highly problematic.

Other factors contributed to the dominance of acquisitions as the means to expansion. One chief executive, at the time managing director of a subsidiary business, notes that his parent company's centralization meant that 'I never had any money of my own, so I could not make the capital investments I wanted. Everything went back to the centre, where the acquisition decisions were taken.'

So the takeover boom ran on through 1986, with companies' immediate Stock Market performance apparently becoming ever more important as a determinant of the corporate future. While the more fickle institutions – the external pension fund organizations, unit trusts and all funds geared for growth rather than income – were a source of constant encouragement to bidders, there was an alternative constituency, whose founder members were the Pearl and Britannic insurance groups, which would not accept hostile bids at any price. The camp that tended to support incumbent management also included more discerning elements. One such was the M&G fund management group, which brought to bear a measured, distinctive and distinguished perspective notable for its absence elsewhere.

Between these two sides was the great open battlefield of the Stock Market, where most bids were won and lost. Dubious tactics were employed by financial advisers in some bids to influence the market. The stakes – whether you were a bidder or target – were big. Commented one merchant banker, defending a company in a particularly closely fought bid: 'The rewards for keeping an independent client are very high. To walk away with your fee for unsuccessfully defending a client is unexciting: at the end of the day, you don't have a client.' Winning was everything. And that end justified the means employed to achieve it.

The methods allegedly employed by Guinness to defeat Jimmy Gulliver's Argyll Group and take over Distillers seem to have been the most extreme reflection of this apparent win-at-all-costs approach. Appropriately and predictably, therefore, their discovery stopped the hostile takeover fad in its tracks. The fashion began to change on that day – 1 December, 1986 – when Department of Trade and Industry investigators descended upon Guinness's London head office and gave the first inkling that something had been amiss. By an entirely apposite historical coincidence, the inspectors arrived precisely one year after that amazing first week of December 1985 which ushered in the age of the megabid. When successive and rapid revelations showed that the investigation was concentrated on Guinness's conduct of the Distillers bid, hostile bids plunged dramatically out of vogue, with BTR's hotly-contested bid for Pilkington the biggest casualty of the swing in sentiment.

Momentous as it is, and the most dramatic memorial to the remarkable 1985/6 takeover boom, the Guinness scandal has concealed more than it has – at least so far – revealed about the vexed relationship between industry and the City.

The fundamental question that preceded the lurid battle which gave rise to the Guinness affair appears to have been forgotten: why, as one leading City figure puts it, was Distillers 'allowed to drift over a decade by institutional shareholders who sensed that it was drifting but did nothing about it, not even strengthen the board'.

Correspondingly, the immediate reaction against hostile bids triggered by the scandal obscured the fact that, below the surface, nothing in the relationship between companies and their shareholders had, in essence, changed. Instead, there was an ephemeral shift in the climate of takeover opinion which could easily reverse itself again.

As things turned out, December 1986 did mark the end of a brief but remarkable takeover era. Acquisitions did not stop – indeed, 1,125 companies were bought in 1987 compared with only 696 in 1986. But the deals were smaller, and more friendly. At constant 1986 prices, the value of 1987 acquisitions was slightly down on the peak of the previous year, at £14.8 billion. Of hostile megabids, there was no sign.

What changed the underlying – as opposed to the superficial – takeover conditions was the financial markets crash of 19 October, 1987, when share prices came tumbling down around the world as the great bull market abruptly collapsed. Worst hit of all the major world stock markets, worse even than New York where the slump had originated, was the London market, already in organizational turmoil because of the 'Big Bang' changes which had abolished its historic demarcation lines and opened it up to full international participation.

The first thing that happened in the backwash of the Stock Market slump was a rash of successful takeover bids where the bidder was offering cash. Scottish & Newcastle Breweries, for instance, had spent several years trying and failing to acquire the regional brewer

Matthew Brown. Now it swallowed Brown in one gulp. The reason was simple: the commitment of many financial institutions to investment in the Stock Market, born of the cult of equity being embraced by younger fund managers who had only ever seen the market go one way, now looked dangerously unbalanced. Many institutions, though not all, were long on shares and relatively short on cash. When October 19's financial hurricane struck, everyone rushed to go liquid. Cash bids offered a perfect exit.

But cash was only king for a while. Institutions rebalanced their portfolios, and fund managers, grown older and wiser almost overnight, determined that they would never over-expose themselves to equities again. Policy-holders' cash flowed into the life assurance companies and pension funds, automatically reducing their relative investment in shares. Unit trust investment sagged.

While this realignment was taking place among the institutional shareholders, a far more profound shift in the balance of takeover power was occurring in industry. Overnight, the October crash wiped out the frothy price-earnings multiples that had fuelled the takeover boom. Ambitious companies could no longer leverage themselves up and up on the back of shares rated massively higher than those of their targets. Numerous companies which had relied on acquisition to produce earnings advances but had failed to establish critical mass, were beached on the corporate shore by the receding takeover wave, left high and dry and gasping to keep their growth alive. The paper chase was over. As a result, while demand for takeover activity by the mergers and acquisitions departments of the merchant banks remained as strong as ever, the main source of supply was choked off.

19 October, 1987 marked the real end of the essentially parochial, mid-1980s British takeover craze. What happened next set a tone which was still growing in strength as the 1980s turned into the 1990s. The British takeover scene acquired an international dimension potentially so enormous that, as the decade drew to a close, its full significance remained untold.

From the outset, this new takeover phase was far more fundamental than the bull market-driven phenomenon of mid-decade. Of the nine hostile bids worth over £1 billion made in

1988, seven included a foreign bidder. In all, 43 per cent of British public takeover volume was accounted for by overseas companies, compared with only ten per cent in 1987 (*Acquisitions Monthly*, January 1989).

Two of the bids – Goodman Fielder Wattie's for Rank Hovis McDougall and Elders IXL's for Scottish & Newcastle – owed at least part of their motivation to the Australian drive, backed by the country's banks, to increase assets overseas. (Both were ultimately barred by the Monopolies and Mergers Commission and the Government.) A third, the near-£3 billion offer by Luxembourg-registered Minorco for Consolidated Gold Fields that beat Hanson's record to become the biggest British bid ever, was driven by the desire of Minorco's South African parent Anglo-American to create an alternative investment base overseas.

The others – the rival bids for York chocolate company Rowntree by Swiss foods groups, Nestlé and Suchard, property group Rodamco's bid for Hammerson, and the Anglo-German electronics alliance of GEC and Siemens against Plessey – all sprang from a common source: the Europeanization and globalization of industry.

And whatever their diverse provenance, the foreign bids made one, unanimous point: outside the United States, it was easier to launch and sustain a hostile takeover bid in Britain than in any country in the world.

That fact highlights the particular potency of the fresh takeover boom. If its internationalism established a new fundamental, this was compounded by a fundamental that was historic: the divide between British companies and the institutions that owned them, which created a massive opening for overseas bidders. The opening was widened still further by the Government's competition and takeover policy, which was thrown into dispute by the eruption of hostile bids from abroad.

The watershed battle that contained and defined the issues in this new takeover debate was over Rowntree. At 8.30 on the morning of 13 April, 1988, the Swiss chocolate and coffee group Jacobs Suchard sent its British stockbroker Warburg Securities into the Stock Market to buy almost 15 per cent of Rowntree (the maximum level permitted by Britain's Takeover Code) in a 'dawn raid'. Barely 35 minutes later, Warburg's mission was accomplished. At least one major fund management group sold its entire Rowntree holding. Other institutions 'top-sliced' – sold part of their stakes. Suchard declared that it planned to raise its holding to 25 per cent, but ruled out launching a full bid for at least a year unless a rival offer was made for Rowntree.

However, that statement of limited – albeit determined – intent distracted no-one from the fact that the York-based maker of Kit Kat, Aero and Smarties had, in the space of little more than half an hour, been transformed from a repository of famous British chocolate snacks into a hostage to Swiss fortunes.

The full force of public indignation fell not on Suchard but on the City, for disposing of such a strategic stake with such startling alacrity. Almost 18 months after the 1985/6 takeover boom juddered to a halt, the air was thick once more with accusations of institutional short-termism and charges that the financiers were selling out British industry. When, two weeks to the day of Suchard's dawn raid, its much larger compatriot Nestlé actually launched a full £2.1 billion bid for Rowntree, the row reached new heights of industrial xenophobia.

The Rowntree controversy could have proved highly enlightening. Instead, unfortunately, it was conducted at less elevated levels, with Rowntree portrayed as the innocent victim of a perfidious alliance between the Swiss and the City, while the cowardly Government looked on, refusing to intervene on the side of right. What made the bid battle such a strange affair was that the many lurid words spilled in the media contrasted sharply with the relative bloodlessness of the fight. Only blatant Government intervention could have prevented Nestlé, whose resources were so vast that it could afford to buy Rowntree for cash, from winning after Day One of its bid. Rowntree recognized as much, and started talking to both the Swiss companies (Suchard having eventually made a bid) as soon as Trade and Industry Secretary Lord Young made it clear that he was not going to block the bid. Nestlé was always Rowntree's preferred buyer, and when Rowntree agreed to accept a £2.55 billion offer on 23 June, it was simply bowing to the inevitable at the best price it could get.

What prevented many of the real issues in the Rowntree bid from being aired was the paradoxical combination of the uninformed public debate – much sound and fury signifying very little – with Nestlé's interest in keeping its hands clean so that shaking on an agreed deal at the end of the day would be easy. Nestlé was so big – its 1987 trading profits of £1.4 billion were as large as Rowntree's total annual sales; its sales of £13.5 billion were almost ten times Rowntree's – that it could simply absorb the populist criticisms of Swiss aggression.

Aggression was absent even from the approach of the more abrasive Suchard. In the end, Nestlé won without really breaking sweat, having quietly made the point, both to the Office of Fair Trading director-general Sir Gordon Borrie and to Lord Young, that, as Borrie later put it 'Nestlé has been in England for generations'. (*The Times*, 27 March, 1989). In other words, that it was a good British corporate citizen which would not do Rowntree, or the British consumer, harm. The conviction with which Nestlé could pursue this line was an ultimate demonstration of truly multinational industrial power that neither Rowntree, nor any other British food company apart from the Anglo-Dutch Unilever (which showed no interest in the situation) could even approach.

Yet beneath the calm surface, as unruffled as the waters of Lake Geneva on which Nestlé's massive glass-fronted head office at Vevey looks out near Lausanne, the Swiss giant had some biting criticisms of Rowntree's 1980s strategy. It questioned Rowntree's commitment to its famous brands; regarded the company's diversification away from confectionery into snacks like Riley's crisps and the American Tom's Foods as erratic, not whole-hearted, and ill-directed – this last on the grounds that a huge distribution network was needed if the diversification was to work; and viewed Rowntree's move into retailing, with the American biscuit The Original Cookie Company and confectionery outlets in Europe, as misconceived. Retailing and manufacturing, Nestlé maintained, did not mix.

This critical analysis, quietly made behind the scenes, was hard but fair. In the early 1980s, Rowntree had tried to expand from its European confectionery base into the huge United States market, but its £162 million bid for the Lifesaver company failed and Nabisco eventually bought the business. After that, Rowntree appeared to divert its attention into counterbalancing the confectionery side with snack foods: it bid for Huntley and Palmer in Britain, but again lost out to Nabisco. Then came the snacks acquisitions. The company, as finance director David Bowden explained on the day that the £140 million Tom's Foods deal was announced, wanted to expand 'both geographically and by product range'. It was not until August 1986 that Rowntree at last made a major acquisition which enlarged the heart of the business: it bought the American sugar confectionery company Sunmark for £155 million. But even that deal had an unfortunate sting in the tail: within four months, E. J. Brach, the third largest United States sugar confectionery group, came on the market. But Rowntree, having just bought Sunmark, could not afford to go for it and had to watch as Suchard bought Brach for $730 million.

In the meantime, Rowntree was plugging away in mainland Europe. KitKat was a genuine world brand (under a 1969 licensing agreement, Hershey handled KitKat in America, paying a royalty to Rowntree). Painstakingly, Rowntree built up Lion Bar in France and After Eight in West Germany. The company made progress, but from a small base insufficient to transform a picture dominated by the maturity of the British confectionery market. Earnings climbed strongly in 1983 and advanced again in 1984, but virtually stood still in the following two years.

The bottom line trend contrasted almost totally with Rowntree's share price performance. During the five years preceding the Suchard raid, the period when Rowntree had outperformed the FT 30-Share Index ran from mid-1984 to mid-1986. It was not anticipation of future strong profits growth which motivated the shares during that time: it was speculation, which focused on the Swiss, about a bid for Rowntree.

The rest of the time, Rowntree's shares were dominated by the market's perception of the confectionery industry as dull and offering little scope for dramatic growth. Before Suchard's raid, Rowntree had underperformed the all-share index by 20 per cent in the eight years from 1980. It had underperformed the food sector by 35 per cent. The institutional investors who sold shares to Suchard on 13 April were making instant decisions, but decisions backed by a history of poor Rowntree Stock Market performance.

One contention by some in the pro-Rowntree camp was that this underperformance could be blamed entirely on the City's blindness to Rowntree's long-term strengths. As Suchard's raid was followed by Nestlé's bid, and Rowntree's share price hit heights undreamed of by even its biggest supporters, the City was lambasted for its alleged ignorance about the value of brands. KitKat, Quality Street, Aero and the rest were jewels in the nation's consumer products crown, international brands of rare and compelling attraction. Except to the shareholders, who had failed totally to appreciate their significance.

Certainly, the speed with which Rowntree lost control of its destiny was shocking. On 27 April, the day of Nestlé's full bid, the company bought 15.8 per cent of Rowntree while Suchard raised its holding to 29.9 per cent. Rowntree had become 46 per cent Swiss. One authoritative estimate put the size of the arbitrage holding in the company – by investors betting on a higher offer – at up to 15 per cent, with institutions and some private shareholders holding the remaining 40 per cent. And all in the space of a fortnight.

Undoubtedly, many in the City – like most commentators – underestimated Rowntree's true worth. Their reasons for doing so were perfectly valid. As the fund manager who sold out entirely at Suchard's 630p a share raid price commented wryly afterwards: 'It was early in the morning, I had ten minutes to decide what to do, and Rowntree had underperformed for years.'

The underlying explanation for the free market's failure to value Rowntree at all accurately was simple: the stock was judged in the purely domestic terms of its performance on the London Stock Market, not in the context of international industry. The Stock Market and others knew little, and understood less, of that global context. That was one reason why the Rowntree bid proved both an education and a revelation. Few appreciated the extent of the rivalry between Suchard and Nestlé, and Nestlé's determination not to see Rowntree pulled into someone else's corporate orbit. Nestlé had little history of hostile takeover bids. Although a Nestlé intervention had seemed quite possible, even Suchard appeared to be taken aback at the alacrity with which Nestlé reacted.

But Rowntree had to carry a large share of the blame for the Market's manifest inefficiency in its regard. Over the years, it had done little really to explain itself to the City. Its chairman, Ken Dixon, was widely respected, but to all intents and purposes, the company appeared closeted in York, where its deep business roots extended into the social realm of the Joseph Rowntree charitable trust, backer of liberal causes. Its headquarters exuded an air of contemplation in character with the group's gradualist strategy, which Rowntree described as one of 'drip, drip, drip and eventually it will pay off'. When Rowntree ventured abroad, it was on the shopping trips which brought back not just confectionery companies but those diversifications which hinted that it lacked some faith in the growth potential of its staple business.

That inference may have been unfair. Perhaps the case was rather that an independent Rowntree did need to spread its business portfolio beyond confectionery. If so, that fact confirmed the fundamental reason why, far from being an outrageous instance of Swiss depredation, Nestlé's takeover of Rowntree was an eminently logical act which made complete international business sense.

The truth was that Rowntree needed a partner with which it could concentrate its resources on the one business, confectionery, where it was internationally strong. On its own, as the diversification showed, it was condemned to divide its resources to avoid over-exposure to the confectionery side, and enter businesses which were less than natural combinations with its core activity.

But this strategic conundrum had a corollary. To a group with the size, spread and resources which could allow Rowntree the comparative luxury of concentrating on the business it knew best, Rowntree could be an immense asset. According to Nestlé's estimates, Rowntree lay fourth in the world chocolate league with annual sales of 300,000 tons. Ahead of it were the American giants Mars (at 800,000 tons a year, the world leader) and Hershey, followed by Cadbury Schweppes of Britain with annual output of 320,000 tons. Suchard and Nestlé were smaller than Rowntree, lying fifth and sixth respectively.

Mars and Hershey were beyond the reach of the ambitious Swiss, but although Cadbury was bigger than Rowntree and in theory more vulnerable, since the American cinema owner and soft drink bottler General Cinema had taken a major stake in the British company, Rowntree presented a unique opportunity to establish its purchaser as the second largest chocolate producer in the world. Cadbury's product portfolio to a great extent duplicated that of the Swiss: it was regional in character – different brands sold in different countries – and limited in geographical scope, with strong positions in Britain and Australia, problems in North America and a minimal presence in mainland Europe. Moreover, despite an innovation effort which had produced Wispa, plus repackaging of older brands, it was quite heavily concentrated in the mature area of moulded chocolate bars. Suchard and Nestlé had much the same problem. But the strength of Rowntree lay in 'countline' products – chocolate-based snack bars – which were the biggest growth area in the business and, with KitKat the supreme example, were brands which could transcend national boundaries. In particular, Rowntree had made some headway in continental Europe, where the Swiss wanted to strengthen their bases prior to the establishment of the European Community's single market around 1992. Concern that as the barriers between EC members fell, those against outsiders might rise was another factor in the situation. Switzerland is not a member of the Community club.

It became apparent very quickly after the intervention of Suchard and Nestlé that both companies had been aware of Rowntree's complementary attractions for several years. Suchard had bought a small stake in Rowntree in 1984 and made overtures to the company about a link-up, but had been firmly rebuffed. Nestlé had also sought either a friendly takeover or a collaboration agreement in which Nestlé would take a significant minority stake in Rowntree.

The Swiss giant held precisely that position in the French cosmetics group L'Oréal, with the prospect of taking full control of the group in the mid-1990s. It had made firm suggestions to Rowntree in the late summer/early autumn of 1987, and accompanied the proposal with a warning that if Rowntree did not accept it as a protective 'big brother', the company could well find itself exposed to someone else's unwelcome attentions.

Immediately after that prophecy came true, with Suchard's 13 April raid, Nestlé renewed its proposal to Rowntree that it take a protective, but minority stake in the company. When this suggestion was again rejected, Nestlé resorted to its hostile bid. Nestlé managing director Helmut Maucher observed tellingly: 'It is very nice to stay independent, but one has to face reality. After Suchard, it was no longer a question of whether Rowntree would be taken over or not, but of who could do it. The company was on the market.'

Rowntree's slowness to appreciate the harsh facts of global business life that had suddenly invaded its smaller world may have been characteristic. At least the City immediately recognized that Suchard's raid heralded the end of Rowntree's independence. What virtually everyone completely underestimated was Rowntree's take-out value. Suchard's successful raid was pitched at 630p a share against Rowntree's pre-raid price of 483p. Nestlé's first offer was 890p a share, and its final, winning bid which topped Suchard's own 950p offer valued Rowntree at no less than 1075p a share or £2.55 billion.

Rowntree shareholders could never, in their wildest dreams, have imagined that the stock would reach such a height. Neither, it appears, did Rowntree itself. At the outset, the board had no conception of what value might ultimately be placed on the company.

The bid was a landmark because of the lesson that it handed out to British industry and British investors, British politicians and the British public – a lesson which Rowntree and those shareholders which sold out early both learned the hard way. Big international business was getting bigger. In this new, global drive for size the choice, as the *Financial Times* remarked in May 1988, a month before Nestlé won Rowntree, was: 'Buy, or be bought'. Those companies doing the buying might have to pay a high price, but those who did nothing would pay a higher one.

For all the particular defects of Rowntree's case for independence – its persistent strategic dilemma, slowness in making headway with its brands overseas, Stock Market underperformance – the company's takeover nevertheless raised real doubts that British industry in general was at a relative disadvantage in this new, globally competitive dimension.

The most fundamental question concerned the Government's approach to industry, as manifested in its competition policy. At the time, most of the competition-related controversy concerned the decision by Lord Young, taken on the advice of Sir Gordon Borrie, director-general of the Office of Fair Trading, not to refer either Nestlé's bid or Suchard's interest to a Monopolies and Mergers Commission inquiry. Criticism of this non-referral focused on the lack of bid 'reciprocity' – the fact that while the Swiss groups could take over Rowntree, they themselves were immune from such a bid because of limits on foreign share ownership (in Nestlé's case) and family control (Suchard). Nestlé produced some not entirely convincing counter-arguments. Against those who said that hostile takeover bids were impossible in Switzerland, it cited the recent merger of Asea of Sweden with Switzerland's Brown Boveri. The ABB agreement, creating the world's largest electrical equipment group, pioneered the transnational European mega-deal of which Nestlé's bid was another instance. But, said Nestlé, anyone who believed it was a merger of equals was wrong: in Switzerland, there was little doubt that Asea was taking over Brown Boveri.

ABB was scarcely comparable with the Nestlé–Suchard – Rowntree situation, and the British proponents of reciprocity had principle on their side. However, their claims lost conviction in practice as it became increasingly evident that Nestlé was going to win. The idea that Rowntree could ever bid for Nestlé was patently incredible. The force of the reciprocity arguments was drained by this basic empirical point.

There was indeed no good reason why the Swiss predators should be blocked by Borrie and Young, particularly given that the central competition policy criterion for judging mergers was the share of the relevant home market that would result from combination of the two companies concerned. Both the Swiss had infinitesimal shares of the British confectionery market (Nestlé's was only two per cent). Borrie commented later: 'In the Rowntree case, public concern was whipped up artificially to influence the Government.' (*The Times*, 27 March, 1989). Young made his disposition to clear the Nestlé bid very obvious at the outset, and an ineffective political lobbying campaign by the Rowntree side did nothing to change his view.

Since the competition authorities viewed Rowntree as an open and shut case for free market decision, what the bid battle needed if all the issues which it involved were to become universally visible was an alternative to the Swiss. It very nearly got one. Shortly after the Nestlé bid was launched, Cadbury-Schweppes and Rowntree held discussions about a possible agreed offer by Cadbury for its main British confectionery rival.

Cadbury's intervention completed a triangle which, if not exactly eternal, did confirm the geometrical relationship between

A FIGHTING CHANCE

Britain's three largest chocolate company owners. It was an isosceles triangle, because United Biscuits, its third component, had a much smaller confectionery business than Cadbury and Rowntree.

UB chairman Sir Hector Laing had courted Rowntree for years. But his overtures had met the same cold reception accorded to Suchard and Nestlé, even when the Terry's purchase made him a York neighbour of Rowntree. After the failure of the Imperial bid, Laing renewed his suit. Rowntree rejected him again. Then, in March 1988, Laing agreed to pay £335 million for Imperial's chilled and frozen foods subsidiary Ross Youngs, which Hanson had put up for sale. The price was regarded by several City securities analysts as high, but the deal was an opportunity which UB could not afford to miss to establish itself as second in the market to Bird's Eye, and one for which Laing had been waiting ever since UB lost out to Hanson two years before.

The hard irony was that the purchase came too late for UB's Rowntree aspirations. Instead, it made them quite unrealizable. When Suchard raided Rowntree only weeks after the Ross deal, UB was already committed elsewhere. Laing could only stand on the sidelines, a spectator as the fate of the British company that he had most coveted was decided by others.

Whether, even without Ross, UB could have mounted a realistic challenge for Rowntree is not certain. But at least it would have been in a position to try. The way UB found itself trapped by the fateful turn of events formed a bond with Rowntree's own American frustration, when the timing of its Sunmark purchase disabled it from bidding for the larger, highly complementary Brach.

Doubling the irony of UB's situation, the group found itself paying a latent, cruel penalty for its defeat in the Imperial battle. Had it won two years before, what might have been United Imperial would now have found itself perfectly placed to outgun Suchard and dispute Rowntree's future with Nestlé. Instead, UB found itself imprisoned by its limited resources. There was a final twist. Until Suchard suddenly descended on Rowntree, Nestlé's acquisitive eyes had been on a different British target: United Biscuits itself.

UB and Rowntree were therefore united, not only by the former's interest in the latter, but also by recent opportunities either lost entirely or gained at the wrong time, and even by the common source of interest they had attracted from overseas. Such was the harsh, global perspective on two major constituents of Britain's food manufacturing sector.

Cadbury's behind-the-scenes intervention into the Rowntree battle added a new angle to the slant given by the affair to the big three British confectionery-related groups. Of the trio, Cadbury had seemed in most imminent danger of receiving a hostile bid because of General Cinema's 17.7 per cent stake in the company. But what rendered Cadbury attractive to General Cinema also made it far more able to withstand a bid than Rowntree.

Cadbury might well have been another, larger Rowntree. Three years earlier, the group had looked ripe for takeover after problems in its North American confectionery business knocked 1985 profits back by 25 per cent from £124 million to £93.3 million.

In fact, by the time the 1985 results were declared, measures to recover the ground lost and to put that setback far behind Cadbury were well in train. Under Dominic Cadbury, chief executive since January 1984 and younger brother of then chairman Sir Adrian, the group was transformed in a corporate restructuring almost as complete as the merger with Schweppes which created Cadbury Schweppes in 1969.

Sweeping changes were made in the American management with numerous dismissals of incumbent executives and their replacement by a new team headed by Jim Schadt. Schadt's was one of three key appointments made in the nine months between December 1984 and the following September, the others being Derek Williams to head Schweppes in Britain, and Neville Bain to run the Confectionery business. All three men played vital roles in the rapid development that followed.

The central feature of Dominic Cadbury's strategy was concentration on the two core businesses – two 'streams', as Cadbury called them: Confectionery and Drinks. The decision marked a historic break with the direction Cadbury had previously followed. Like Rowntree, only earlier, the company had resolved that it must diversify from confectionery. 'If we are to continue to grow, we must look at ourselves not as a chocolate firm but as a food company,' remarked Adrian Cadbury in the early 1960s (quoted in *The Strategy of Takeovers* by Anthony Vice, McGraw-Hill, 1971). This strategy led to the development of Smash instant mashed potato and Marvel milk powder and, in March 1969, to the Schweppes merger, which was the biggest deal of an eventful year for bids. Aside from its carbonated soft drinks, Schweppes brought in Typhoo tea and Kenco coffee. Three years later, the group started a Health and Hygiene division by buying the Jeyes disinfectant business and got further into it in 1982, paying Reckitt and Colman almost £8 million for its industrial cleaning division which included toilet roll manufacture.

Four days in December 1985 encapsulated Dominic Cadbury's dramatic redirection of the group and testified to the end of the diversification era. On 16 December, Cadbury agreed the sale of Health and Hygiene to a management buy-out; on 19 December, it announced agreement in principle with the world leader Coca Cola to form a joint British soft drinks company, Coca Cola Schweppes Beverages. Five months later came the biggest single disposal: the £97 million sale of the (non-Schweppes) Beverages and Foods business, including Smash, Marvel, Drinking Chocolate, Kenco and Typhoo to another management buy-out called Premier Brands.

And after the disposals came the core business acquisitions. In soft drinks, Canada Dry – including the Sunkist brand – was bought in July 1986 for $140 million. Two months after that, Cadbury acquired 30 per cent of the American soft drinks company Dr Pepper. Soft drinks was clearly the principal dynamo – so much so that the City joked about renaming the company Schweppes Cadbury. But Cadbury did not neglect confectionery. In December 1987 it made its first major move into mainland Europe by buying the French company Chocolat Poulain.

Then came Suchard, Nestlé and Rowntree. Just as General Cinema used the Rowntree developments to stoke up speculation about its Cadbury intentions (it made an enigmatic statement which carefully excluded no eventuality), so Cadbury fastened on to the situation to raise public and political consciousness of the perceived threat to Britain's chocolate companies.

Behind the scenes, however, Cadbury went further. It and Rowntree explored the possibility of an agreed merger. This was not the first time that a Rowntree-Cadbury merger had been mooted. Indeed, the situation was uncannily reminiscent of events 20 years before, when the notion had been debated for the first time. Then, it was a hostile bid for Rowntree from the United States giant General Foods which provided the catalyst. While a rival offer for Rowntree by Schweppes was ruled out by its connections with the drinks trade (*The Strategy of Takovers*, Vice) Cadbury considered a bid, an emergency Cadbury board meeting being held immediately after General Foods launched its attack.

In the event, Rowntree repulsed General Foods thanks to the support of the Joseph Rowntree Trust, which had a controlling shareholding, and merged instead with Mackintosh, creating the company that attracted Nestlé and Suchard so many years later. Cadbury did not bid for Rowntree, merging with Schweppes the following year. But not before Adrian Cadbury had observed about Rowntree's defence against General Foods, in terms almost identical to those he used two decades later: 'Obviously this is a matter of great interest to us.' His comment came after another Cadbury board meeting which he had had to fly back from holiday to attend. He had been skiing – in Switzerland.

Twenty years later, the one-time majority holding of Rowntree's trustees had dwindled to 6.5 per cent. The attraction of a Rowntree-Cadbury merger, however, was as strong as ever. At first sight, the idea seemed totally out of the question. Together, the two groups would have about 60 per cent of the British confectionery market – something which the competition authorities would surely not tolerate.

However, the Rowntree bid had created an extraordinary atmosphere in which the apparently impossible suddenly seemed tantalizingly close to realization. Suddenly, everyone was talking about Europeanization and the need to judge the effects of takeovers on market shares and competition in a European, not a purely British, context. Young gave an exposition of Government competition policy which was presented as a restatement of existing attitudes but did explicitly recognize the European dimension. More than one insider close to the Rowntree–Cadbury talks believes that the Government was prepared to look kindly on a proposed merger of the two companies.

What killed the idea were the sheer practicalities of the situation. Whatever the Government's attitude, Borrie of the OFT, that champion of the British consumer, would without a doubt have recommended that a proposed Cadbury-Rowntree merger be referred to the Monopolies Commission. Almost equally certainly, Young would have had to take Borrie's advice. Since the aberrant days in the early 1980s when Lord Cockfield was Trade Secretary (before Trade and Industry were merged) and several times overruled Borrie, there had been few cases of Borrie's recommendation being disregarded by the Secretary of State. The only recent case, when Young's immediate predecessor, Paul Channon, had rejected Borrie's advice to refer the Cannon cinema group's proposed takeover of the EMI film business, was an unhappy precedent since Cannon had subsequently hit severe financial difficulties.

Even so, a Monopolies and Mergers Commission inquiry need not have formed an insuperable obstacle to Cadbury and Rowntree. Had a merger been proposed, Nestlé's bid and Suchard's share-holding might quite easily have been sucked into the ensuing inquiry. In the way of things politically, it was the absence of a British alternative which ensured that the Swiss would not be referred.

Stock Market realities played a more decisive role. By the time Cadbury surreptitiously entered the field, almost half of Rowntree was in Swiss hands. Since even a Government determined to bless a Cadbury-Rowntree deal might have had a hard time blocking both Nestlé and Suchard at the same time, the existing concentration of Rowntree shares would have given Cadbury a mountain to climb.

But the clinching factor was simple and twofold. Nestlé would pay almost anything but a silly price to win Rowntree. Cadbury could only afford to come anywhere near matching that price if it could make substantial post-merger cost savings. That meant job cuts and plant closures – the inevitable consequence of combining two strong domestic groups. This imperative inevitably invested Cadbury's approach to Rowntree with the air of a takeover rather than a friendly merger. And Rowntree reacted against it. In the end, it appears, chairman Ken Dixon and his colleagues preferred to deal with Nestlé (but not Suchard). Nestlé's sheer enormity held out the promise that Rowntree would retain a fair degree of autonomy; the British alternative, a Cadbury merger, would have been altogether less palatable.

The fact that, for very good reasons, a Cadbury-Rowntree merger plan never happened, should not distract attention from the flaw in British competition policy which meant that by the time such a deal was considered, the odds against it were too great.

Despite Lord Young's belated clarification of competition policy, the impression remains that the authorities were trapped in a time-warp entirely and unfortunately symptomatic of the prevailing 'hands-off' attitude to British industry. Essentially, competition policy's emphasis on the domestic consumer opposes the international industrial trend towards globalism. Despite protestations to the contrary, there exists a strong suspicion that the British authorities take insufficient account of business internationalization when assessing combinations of British companies which would create a large home market grouping.

Related to this doubt about competition policy, and reinforcing it, is the question of its readiness to anticipate changes in the business framework which were foreseeable at the time a particular judgment was made, even if they had not yet occurred. Borrie's attitude is straightforward: he has to make decisions based on existing circumstances, not indulge in bouts of crystal ball-gazing.

However, Borrie does not have the final say in whether a deal proceeds or not. That decision lies with the Monopolies Commission and the Government. And a lack of responsiveness to external business stimuli is all too entrenched in those quarters, too.

Essentially, Thatcherite non-interventionism was institutionalized in mergers policy in 1984, when the then-DTI Secretary Norman Tebbit published guidelines which established competition as the primary criterion for determining whether a deal should be referred to the Monopolies Commission. The Tebbit guidelines endured throughout the rest of the decade, including a restatement by Young in a 1988 Blue Paper. The Paper declared categorically: 'It is the exploitation through market power of UK customers – whether other UK industries or the final UK consumer – that is the appropriate touchstone for UK merger policy.' Young followed up, in a speech to the London Stock Exchange: 'My responsibilities are for the United Kingdom, not Europe nor the wider world. I look at mergers from the standpoint of the United Kingdom customer. It is competition policy which is the great shield of the consumer.'

There was one very good reason for the Tebbit guidelines. They were produced after the chaotic Cockfield period when the unpredictability of merger referrals had raised a chorus of pleas for greater consistency in decision-making. Establishment of domestic competition as the crucial factor enabled the Government then to hand the merger issue over to the OFT on one side and the Commission, if needed, on the other. The problem is that this structure has replicated in mergers policy the vacuum in industrial strategic awareness of which the Government has made such a virtue. By giving mergers policy a competition bias in the cause of consistency and non-interventionism, the Government has created a risk of one-sided and short-sighted decision-making.

Coincidentally, this danger was highlighted by a Monopolies Commission judgment of March 1984, three months before the Tebbit guidelines formalized what, by then, had become normal practice. The bid concerned was by GKN for the engine components maker, AE. Originally, AE had recommended the bid but subsequently changed its mind and the whole thing had ended up in the Commission. There it was ultimately roadblocked, primarily on the grounds that the huge share of the home market that a combined group would hold in bearings (94 per cent) and cylinder liners (86 per cent) would lead to an increase in imports to the detriment of UK home market share. The Commission brushed aside GKN's arguments that the whole rationale for the deal was to establish one strong British engine component maker to compete in the European and world markets where component sourcing was becoming increasingly multinational – even though, most significantly, that argument was endorsed by the three major international vehicle companies active in Britain. Ford, Vauxhall and Talbot (now Peugeot) all told the Commission that the merger was in the British industry's best interests.

As a result of the Commission veto, GKN abandoned its drive into engine components and redirected its attention towards axles and suspension systems. But that was not the end of the story. In late 1987, AE was taken over by the Ferodo brake and clutch lining company T&N after one of the most bitter and protracted bid battles of the decade. The day that T&N announced its bid, one motor industry analyst commented cynically, 'This bid has no industrial logic: that is why it is bound to be cleared by the competition authorities.'

In fact, the bid made enormous sense for T&N, which had almost been dragged under by its exposure to asbestos in building materials and which had to upgrade the quality of its earnings, much of them derived from South Africa and India. No T&N interest overlapped with AE, so the bid sailed through the OFT. The following year came a telling postscript. T&N bought GKN's engine bearings business Vandervell, and the OFT waved through a concentration of manufacturing capability which less than five years earlier it had found to be a prime reason for referring GKN's AE bid to the Monopolies Commission. Borrie's explanation was straightforward: the situation had changed, and the British components industry was now open to international competition. This, he said, had not been the case when the GKN bid was referred in 1983. GKN, of course, had told the OFT, the Government and the Commission precisely that the bid was intended to position the combined engine components business to take advantage of this internationalization trend, which both it and the major vehicle manufacturers foresaw at that time.

The failure of mergers policy to acknowledge such wider industrial realities as were evident in the GKN-AE-T&N case speaks volumes for its continuing limitations. The Cadbury-Rowntree case-that-never-was provides further evidence of the policy's shortcomings. Cadbury and Rowntree had not entertained thoughts of a merger in the months and years prior to the arrival of the Swiss because they took it for granted that the British authorities would not permit such a concentration of market share. When, after Nestlé's bid, a chink of an opening for a merger suddenly appeared, it was already too late: the circumstances which had shifted the Government view also made a Cadbury-Rowntree deal practically impossible. And after it became clear that the merger idea would not get off the ground, the Government barrier descended again: confectionery, it was said, was a local, domestic market which was not susceptible to imports. Competition rulings therefore had to be made entirely on the basis of British, not European market shares.

That judgment was, to put it mildly, contentious. There are clear signs that in the future, confectionery kiosks will carry an ever-increasing variety of countline products (ie. snack-type confectionery rather than moulded bars) of different nationalities. And even in present conditions, the British consumer would have been protected from ruthless chocolate barons by Britain's retail chains, whose purchasing power is such that if a combined Cadbury-Rowntree had abused its market strength, it could have found its products excluded from supermarket shelves. In any case, the competitive presence of the giant Mars would have exerted a mighty restraint on a new, predominant British group.

The home market strength of a combined Cadbury–Rowntree would have provided a perfect springboard for international expansion. It would have given Britain a new European-scale commercial enterprise, and this country has few enough of those. The real tragedy of Rowntree is that Government policy made such a creation quite impossible, and nothing in that policy has changed.

Instead, the combination of mergers policy and the highly active Stock Market means that British industry remains most vulnerable to hostile overseas bidders. In 1988, it looked to many as if Nestlé's takeover of Rowntree was the harbinger of a spate of foreign acquisitions of British companies.

The number of companies acquired in Britain in 1988 totalled 1,224 – higher in sheer volume terms than the previous peak year of 1972. By value, takeovers far exceeded the megabid record year of 1986. At current prices, the total worth of deals was £22.1 billion, compared with 1986's £14.9 billion (*DTI Business Monitor*).

It was hard to escape the conclusion that the advent of the foreign bidders marked the start of a fundamental shift in the nature of takeovers in Britain. Of course, as was frequently pointed out, the number of overseas acquisitions of British companies (72 in 1988, worth £5.62 billion – *British Business*, 17 March, 1989) was dwarfed by British companies' takeovers abroad, particularly in the United States where British groups embarked on an acquisition binge in the mid-1980s. Between 1986 and 1988, the number of British acquisitions overseas almost doubled in volume and value, from 317 purchases worth £8.9 billion in 1986 to 595 deals worth £16.6 billion in 1988. Almost £14 billion of that last figure was spent in the United States.

However, although British companies bought 186 firms in the European Community countries, the total value of those purchases was only £1.65 billion – £900 million less than the value of the Rowntree takeover alone. And the number of hostile acquisitions by foreign firms in Britain – six – actually exceeded the five contested takeovers completed by British firms overseas. Moreover, the Americans were largely absent by choice from the British bid scene. They had been scarred by British opposition to their UK takeover bids in the 1970s and deterred by the 1981 Government bar on Enserch's hostile bid for the process plant contractor Davy Corporation.

It was, therefore, primarily a foreboding about the future, based on a limited but growing weight of evidence, which fuelled a resurgence in 1988 of the furious 1986 debate about takeovers. The presence of UB's Sir Hector Laing in the forefront of the new controversy, which amounted to an attack on hostile takeover bids, completed an indelible connection with the events of 1986.

Except that this time, Laing went much further. All concession to the interest of those institutional shareholders seeking earnings per share growth was jettisoned. Instead, Laing declared in *The Times* in June 1988: 'Considering the number of major British companies currently the subject of takeover speculation, it seems that in the present climate any and all of British industry is for sale if the price is right. Prostitution is not a pretty word, and I am sure we will not sell ourselves cheap – but at any price it is still prostitution.'

The gap between industry and the City suddenly looked wider than ever. Asked if the fund management group he headed would receive an offer for Cadbury Schweppes as favourably as it had the Swiss bid for Rowntree, a fund manager replied: 'It would depend on the price.'

Laing carried on regardless of the bitter feelings he was arousing in the City, where it was quite apparent that many fund managers would have liked nothing better than to see his dire prophecy come true in the most personally relevant manner – through a foreign bid for United Biscuits.

He asked the Royal Bank of Scotland for a written assurance that it would not back a hostile bid for UB – this after the Royal had joined the consortium of banks funding Elders' bid for Scottish & Newcastle Breweries, and had been sacked by publisher William

Collins because its merchant banking subsidiary Charterhouse was advising hostile bidder Rupert Murdoch's News International.

At the same time, Laing led a takeover debate at the CBI's annual conference. He scored a bullseye when he noted that, for all the wave of British takeovers of American companies, less than five per cent of American manufacturing industry's gross domestic product was foreign-owned, against more than 20 per cent of Britain's manufacturing GDP. He also waded into the City: 'The City and industry have a complementary symbiotic relationship – we need each other. We need to operate as partners and partnerships aren't built by stabbing each other in the back.'

Although the CBI conference was divided down the middle on the hostile takeover issue, Laing's onslaught was endorsed by its director-general, Sir Terence Beckett's successor John Banham. Banham declared that: 'Whenever the price is even vaguely respectable, control of company after company will fall to owners not just outside these islands, but outside the [European] Community.' Banham proposed a series of changes to the City takeover rules to make life harder for aspirant or actual hostile bidders.

The Government's obvious determination to maintain the competition-orientated basis of its mergers policy meant that any structural changes to influence the incidence and course of hostile bids had to be made through the takeover rules and Companies Act regulations on disclosure of shareholdings. This fact in a sense brought the takeover debate full circle back to the basics of company-City relations debated two years earlier before the Guinness scandal and the October 1987 Stock Market crash clouded the issue.

The CBI's previous contribution to the great City-industry debate had been somewhat inglorious. A year earlier, in November 1987, it had produced a report, 'Investing for Britain's Future', by a 'Task Force' of 29 representatives of the City and industry. The mettle of this Task Force did not match that of its larger namesake which reconquered the Falkland Islands. Its report made many worthwhile points of detail, but its overall tone was bloodless. It bore all the signs of a compromise between widely divergent opinions.

On the key issue of whether the City was pressurizing companies into short-term decisions, the report observed: 'Although there has been much concern that short-term pressures from financial markets affect business decision-making, the evidence does not seem to indicate that this is generally warranted.' Having published statistics showing that financial institutions' rate of turnover of shares had accelerated overall by about 50 per cent between 1980 and 1986, the report commented lamely: 'Undue alarm should not be registered at increases in share turnover.' Moreover, publication of the report was followed by a debate at the 1987 CBI conference in Glasgow which, albeit preoccupied with the implications of the October financial crash, nevertheless teetered on the brink of sheer complacency until it was saved by some robust observations from the floor.

Twelve months later, the CBI had to eat some of the words of that report. A poll of 249 member firms published on the conference eve revealed that almost two-thirds were not satisfied that the financial institutions made 'a long-term and strategic evaluation' of their companies. The CBI noted: 'The perception of a short-termism problem is perhaps more widespread than last year's Task Force Report suggested.'

All that had really changed in the year between the CBI conferences was the sudden awakening of British companies by the Rowntree battle to the fact that they were part, and a vulnerable part, of a great business *jeu sans frontières*' caused by industrial globalization. This added an international dimension which the takeover debate of 1986 had lacked.

Fundamentally, however, the issue was the same as it had been then and would be in the future: how to change the relationship between industry and the City for the better.

To this end, the man who had really raised people's consciousness about what became tagged as short-termism had long since moved the debate on. In a February, 1987 speech to the National Association of Pension Funds annual conference, David Walker of the Bank of England sought to close the first chapter in the discussion: 'I am inclined to think that the short-termism debate has now cast as much light as it is capable of doing and that the debate on relationships between financial institutions and industry needs to be developed in a more down-to-earth and pragmatic way.'

Walker devoted the rest of his speech to suggesting ways in which fund managers could, and should, involve themselves more closely and consistently in the affairs of the companies where they were shareholders. The heart of the problem, and the source from which the 'short-termism' accusations sprang, was as Walker himself diagnosed, the fact that in the vast majority of cases, a takeover bid was the only means that institutions used to rid themselves of an underperforming management. Until and unless a takeover bid was forthcoming, the institutions which could not sell their shares merely sat back passively and suffered while the performance drift continued. This fact helped to explain the element of collusion between bidders and the shareholders of target companies. Every buyer needed a seller. The financial institutions' dependence on takeovers for an exit route was the corollary of the use of takeovers by ambitious companies as the prime source of growth, in preference to organic investment-led expansion.

When the supply of British buyers – hostile bidders – dried up after 19 October, 1987 because of the slump in their share ratings, the industrial side of the City-industry equation started to change. But nothing on the institutional – the *demand* side – had altered. The supply gap was filled by the onset of the overseas bidders. That was the subliminal reason for the furore touched off by the Rowntree battle.

Through the comparisons with Continental industry that it invoked, the Rowntree contest also deepened the British City – industry debate, focusing attention on the contrasting contribution made to industrial investment by the UK's financial system, essentially based on Stock Market ownership, and the mainland European system which was built on bank ownership.

Research by Professor Colin Mayer of the City University Business School, first published the previous year and subsequently developed, had examined the sources of finance for physical (capital) investment in Britain, the United States, Japan, West Germany and France between 1970 and 1984. The findings were striking, and went right to the heart of the takeover-inspired debate about British industry and the City.

Mayer (*New Issues in Corporate Finance*, May 1987) identified that in none of the five countries did new equity finance contribute significantly to the funding of physical investment. That was scarcely surprising in France and West Germany, with their minor stock markets, but eyebrow-raising for the hyperactive financial markets of

Britain and America. But Mayer's research went further. It showed that the underdeveloped stock markets of the two Europeans had actually contributed more to domestic investment than had new equity in Britain and the US. Indeed, the British and American markets had made a negative contribution to investment. In net terms, almost all of the investment by British companies was funded by their own cash retentions.

The country whose stock market had contributed most to industrial investment was Japan, which appeared to enjoy the best of both equity and loan funding worlds. The reason is clear: Japan has a stock market as active as London's and New York's, but takeovers – and, in particular, hostile takeovers – are practically unheard of there. Competition is the law of the Japanese industrial jungle, and companies which cannot stay the pace are simply driven out of business. A classic case was Honda's obliteration of Tohatsu from the domestic motorbike market in the late 1950s (quoted in *The Reckoning* by David Halberstam).

The contrasting reliance of British and American industry on growth by acquisition explained why their financial markets' contribution to net capital formation was actually negative: repurchases of shares, through takeovers for cash, exceeded new share issues.

From this point, it was not far to Mayer's judgment on takeovers themselves: 'Even if the takeover process operates efficiently in a current period sense of augmenting shareholder wealth (and share price studies will suggest that the takeover process is indeed efficient), it can be seriously detrimental over a longer horizon through discouraging capital formation and risk-taking.' And Mayer diagnosed the root of the short-termist accusation against the Anglo-Saxon financial markets as being 'not, in all probability, a fundamental deficiency in pricing assets correctly (though this may indeed also be a feature of investors with limited information). Instead, what underlies the short-term concern is the lack of commitment of market investors.' Takeovers, Mayer implied, were at the centre of a vicious short-term circle in which companies expanding by acquisition called on the financial markets to provide cash for further takeovers which offered the investors an instant get-out. Short-termism was built into this climate of complicity between industry and the City. And although the circle was broken when the stock of (hostile) British bidders

A FIGHTING CHANCE

dwindled after October 1987, this change did nothing to deepen investor commitment.

On the contrary, in the demonstrably more successful manufacturing nations of Japan and West Germany, the lead role in corporate financing had been taken by the banks, which over a long period maintained consistently close and constructive involvement in the affairs of the companies that they were funding and, notably in Germany, in which they were shareholders.

In contrast with West Germany and Japan, said David Walker in February 1988 (Bridge Lecture to the Worshipful Company of Engineers), 'there is much less certainty about relationships in this country and in the United States, with an increased and perhaps increasing orientation of banks toward individual deals in place of continuing relationships, and with the probability that institutional shareholdings will be traded now at least as high as that they will be firmly held.'

Walker noted that 'while primary provision for the funding of British industry in general compares very favourably with that in other developed countries, the quality of relationships between industry and its suppliers of loan and risk capital is deficient.'

Walker made the challenge manifest: if those relationships were not improved, British industry's grounds for long-term success would be undermined. 'The ideal,' said Walker, 'would be to achieve a structure in which British business continued to enjoy the full benefits of an efficient and liquid institutional and market structure alongside much more positive and constructive relationships of the kind seen in Germany and Japan.'

Until that tall order is fulfilled and City-industry Utopia is reached, takeovers friendly or hostile will remain the prime instrument of company-initiated, institutionally-enforced change. Provocatively, paradoxically, the 1980s experience of one major British company suggests that Britain's continued addiction to the takeover – however out of line with the culture of the most successful manufacturing nations – does not necessarily spell gloom and doom for this country's future.

the recent history of APV is any guide, then it may prove that the ost effective agent of dynamic corporate change is the hostile id that fails.

In April 1986 – the zenith of the takeover boom – APV was a manufacturer of process plant for the food, drink, chemical and mining industries, which was just recovering from a 1984 trauma when its chief executive departed amid a group profits slump.

Three years later, APV had established itself via two changes of company name, two major takeovers, one significant disposal, and numerous smaller deals as the overall world leader in the manufacture of food and drink producing equipment. Pre-tax profits had more than trebled from £15 million to £51 million on sales up by 150 per cent from £400 million to almost £1 billion. The group stood out as one of the very few British multinational manufacturers actually created during the decade.

The single event most responsible for this remarkable transformation was the £182 million hostile bid that APV received on 24 April, 1986 from the diversified engineering group Siebe, which was dominated by its autocratic chief executive Barrie Stephens.

Stephens and Siebe were everything that APV, a blue-blooded member of the British engineering establishment, was not. When Stephens had joined it 23 years earlier, Siebe Gorman was a manufacturer of diving apparatus with annual sales of about £1 million. For 18 years, the company grew steadily, doing one sizeable deal along the way. But when, at the start of the 1980s, Stephens did get the urge to merge, he acted with exceptional zeal. Five takeovers in five years increased the group's size ten-fold to annual sales of more than £500 million, and made Siebe an archetypal bull-market consumer of other companies. No-one questioned the short-term impact of Siebe. What they did wonder about was longer-term growth. 'Everyone should have one year of Barrie Stephens', commented an executive of one company swallowed by Siebe. 'But that is all they should have. Siebe is like a comet – you start at its head and are burnt out through its tail. Then it's on to the next thing.'

In complete contrast, APV's chairman Sir Ronald McIntosh, a former director-general of the National Economic Development Office in the 1970s, eschewed hostile takeovers. Indeed, its recent acquisitions had been minor affairs as McIntosh's relatively new chief executive Fred Smith concentrated his efforts on getting APV's existing operations into shape after the earlier loss of management focus. Smith's name may have been ordinariness personified, but he

A FIGHTING CHANCE

brought to his job an extraordinary talent for motivation and a global understanding and vision of APV's market. That internationalism was the product of a multinational family and business upbringing: Smith was an Australian who was born in South Africa, later returning to Australia where he eventually took charge of APV's operations before moving to run the group's American business. Thence he was plucked in mid-1984, aged 52, to revive APV in its hour of need from a nadir in which operating margins had plunged to two per cent.

As it turned out, McIntosh and Smith had made sufficient progress by the time of Siebe's bid to be able to forecast an 80 per cent rise in 1986 profits. This, together with the support of institutions headed by Warburg Investment Management, a major APV shareholder, was enough to bury Siebe's increased £220 million final bid. APV had to strain every sinew to meet that forecast, and it had a reaction in 1987 when its ongoing businesses actually suffered a profits fall. But by that time Siebe and Stephens were long gone on to new pastures, having joined the great British takeover trail west with two mega-deals in America.

The APV-Siebe battle produced one memorable line – McIntosh's disparaging comment that 'the only synergy between Siebe and APV would be if someone wanted to build an underwater dairy' – and two quite invaluable benefits for APV. First, in the space of two months Smith gained experience of the City which would otherwise have taken him years to accumulate.

Similarly, but more importantly, the bid engineered a massive overnight re-rating of APV's shares. APV's share price was almost doubled from 350p on the eve of Siebe's attack to 673p after its final offer. Although the price slipped back when the bid failed, it still settled around the 600p mark – more than 70 per cent higher than it had been before the bid.

The hardest task that most companies faced when they approached the City was to change its entrenched opinion of their shares. Thanks to Siebe, APV had suddenly and hugely heightened its profile. What it achieved subsequently would almost certainly not have been possible without that sudden, stupendous uplift.

Just over six months after its defeat of Siebe, APV won the agreement of Peterborough-based Baker Perkins to a £147 million offer of APV shares for Baker's paper. Baker had a strong niche in printing equipment, but its core business was process plant manufacture for the bread, biscuits, snack foods and confectionery industries, which perfectly complemented APV's drink and liquid (milk, cheese, ice cream) foods expertise.

Agreed the deal was, but the enabling influence on it of the hostile bid climate extended beyond the share purchasing power which APV had acquired from Siebe's bid. APV had first mooted a merger with Baker ten years earlier, but Baker had always stuck out for its independence. One factor which had changed its disposition, when APV made its initial approach in October 1986, was the concern that, in the welter of unsolicited bids, Baker might arouse the interest of a less congenial partner than APV.

Just such a party emerged shortly after the deal was announced, in the unmistakable form of Robert Maxwell. Maxwell bought almost five per cent of Baker and tried to stir up a rival bid for the company, albeit to no avail. But while Maxwell came and went, unforeseen cost overruns on an American contract in Baker's BCS (Biscuits, confectionery, snacks) division triggered a series of moves which made the deal look increasingly like an aggressive takeover by any other name. APV cut both its offer price (by £30 million), the number of Baker directors it was taking on to the combined board, and the seniority of the positions the Baker people would occupy. Eventually, after a decent interval, APV dropped the Baker and returned to its original name.

It also continued its rapid international expansion. Less than three months after completing the Baker Perkins purchase, APV bought the Danish company Pasilac for less than £16 million. In many ways, the deal was even better than the Baker acquisition: Pasilac was strong in dairy product and brewing technology, offered immense scope for margin improvement on its £130 million sales, and expanded APV's multinational manufacturing infrastructure. Smith's strategy was to establish factories making similar products in both the United States and Europe, to protect the group against currency shifts while at the same time taking it close to its customers. Although gaps in APV's product portfolio remained after Pasilac, the acquisition effectively completed APV's transformation from British-orientated international group to true multinational. This corporate evolution was symbolized by APV's 1988 closure of its previous headquarters site in Crawley, near Gatwick Airport, where manufacture of plate heat exchangers, a core process plant component, had been concentrated. APV shifted European heat exchanger production to a Pasilac factory.

Two events in 1989 confirmed the group's single-minded global drive. APV embarked on a war of attrition in West Germany in an effort to obtain control of SEN, a maker of bottling equipment which would fill one of the two major holes in APV's product range. And during the SEN affair, the group sold Baker Perkins' printing machinery business for £85 million to Rockwell of America. At the time of the Baker deal, APV had specifically committed itself to retaining the printing business. Its disposal both highlighted the process of industrial globalization – substantial resources were required by the Baker printing operation if it was to match the commitment of the major international players, of which Rockwell was one – and re-emphasized how the agreed deal that Baker Perkins chairman John Peake had called 'a happy marriage, but not a shotgun marriage' had left APV very much in charge.

McIntosh retired in September 1989, after a momentous 7½ years in the chair during which APV had become that rare animal, a British-owned world industrial power in its sector. His succession by an executive of British Petroleum, Britain's biggest company, added a kind of official seal of recognition to that achievement. Throughout, McIntosh adhered to the conviction he expressed after the Siebe bid, that 'by and large, hostile takeovers are a rotten way of restructuring British Industry. They divert management time to unproductive activities and stir up all sorts of resentments which make it difficult to run the combined company if the bid is successful.'

As McIntosh noted almost three years later: 'APV has been transformed in five years from a conventional British engineering company with good technical products but becoming gradually less competitive internationally, into a genuine multinational which is a leader in its field.'

Yet APV owed that great rise to the twin impulses of a hostile bid for the group which failed and an agreed bid which, by force of exceptional circumstance, freed it to take executive action untrammelled by the concessions to the consenting party that friendly deals habitually entail. As APV entered the 1990s, its close observers had little doubt that if the situation so demanded, the group might be ready to go hostile in pursuit of its global ambitions.

CHAPTER FIVE

NATIONAL CHAMPIONS

In the middle of British Steel's massive integrated works at Port Talbot in South Wales stands the only surviving wall of a Thirteenth Century Cistercian monastery. According to local legend, if the wall falls down then steel-making at the plant will cease. So Port Talbot's management have guided destiny's hand: they have reinforced the wall with home-produced steel to ensure that myth never becomes reality.

During the 1980s, British Steel mastered a greater fate. Its remarkable odyssey from the brink of bankruptcy to a successful Stock Market flotation valuing the company at £2.5 billion makes it the decade's greatest single story of manufacturing resurrection.

On 2 January, 1980, almost all the 166,400 employees of the then-nationalized British Steel Corporation (renamed British Steel plc in 1988) walked out on the first national steel strike for 70 years. Behind them lay an over-manned, underperforming business with too much capacity and too little product quality to withstand the cost and price storms buffeting the world industry from at least three points of the steel compass: a vastly over-supplied European market; a protectionist America; and fast-rising Far East competition.

Eight years and 11 months later, at 2.30 on the afternoon of 5 December, 1988, dealings began in London, New York and Toronto in the shares of British Steel, the world's fourth-largest steel maker with 1988 output of 14.7 million tonnes, and the lowest-cost producer not only in Europe but also, according to one American stockbroker's analysis, in the world.

The stock market flotation of British Steel marked the ultimate seal of approval for the group's astonishing recovery and the culmination of the Thatcher Government's successive sales of State-owned manufacturing assets. Although denationalization was nothing new, Thatcherism did more than merely invent a new name – privatization – for the process. With the public offerings of shares in British Aerospace, Amersham International, Jaguar, Rolls-Royce and British Steel, the management and leveraged buy-outs of such as Allied Steel & Wire and Vickers Shipbuilding and Engineering, and the sale to existing British and overseas companies of businesses including much of what had been British Shipbuilders, Thatcherism redrew the British manufacturing map, obliterated the old boundaries between the public and private sectors – and exposed several keystones of British industry to the harsh but honing edge of real competition.

To a large extent, British Steel was the exception to this norm because so much work had been done in the years preceding privatization to make it fighting fit. Coincidentally or otherwise, the flotation was itself imbued with this sense of maturity.

Unlike some of the earlier manufacturing sales – notably Amersham and Jaguar, though these paled beside service sector privatizations like British Telecom and British Gas – British Steel was no great bonanza, either for Stock Market stags in and out for the quickest profit, or the longer-term investor who nevertheless liked to see a large immediate price appreciation.

This fact was partly due to the nature of the investment offered by British Steel, which was sold on the dividend yield it could offer rather than as a capital growth stock. Still more influential was the Stock Market environment into which British Steel was launched: the October 1987 crash in markets worldwide was followed (except in Japan) by 14 months of fear and caution which was most pronounced in London. The halcyon days of the bullish mid-1980s had become a distant memory by the time British Steel began its run up to privatization.

On the very eve of the British Steel sale, atop the underlying bearishness, was heaped the alarming sight of a massive British trade deficit for the month of October. The figures vindicated the decision by the Government and the financial advisers to the float to price British Steel at the bottom end of the range – between £2.5 billion and £2.8 billion – that they had previously laid down. But they also appeared to dash all hopes of strong public – as against professional – interest in the privatization.

152

For despite the prevailing Stock Market sentiment, hopes among the British Steel marketeers had been very high. Their aim in advising a lower-end price – £2.5 billion meant 125p a share, of which 60p was the first instalment – had been to achieve an enormous 'conversion' rate: more than 1.5 million people had registered an interest in the sale; it was thought, with 125p a share and a fair wind, that this could be translated into more than a million applications for shares.

But British Steel had a surprise in store. The great British investing public did not lose its nerve and run a mile at the gruesome sight of the trade figures. Instead, 650,000 people applied for three times the number of British Steel shares on offer, triggering both 'clawback' thresholds under which shares provisionally allotted (to overseas markets and domestic financial institutions) could be reallocated to the private British investor. Early trading in the shares was glum, with a marginal premium quickly evaporating and a slight discount setting in before the first week of dealing was over. But underpinned by its yield, particularly in the ten months before the second instalment of 65p was due, British Steel remained a stock to hold, not sell.

That private investors had gone into British Steel in such numbers with their eyes open said something for the increased sophistication of the new generation of individual shareholders conceived by, and weaned on, the privatization programme. British Steel's privatization constituency was populated by this new but informed investor, dubbed 'Sidney' by Tony Carlisle of Dewe Rogerson, the financial public relations advisers to the sale, in a middle-class variation on 'Sid', the mythical target of the populist British Gas sale.

The character of the shareholders fitted the company in which they had invested. Pre-privatization, British Steel's chairman Sir Robert Scholey may have likened the company to 'the Nubian slave stood on the block, well-oiled and looking pretty', but there was nothing passive about the way Scholey, his fellow executives – chief executive Martin Llowarch, managing director of personnel David Grieves, business chiefs Gordon Sambrook and John Stewart, and managing director of finance Brian Moffat – and some of their immediate predecessors had made British Steel the greatest turn-round of the decade.

In the 12 months to March 1980, the year of the strike, British Steel lost almost £1.8 billion before (almost non-existent) tax. In 1988/9, its pre-tax profits totalled almost £600 million. The company did not get into the black before tax until 1985/6, and its ensuing profits eruption derived partly from the happenstantial and highly favourable sterling exchange rate conjunction of a weak dollar – which cut the price of British Steel's raw materials – and a strong Deutschmark, which enabled the company to maintain selling prices against its principal, West German competitors. The consequent boost to margins was dramatic. While sales increased by about 19 per cent to £4.1 billion in 1987/8, pre-tax profits soared 120 per cent.

British Steel deserved the slice of good fortune that helped to make that profits *annus mirabilis*. In its struggle for survival during the first half of the decade, it had to overcome not just its own internal barriers to success – a bitter harvest sown by years of political interference and procrastination, management frustration and union reaction – and unfavourable world steel industry conditions, but the external hazards of rail disputes and the epic 1984/5 miners' strike, which cost British Steel about £180 million. The story of British Steel's resurrection is that of British manufacturing industry writ very large.

The company's nine-year, £2.4 billion losses-to-profits turn-round was only one aspect of its vast recovery. Equally remarkable, and much more painful, was the extent of the job cuts that fuelled the profits resurgence by radically shrinking British Steel's cost base. The workforce dropped from 166,400 at New Year 1980 to little over 50,000 by March 1989, a reduction of almost two-thirds. In contrast, the total job loss in British manufacturing over the decade was little over 33 per cent.

Almost 46,000 steel jobs went within a single year – most of them in the six-month period following the ending of the 13-week strike on 3 April, 1980. At the two South Wales integrated works of Llanwern and Port Talbot, the rate of job-cutting was incredible. After three months' discussion immediately following the strike, the total workforce was more than halved from 21,900 to 10,600 in the space of one month.

The post-strike cuts created an efficiency 'floor' which underpinned productivity and cost improvements in British Steel throughout the decade. Its pre-existence meant that when the upturn in demand came in the mid-1980s, the company's profits could take off like a rocket as the lion's share of booming output flowed straight through to the bottom, profits line. Completing the virtuous circle, rising demand – notably from the construction and motor industries – reinforced productivity progress.

Figures tell the story vividly. In 1980/1, it took British Steel 14.5 man hours to produce a tonne of liquid steel. Seven years later, productivity was up by two-thirds to five man hours per tonne. Over the same period, labour costs were reduced from 37.7 per cent of sales to 20.3 per cent. They were cut again in 1988/89 to below 14 per cent. Total pre-tax costs of steel shipped, $568 a tonne in 1981, were $415 a tonne in 1988 – slightly lower even than those of South Korea, Brazil and Taiwan. Energy use per tonne of steel produced was cut by almost 20 per cent between 1980/1 and 1987/8. Yield – the amount of saleable product obtained from a certain quantity of raw material, which is the prime measure of plant efficiency – fell back in 1982/3 from early 1980s levels, but has since improved by almost 8.5 per cent. The yield enhancement alone may be worth £75 million over the five years since 1982/3. (Warburg Securities estimates.)

In sharp contrast, international standards of efficiency have been harder to achieve, and later to arrive, at the other manufacturing giant privatized during the decade. Surveying British Aerospace in summer 1988, when the group had just exploded on the world the bombshell news that it planned to take over the struggling State-owned car company Rover Group, a senior investment manager and long-time City follower of BAe commented: 'The reconstruction of UK industry started in the late 1960s with the creation of GEC. It has involved virtually all of the manufacturing sector. British Aerospace is the last great unreconstructed company in UK manufacturing.'

For years, British Aerospace struggled to reshape itself into the lean, mean form taken by British Steel after the big bang of its 1980 strike blew away the clutter accumulated since renationalization. One lesson of its long, slow grind was that privatization as an act in itself made little difference – privatization was what BAe made of it. The other, which applied equally to British Steel and Rolls-Royce, was that change in the corporate structure was indivisible from fully effective commercialization; indeed, that the former was a crucial precondition of the latter and the true road to international competitiveness.

The same went, in smaller measure, for innumerable private sector companies. But it stood out like a giant sore thumb in the State-owned manufacturers, with their fragmented pre-nationalization provenance compounded by the artificial insularity of political ownership; cossetted by State support on one hand, constantly exposed to political and bureaucratic intervention on the other.

All three groups – BAe, Rolls and British Steel – were, by definition of their history, characterized by factionalism. In British Steel, the driving force was the so-called 'Sheffield mafia', the former management of United Steel, one of the pre-nationalization companies – at least until very recently, when followers of the company detected a power shift towards executives reared in South Wales. But the Sheffield steel men, led by British Steel's present chairman Sir Robert Scholey, used their influence to foster a spirit of common enterprise and to encourage decision-making devolution. The first of a series of efficiency studies code-named OPERA (Overheads: a plan for the examination and reduction of activities) implemented between 1980 and 1984 included the objective of encouraging steelworks in different parts of the country, and different steel businesses in the same area, to share services. The aim was to 'break down the castle walls'.

Sir Raymond Lygo, the former Royal Navy Admiral and therefore industrial outsider who has played the largest single role in dynamising British Aerospace, recalls that when he became managing director in 1983, the different power blocs in the group 'all had their walls around them'. The centrifugal forces at work in British Aerospace made the group a parallel but larger version of Rolls-Royce (in several cases, like de Havilland and Blackburn, BAe's constituent subsidiaries had taken the airframe side of a company while Rolls had acquired the engine business through its 1966 takeover of Bristol Siddeley Engines).

In Rolls-Royce, the separatist power bases were broken down by Sir William Duncan, the Rolls chairman who died suddenly in 1985 after only 20 months in charge. Before his arrival, 'the military engine side didn't talk to the civil side, and vice versa, and helicopters was left struggling along on the edge,' as stockbroking analyst Pete Deighton puts it. 'Each business was very powerful; they had their own expenses, for example. Duncan said: "you aren't going to have it this way". He brought the power into the centre.'

Under chairman Sir Austin Pearce at British Aerospace, Lygo also initially followed the centralization course – when he was given the chance. He joined the group's missile-making Dynamics division in 1978, but was not promoted to the centre until 1983 when he was made managing director. By that time, the majority of BAe had been privatized through the £148 million Government sale in 1981 of 51.8 per cent of the company.

The shares sale came only four years after BAe was actually created, in the 1977 nationalization of the aircraft (and shipbuilding) industries, by the combination of Hawker Siddeley Aviation, the British Aircraft Corporation and Scottish Aviation. In a sense, however, the genealogy of BAe's constituents made nationalization less of a shock to the system. They themselves were the result of more than a dozen post-war mergers and takeovers of British airframe companies, like Avro and de Havilland – both part of Hawker Siddeley – and the BAC consortium of the former Bristol Aeroplane and the aircraft interests of Vickers and English Electric.

But this background only conspired with the ultimate amalgamation into British Aerospace to reinforce the sectional barriers against unification and streamlining. And privatization in itself brought little incentive to remove these fiefdoms, because the entrenched demand for military aircraft at 'cost-plus' prices (an order price incorporating a guaranteed inflation-proofed profit for the manufacturer) cushioned the group against the market forces to which privatization theoretically exposed it. As a result, BAe reported profits throughout the recession, save in 1982, and in May 1985 approached the Stock Market for the second time apparently unchanged from the same unwieldy, faction-ridden, but highly profitable, corporation which had been floated four years earlier.

Market forces had threatened to break in on BAe the previous summer, when first Thorn EMI and then GEC approached the group with a view to taking it over. But BAe turned them both down and the Government completed its privatization by selling its outstanding 48.2 per cent shareholding for £363 million and taking out a golden share protecting the group against takeover, while BAe strengthened its balance sheet by raising £187 million from investors.

The following month, Lygo was appointed chief executive as well as managing director. Below him was a collection of operations which in their determined independence resembled a set of feudalistic industrial baronies with an over-manned, low-productivity workforce which was 76,000-strong, having shed only 8,000 employees in the previous five years. BAe's finance director Bernard Friend acknowledged that it should be 16,000 lower at no more than 60,000: 'There is no doubt about the over-manning, and we are trying to improve it . . . but we cannot achieve it overnight. In the next few years you will see major improvement in productivity and performance ' (*The Times*, August 1985).

Lygo faced the Herculean task of fulfilling such promises. British Aerospace had, he said, 'inherited a rundown, dispirited, and wrongly motivated organization' (*The Sunday Times*, 9 July, 1988). 'The divisions between management and workforce were incredible. There was no communication; total secrecy; an unfortunate history of relations with the unions.' Within the Dynamics divison, he found that managers had received no training.

He immediately began unaccompanied office and shopfloor walkabouts, soon encountering one 35-year company veteran who told him: 'You are the first director I have ever spoken to.' He also discovered that 'none of our drawings had marked on them what the end product was, so the worker didn't know if he was making a piece for a 146 jet or a Rapier missile system. There was no connection between what the man was doing and the product at the end of the line.' Changing all that was a long slog. Even after six years in the Dynamics division, his effort to implant a spirit of communication and purpose had not taken root. He told an Industrial Society conference in 1984 that on a recent visit to one of the component factories, he had picked up a drawing and found that there was still no indication on it of the end product in which it would be used.

To knock BAe into shape, Lygo first concentrated authority and then devolved it. The management restructuring process began with an announcement on 4 November, 1985 and was not completed for more than three years. It spearheaded a five-year cost-cutting drive, started in 1987 and intended to be sustained until 1992. It also caused some mirth in the industrial community: no year is complete, the joke ran, without a corporate reorganization by British Aerospace.

The first move, which took effect on New Year's Day 1986, abolished the structure of only two groups – Aircraft and Dynamics – with which BAe had been privatized in 1981. Both groups had their own headquarters not many miles apart in the Home Counties. Together, they contained no less than 11 subsidiary divisions, centred on geographical manufacturing sites – including Warton in Lancashire for the Tornado fighter; and Dunsfold in Surrey where the Harrier jump-jet was built. The organization made sectionalism an institution. Lygo closed the two headquarters and concentrated all operational direction on BAe's corporate headquarters in London and Weybridge. Two deputy chief executives were appointed, one to cover all BAe's manufacturing operations, the other responsible for engineering. Below them, the aircraft division was split into civil and military divisions.

Seven months later, BAe announced the closure of its Weybridge components plant which employed 4,000 – its first major plant shutdown. The rationalization, in which 2,500 of the jobs were lost altogether, appeared to be a straw in the wind of change blowing through the group.

But it took Lygo another two years to establish the final platform from which BAe could approach the 1990s. On the weekend of July 2/3, 1988, BAe's workforce was given notice of the planned total de-centralization of the group. This reorganization, phased in from the following autumn, established eight profit-centred businesses comprising the major historic BAe businesses – Commercial Aircraft, Dynamics and Military Aircraft – the group's three big acquisitions since 1987 – munitions maker Royal Ordnance, construction group Ballast Nedam, and Rover Group – and the two smaller businesses of Space Systems and BAe Enterprises. The London head office, built up in 1986, was to be halved in size. Each of the eight organizations had its own chairman and board of directors.

The restructuring made BAe more lucid in other ways, too. Until then, the company's marketing of aircraft was done by one group, selling both civil aircraft – like the 146 regional jet and the

Jetstream – and military planes including the Tornado, Harrier and Hawk. Conflicts of interest and customer confusion frequently ensued, noted BAe executive Dick Evans (In *Jane's Defence Weekly*, 24 December, 1986). Meanwhile, different defence equipment divisions competed for the same export customers. Under the new organization, Evans chaired an umbrella group of BAe Defence Businesses (military aircraft, missiles and Royal Ordnance) with a newly unified central marketing organization.

Ostensibly, the most remarkable aspect of the new BAe structure was its return to devolution after several years when centripetalism ruled. Lygo explained that two principles underlay the move. First, it had been required by the 'change in scale and size and nature of the company. The plan was to get ourselves into a position so that, whatever else we did in diversifying, then the organization of the company would be able to absorb it and handle it. In the old BAe, everything was totally integrated into individual businesses with little or no profit accountability. You couldn't get a commercial sense into that organization; no matter how much you said it, it didn't work and wouldn't work because it was like nationalization: the minute you take profit away from an organization, what do you put in its place?'

Still more fundamentally, said Lygo, BAe centralized only in order to decentralize. Lygo maintains: 'Starting from where we did, the only way I believe it could be done was to drag all the power into the middle, to take all the power myself, so that I could then redistribute it. People suspected my motives, but if I had not done it then the old management would have protected their empires.'

The devolution now in train is dedicated to 'giving a complete focus on the commercial aspects of running a business', a process both aided and made more urgent by the British Ministry of Defence's adoption of a tough competitive procurement policy and the elimination of cost-plus comfort. 'We still had to achieve a vehicle to develop better businessmen and women in the company. There is no better way of doing that than by creating separate businesses in which they can flourish,' says Lygo.

In tandem with, and resulting from, BAe's post-1985 restructuring was a sustained effort to thin out the legions of managers in the company. In early 1989, Lygo estimated that about 3,000 managers had been taken out during this period. The process began with the scrapping of the two entrenched Aircraft and Dynamics divisions, which cut a whole chunk of top management, and moved on to address the proliferation of lower-to-middle managers. Lygo believes the problem was not peculiar to BAe or nationalized industries: 'I suspect that this was a direct result of that period of wage restraint in the 1970s, because the only way to give somebody extra money was to promote them.'

But if a company the size of BAe or British Steel resembles an army – a comparison made by British Steel chairman Scholey – and that army marches on its stomach, then Lygo's long march away from hierarchy and towards efficiency is encapsulated in one pungent detail. Only months before he retired at the end of 1989, ten years after joining the group, were dining facilities at each of BAe's 39 sites finally rationalized to one, all-embracing canteen. In their unreconstructed heyday, some plants had boasted five different dining areas. Single-status eating – or messing, as Lygo calls it – had at last been achieved.

That sprawling collection of sites represented BAe's internal Rubicon. Over it lay an invaluable source of cash flow in the form of property profits just waiting to be tapped – and too important to be ignored by a company whose stockbroker, Hoare Govett, forecasted in January 1989 that it would suffer (albeit diminishing) cash outflows at least until 1993.

The surplus property treasure trove, worth £1.13 billion according to an August 1988 estimate by analysts at Warburg Securities, was an alluring, but nonetheless subsidiary, reward awaiting BAe once it crossed that Rubicon. The prime motive for so doing was the most basic reason of all: the need to drive up productivity and persistently improve cost-competitiveness.

Despite the Weybridge closure, BAe did not really begin to grasp the rationalization nettle until June 1987, 18 months after the first major step towards corporate reorganization. At that point, Lygo set a target of cutting total group costs by one-third over the following five years to 1992. The efficiency programme was broken down into two phases, with a 20 per cent cut to be achieved by 1990 and the remainder thereafter. Its mainspring was a long-term drive for competitiveness, in the process closing what BAe had identified as a productivity gap between itself and its American rivals Boeing and McDonnell Douglas which were reckoned to be ten or 15 per cent more efficient. Immediacy was injected into the programme by the weakening dollar – the world currency for civil aircraft sales – which placed BAe (with predominantly pounds sterling manufacturing costs) at a price disadvantage in the commercial airframe sector. By jeopardizing its margins, the movement highlighted its need to reduce costs. Indeed, the exchange rate shift forced BAe to provide £320 million in its 1987 accounts against potential losses up to 1991 on civil aircraft manufacture, leaving the group with a 1987 after-tax loss of £110 million.

The efficiency programme extended to BAe's suppliers and embraced a switch to more dollar-based manufacturing to offset the exchange rate fluctuations. Internally, the productivity drive bore almost immediate fruit with aircraft assembly times cut in 18 months by anywhere up to 54 per cent, and the most astonishing improvement in the manufacture of wings for the European Airbus A-320 airliner, where the number of days taken to produce one wing was cut from 67 to 23 (*Financial Times*, 20 February, 1989).

Then, in February 1989, BAe's new structure finally demonstrated that it was ready to address the rationalization issue, when the Dynamics subsidiary announced a reorganization involving site closures and concentration of operations which would lose 2,500 jobs by the end of 1990. The move came several months after a cleverly orchestrated union and Opposition party campaign designed to pre-empt widespread BAe rationalization by harping on the property profits that the group stood to realize as a consequence of closures. The campaign achieved a temporary success by embarrassing BAe, now chaired by Professor Roland Smith who succeeded Pearce in September 1987. But the Dynamics decision proved that the group, in its new profit-centre form, was ready to tackle the excessive overheads that constituted the main barrier to increasing competitiveness.

It had taken a long time. Indeed, BAe's rationalization experience was almost diametrically opposed to that of both Rolls-Royce and British Steel, and most other private sector companies which had cut and cut hard in the first half of the decade. Its late timing was even more surprising given the perennially loss-making civil aircraft business, which as Nomura Securities analysts remarked in September 1988, had not made 'a proper profit this decade'. However, as Lygo noted, the cardinal difference between BAe and other manufacturers was the group's almost uninterrupted overall profits strength, carried along by constant annual increases in British defence spending: 'The difficulty we've had, one I don't think is appreciated generally, is we've had to do this [lowering costs] in an environment where the company has been continuously profitable and full of work. We haven't had to face a situation where if we didn't do something, the doors were going to close. It is much more difficult to change an organization with a group of people who say, "Why change? We are doing well".'

In complete contrast, Rolls-Royce has been historically much more dependent on the civil aircraft market, and therefore constantly exposed to competition from its two main and larger rivals, the Americans Pratt & Whitney (part of United Technologies Corporation) and General Electric (no relation to Britain's GEC). Indeed, the very origin of the company that rejoined the Stock Market on 19 May, 1987 lay in the incessant battle for aero-engine market superiority. It was the development by GE and P&W in the late 1960s of new, large engines that forced Rolls to undertake development of the RB211-22B, and it was the project's technical problems which so drained Rolls of resources that it called in the receiver on 4 February, 1971 and was nationalized 19 days later. Two years after that, its Rolls-Royce Motors car and diesel engine side was floated on the Stock Market, leaving Rolls in the form in which it was eventually privatized.

Rolls' route to greater efficiency was rather different from BAe's, and despite the constant stimulus of external competition, strangely uneven – possibly because attempts to improve cost-effectiveness actually pre-dated belated organizational change. In basic manufacturing, the foundations for productivity improvements were well laid. In an imaginative 1978 move, Frank Turner – later Rolls manufacturing director civil engines – and a group of senior shop stewards toured competitors' and suppliers' factories in the United States to study productivity levels there. They returned with a joint report which said that Rolls was about 35 per cent less efficient than the Americans, and falling further behind.

Having achieved workforce recognition of the need to sharpen up, Rolls proceeded to develop a manufacturing efficiency programme using the tools of design, procurement and automated manufacturing technology (AMT) to make up for its inability to match the

Americans' economies of scale (because of the huge size of their home market and the American defence budget). Rolls focused on components, production processes and its business with sub-contractors (*Financial Times*, 15 April, 1985).

It concentrated its in-house manufacture on high-cost, high-volume components or parts critical to engine performance and reliability. By standardizing its component designs, it cut the number of tools used for manufacturing in its main, Derby factory from 100,000 in the late 1970s to 2,000 in 1985. And it became a British pioneer in the use of AMT, despite having to introduce automation in highly straitened circumstances. After two years of big losses, the company almost reached breakeven in 1981. But the delayed impact of the second oil price shock and the recession then ate into aircraft demand, and in the next two years the group ran up net losses totalling £330 million. Consequently, AMT had to be developed within a financial strategy which would only approve a project paying for itself in one year or less. Of the projects that did meet this exacting criterion and that therefore proceeded, one cut inventories of engine casings by 70 per cent, another – the 'robot line' – dramatically lowered the lead times for grinding a batch of 250 turbine blades from six days to one, and a third slashed the reject rate on turbine blade grinding.

As financial conditions eased with a return to taxable and net profits in 1984, Rolls at Derby moved on to the most ambitious phase of its AMT programme. This, a £10 million-plus project called AIMS (advanced integrated manufacturing system) cut total production time of engine discs and wheels – a major integral part of an engine – from six months to six weeks (*The Engineer*, 13 February, 1986). It cut stock value from £11.5 million worth in 1978 to £6.9 million in 1983 and to £2.3 million in 1986 (*Financial Times*, 20 February 1986) and boosted labour productivity by 40 per cent.

As a result of the cost-cutting drive, Rolls' group workforce was slimmed by more than 30 per cent between 1980 and 1983. Sir Francis Tombs, a non-executive director for four years before stepping into the gap left by Duncan's sudden death in 1985, credits Duncan's predecessor Sir Frank McFadzean with inspiring the improvements in output per man. McFadzean also established the currency management capability that plays a vital role in the group's financial planning by mitigating the impact of fluctuations in the pound-dollar exchange rate.

Labour productivity was only one part of the picture, however. When Tombs joined the board, he rapidly discovered that after ten years in the State sector, Rolls was badly deficient in some business basics: 'The forward planning was very unrealistic, and so the corporate plan showed rates of return above 50 per cent. Very early on, I pointed out that that sort of thing just didn't exist in the market because if you reach that sort of return competitors cut their prices. The market is dynamic, not static and in that rather artificial nationalized environment that sort of market movement was not foreseen at all.'

Things improved over the next four years, with Duncan's arrival removing other fundamental flaws. He laid the foundations for true commerciality through a new management structure to eliminate duplication of activities, create clear lines of accountability with profit centres for individual directors and other top managers, and thus provide for a new cost-conscious procurement policy. The difference was soon recognized by Rolls suppliers. According to one long-time components manufacturer: 'Before 1984, Rolls-Royce was like a philanthropic organization. There were industry prices, and Rolls-Royce prices. And once you were in, you never left. All that changed in 1984.'

Even so, Tombs faced a considerable task when he agreed to become chairman in 1985 on the sole condition that Rolls should be returned to the private sector. The preparation for, and process of privatization was, Tombs believes, the vital incentive and driving force of the reformation that followed. 'It was enormously educational for staff who had been sheltered for 17 years. We had 19 versions of the privatization prospectus. Having to pick over every word, and justify every word, was good for us. The fact that our results were at last going to be subject to critical scrutiny focused minds in a way they hadn't been focused for 17 years.' Financial controls were improved, and suppliers again felt the effect of procurement tightening in 1987, the year of privatization. In fact, Rolls was ready for flotation the previous September, but the Government held over the sale to late the following spring.

Rolls' announcement in its first full year as a privatized company that it would be cutting a further 2,000 jobs over two years was a reminder that the efficiency process goes on. The group still has 11 sites, the legacy of its origins, although it has made a virtue of the fact by designating different plants as centres of excellence for different work.

But no privatized company, not even British Steel – for all its global pre-eminence in low-cost manufacturing – has left the public sector without carrying over some burden from its days of State ownership. The Government may have written off hundreds of millions of pounds in balance sheet debts and deficits accumulated in the days when British Steel was technically bankrupt, but the group was not privatized with a clean slate. Of its five integrated steelworks, industry observers believe that at least one, and quite possibly two, will be closed within the next decade.

What British Steel has achieved as a result of the sweeping, post-strike rationalization nevertheless remains remarkable. The initial impact of the cuts was, scarcely surprisingly, shellshock. Colin James, in 1988 works manager at the Port Talbot mill, recalls: 'I think that maybe the management was almost as depressed as the workforce'. David Grieves acknowledges that 'morale did suffer to start with,' not just because of the spaces that were left by those who departed, but because the exodus was to some extent indiscriminate. 'There was a period of time when we tended to let the older people go rather than the younger people. People had moved up the seniority lines and were doing different jobs in different places. There was a period when people were settling down to the new working practices which had to be got through. It was quite a task virtually to reallocate the jobs of the whole labour force, because almost everyone was doing a different job.'

Generous severance terms facilitated this astonishing trans-formation. So did the development of the British Steel industry, which worked to foster new ventures and jobs in the steel closure and cutback areas like Consett, County Durham, where 3,900 jobs were lost when the steelworks closed in 1980, and Deeside in North Wales, which lost 8,000 jobs when steelmaking at Shotton was halted in the same year.

Shotton was the biggest single closure in British Steel's Slimline programme and at the time, the largest individual shutdown in Western Europe; Consett, on Derwentside, was a comparatively remote location. Yet, by the end of the decade, new investment in both areas by companies in a wide variety of industries had created as many jobs as had been lost when the steel works closed.

What also helped to realize British Steel's de-manning programme, unprecedented in its scale and speed, was the feeling among steelworkers themselves. In their book *Creating a Committed Workforce* (Institute of Personnel Management), Peter Martin and John Nicholls quote one strip mill worker who lost his job: 'We knew that things could not go on as they had been. Our wives used to tell us that we never did a full day's work for our money, and they were right. It had to change. People had to go or there would have been nothing left – nothing for anybody. I was sorry to go, but it was the right thing.'

The strike and its outcome provided the catharsis that gave free rein to such sentiments. The dispute itself appeared from the outset as a last stand by the steel unions – but particularly by the largest, the Iron and Steel Trades Confederation headed by Bill Sirs – against changes that British Steel simply had to make if it was to survive. If the unions had their backs to the wall in the dispute, that wall was dwarfed by the mountain of losses towering over the Corporation.

The flashpoint for the strike was management insistence on the linking of pay with performance through a new system of locally-determined lump-sum bonuses which would to a significant extent supersede the traditional, centrally-negotiated award of a national wage rise. The unions responded with a 20 per cent pay claim under the old system. The management rejected it, and the unions called the strike.

Grieves, whose department was given the responsibility of developing the lump sum bonus scheme, believes that beneath union opposition to the idea lay resistance to plant closures. A closure programme had been introduced in 1978, after a Labour Government White Paper which detailed a new corporate strategy of rationalization to deal with loss-making over-capacity. The White Paper, produced by Eric Varley, Industry Secretary in the Callaghan Government, at last reversed the expansionist forecasts set down in a 1973 Conservative Government White Paper which had been officially maintained during the ensuing five years despite being rendered almost immediately obsolete by the first oil crisis. The 1973 White Paper envisaged a rise in United Kingdom steel demand from 19.8 million tonnes that year to 35 million in 1978. The actual 1978 figure was 15.7 million tonnes.

Closure decisions had been shelved for years – ultimately for the simple political reason that the Wilson-Callaghan Labour Government of 1974 to 1979 contained numerous ministers with seats in or near steel plants. But in the two-and-three quarter years from the start of 1978 to the day the strike began, the 208,000 workforce was cut by 41,500. Grieves notes: 'There was a great antipathy toward the closures which were increasing in size and intensity, and there was a feeling that these had to stop somehow.'

Instead, the unions' defeat on the issue that triggered the dispute – performance-linked pay being introduced in return for a slightly higher national pay increase than British Steel had originally offered – left British Steel managers a clear field over which to press ahead. At a stroke, the outcome gave British Steel the opportunity to rebuild from the ground up – not so much in terms of capital investment, which had been relatively well maintained considering British Steel's mounting problems through the 1970s, but in the far more critical area of efficient operation to maximize the returns on that investment.

The strike was the first major dispute of the Thatcher era. After years of political concession and compromise, the Government's support for British Steel management was immensely reassuring. 'She was very good in it. She was like the rock of Gibraltar really ,' says Scholey, adding a hint that the Government may nevertheless have had its doubts as the dispute dragged on: 'There's a limit to patience; strikes like that are a big test of government.'

Nerves held, partly because British Steel's customers averted widespread shutdowns throughout manufacturing industry by turning to steel imports. British Steel's share of the total home market slumped from 49.5 per cent in 1978/9 to 44.1 per cent in the strike year and edged up only slightly to 46.1 per cent in 1980/1 as steel users stayed with imports, either through concern about security of British Steel supply or because they had signed long-term contracts during the dispute (Monopolies and Mergers Commission report on British Steel, July 1988).

The surge in imports brought home to the steelworkers a lesson in competitiveness as salutary as that learned by the Rolls-Royce shop stewards on their 1978 visit to the United States.

The steel men knew now that British industry could live without British Steel – it was a prime factor in their strike defeat. In the strike's aftermath, it was a small step from there to the recognition that sheer commercial survival dictated both the draconian measures now being taken by the management, and a constant effort to improve competitiveness thereafter.

With the strike over, other factors peculiar to the steel industry and conducive to the new management drive came into play. Grieves comments: 'Although there was a locking of horns nationally, the relationships in the works between management and workforce were quite good and still are. In a way, it's a man's world; it's a bit like mining: a slightly masculine identity which gives a certain feeling of strength about it.'

Unlike the later miners' strike, the steel strike was a purely industrial dispute with no political undertones save the basic break that it entrained with past years of State intervention in the business. In that sense too, it was a 'clean' strike. Inevitably, it left a residue of rancour among some of the union leaders – which surfaced a month after the strike ended when the ISTC called on new British Steel chairman Ian MacGregor to remove Scholey as chief executive – but when it was over, the corporation's way ahead was clear. 'The management knew what had to be done, and did it,' Grieves says.

Almost all the key elements in British Steel's advance, from the vicissitudes of the world steel market in the early 1980s through its return to profit in mid-decade to its late-1980s prosperity, were established in the immediate wake of the strike. They were embraced by the grassroots policy called 'Slimline', which was initiated by management in the two major South Wales integrated works of Port Talbot and Llanwern and subsequently disseminated throughout the group, and which continues today.

De-manning was an absolute precondition of Slimline in 1980, and the performance-linked payment of lump sum bonus schemes constituted the programme's first principle. But Slimline contained a string of other, closely related ingredients which made it a compendium of the new 1980s flexible working practices and a blueprint for industrial revolution. It aimed to break down traditional demarcation lines between departments and occupations, to establish a 'group working' approach. The number of management levels was reduced, and flexible working arrangements agreed between craft and process, and manual and staff grades. Slimline established the precept that ongoing manning levels were determined not by previously agreed 'standards', but by management decision pure and simple. Hence, it included a commitment to introduce labour-saving automation wherever practicable and cost-effective.

The policy extended to all aspects of plant management and shopfloor operation. The role of first-line supervisors was reassessed and new responsibilities devolved to senior machinery operators; shift patterns were changed to match manning to workload; Slimline ensured minimum manning by using so-called 'light manning' wherever possible, and 'challenged' the need for particular functions and services – like work study, which has been drastically reduced since 1980. It involved 'contractorization', in which some services were taken out of house and handed to external contractors. Catering, office cleaning, general amenities, transport, some building and civil engineering maintenance, were all contracted out at many works. Even mainstream activities like refractory brick-laying went out of house, while use of contract labour for 'peak-lopping' (covering irregular peaks in workload) was increased.

Slimline's benefits were succinctly described in 1983 by one Port Talbot electrician: 'I find more job satisfaction that I have had for many years. We are a smaller workforce now and yet more integrated. There are no craftsmen's mates within the works now, and the various craftsmen help each other out. Even the production workers help the craftsmen out as well, so there is a greater sense of purpose about it' (Quoted in *All Our Working Lives* by Peter Pagnamenta and Richard Overy, BBC Publications).

The steel thread that bound together this new British Steel was the lump sum bonus system, which meant that the workforce was rewarded for the profitability benefits that Slimline bestowed. Grieves describes the scheme as 'a significant move for a public corporation.' But that is an understatement. One basic premise of the new pay

A FIGHTING CHANCE

system most vividly conveys the extent of British Steel's 1980s break from its, and British manufacturing's, inflationary past: improvement in physical and financial performance has to precede any bonus payment.

The system has engineered other breakthroughs, including the coherence of British Steel's multiplicity of almost 20 unions into three basic negotiating groups – 'so in reality our industrial relations life is simpler,' Grieves comments. The criteria that determine the bonus have fostered worker awareness of the importance to profitability of quality, delivery on time and overall customer satisfaction. At the Port Talbot strip mill, Colin James notes: 'We have tailored the operation so that it is very customer-conscious.' Like Slimline itself, the bonus system has evolved during the decade since it was introduced. Allowing for local variations, today's system embraces four criteria: productivity, product cost, delivery on time and quality – the last ensuring that quality is not sacrificed to quantity. At Port Talbot, around 96 per cent of deliveries are now on time: many competitors are still below the 90 per cent level, as British Steel was at the outset of the decade.

It's a democratic system: the same bonus rate (though not the absolute money figure) goes to every employee except the plant manager. Psychology plays a part: the bonuses are paid quarterly – at Christmas, in the summer, and on two other occasions – and can total £300 or £400 a time. Port Talbot's works manager John Madden observes: 'With those kinds of sums, the bonus really makes a difference. If it was paid weekly, people wouldn't notice.' At the same time, the variability of the bonuses is very real. The difference in bonus rates between the various businesses can stretch from seven per cent to 15 per cent. And within a business, performance fluctuations can mean the bonus ranges from as little as two or three per cent to 18 or 20 per cent of total pay.

By definition of its objective – to sensitize steelworkers to conditions in the outside world that they serve – the scheme makes no allowances for external factors beyond employees' control. During the miners' strike, bonuses at the Scunthorpe plant, which was hit hard by the dispute, were negligible; as they were in particular at the hot strip mills, which suffered most from the appalling winter of 1981/2. Grieves declares: 'If you have one of these bonus schemes, you have to be absolutely rigid in what you've agreed: to be fair but firm.'

For all its 1980 pioneering radicalism, on privatization the pay system was still something of a hybrid, divided into three tiers: a nationally-negotiated basic pay rise, a tonnage-related payment made to all manufacturing operations; and the lump sum bonus. British Steel management is determined that the present two-year national deal which expires in March 1990 (and which was increased in its second year from 4.5 per cent to 5.5 per cent because of inflation) will be the last. 'We are talking about the extent to which you can maintain a monolithic situation,' observed Scholey just prior to privatization. 'Possibly, you can integrate the system more than it is at present.'

And despite its efficiency transformation, British Steel has a clear need, and opportunity, for further streamlining. In 1988/9, its labour costs, while substantially lower than those of some European rivals where costs approached one-third of sales, still lagged far behind the South Korean level of around 12 per cent. Performance levels within the company remain uneven. At Port Talbot, it took only 3.7 man hours to produce a tonne of liquid steel in 1987, well ahead of the company average of five man hours per tonne and up with best international practice where the Japanese remain widely recognized as overall industry leaders. But although British Steel's productivity gains have been immense, it has not quite cast off the handicap that MacGregor recognized at the press conference in December 1980 when he stated his determination to hold capacity at the 'Maginot line' of 14.4 million tonnes a year: 'The only trouble is they (the other steel companies) are about three laps ahead of us now. We have a lot of catching up to do.'

British Steel's past achievements, present paradoxes and future challenges in this race for supremacy are all encapsulated in its increasing use of continuous casting for steel making. This method is estimated to be at least £10 a tonne cheaper than the older ingot technique, but its installation is a long and costly job. In the 1980s, the proportion of British Steel's output made by continuous casting trebled from 27 per cent to about 82 per cent. But at that level, it was still behind West Germany and Italy (both 90 per cent of output), France (93 per cent) and Japan (95 per cent).

Moreover, the British Steel figure was only as high as 82 per cent because of the continued operation of the Ravenscraig plant in Scotland, the only works in the group which makes virtually all its steel by continuous casting. Yet in the longer term, Ravenscraig would seem the biggest potential casualty of British Steel's drive for cost- effectiveness.

As Scholey acknowledged in the run up to privatization, the group's proliferation of integrated works builds in a competitive disadvantage. 'We are a five-site company competing with companies that are on one site. That's a big difference in overheads and so on. When you are politically controlled, every MP wants money put into where he is, and you can't run a business like that. You've got to put the money where it is going to enable you to compete and become more single-pointed in your attack on markets.' As a result of privatization, he believed: 'These are the sort of changes that will be possible. Our investment programme can be more selective.'

While the rationalization and concentration of tinplate operations in South Wales early in 1989 bore Scholey out, that move was peripheral to the five-site issue. Analysts believe that British Steel's optimal plant configuration may consist of only three integrated works, including the two Welsh sites. Ravenscraig was the focus of attention immediately following privatization. Steel making at the plant was guaranteed, 'subject to market conditions', in August 1988 for seven years to 1995. But the same pledge was not given for the hot strip mill, the continued operation of which was promised only until 1989 in what looked more like a stay of execution.

Closure of the Ravenscraig mill would help to eliminate over-capacity which at the time of privatization meant that the ultra-modern, £171 million Port Talbot facility was operating at only about two-thirds capacity. Apart from ending Ravenscraig's history as an integrated works, a shutdown would finally excise the memory of one of the most wrongheaded instances of blatant political interference in industry.

The strip mill was only built, in 1958, because Prime Minister Harold Macmillan wanted to appease the Scottish lobby in the Conservative Party in a pre-election year. Macmillan commandeered a plan to build a three million tonne a year strip mill at Llanwern – the minimum size reckoned to provide necessary economies of scale – and split the project between Llanwern and Ravenscraig. Macmillan's critics derided the decision as 'the judgment of Solomon'. It was the height of industrial stupidity. It sacrificed the project's whole rationale on the altar of political expediency.

As for Ravenscraig as a whole, with the diminution of the Scottish engineering industry in the 1970s, the plant appeared ever more out on a limb in cost and market terms. It remains the nub of several issues, a living monument to the post-war politicization of British manufacturing industry – and not just because of the politics that dictated the strip mill's construction. Ravenscraig's survival through the 1980s is eloquent testimony to the difficulties that the Thatcher governments have encountered in their struggle to shed the legacy accumulated by years of interventionism in industrial decision-making.

At first, Thatcherism found itself perpetuating the interventionist inheritance of Ravenscraig. MacGregor wanted to shut the plant in 1982, when British Steel suffered the second phase of the early 1980s slump in demand. But the imminence of the next general election meant that ministers ruled out closure on political grounds. The 1983 election was followed by the 1984/5 miners' strike, during which Ravenscraig steelworkers defied intense pressure from the Scottish area of the National Union of Mineworkers and continued to work flat out. Their action influenced a three-year Government commitment to maintain steelmaking at all five integrated works. In taking its hands off the over-manned mining industry, Thatcherism found itself paying a hands-on debt to Ravenscraig. British Steel management subsequently gave the seven-year pledge to maintain steel-making at the five works.

Ravenscraig started to pay its way when steel demand began to boom. At the time of privatization, British Steel clearly needed its capacity to meet demand. But if demand should fall away, the crunch will come. Ravenscraig will be exposed. British Steel will want to close it and the Scottish Labour movement will oppose such a decision with all the weapons it can muster. That will leave the politicians. Whatever government is in power, its attitude to a planned closure of Ravenscraig will be a final judgment, not just on the plant, but on the whole doctrine of non-interventionism.

No single potential act of rationalization in British Aerospace remotely approaches the political sensitivity of Ravenscraig. But the Dynamics division overhaul of February 1989 showed that the group was embarking on a major structural change which will have

A FIGHTING CHANCE

widespread impact. The logic, expounded by Lygo, is simple: 'We have a chicken pox of sites, many in the South of England. You don't want low-value manufacturing facilities in high value sites. It's an absolutely natural step to put your manufacturing into areas where manufacturing is best suited. It doesn't follow that your engineering and design will go there too. The software revolution has enabled you to be on line to anybody, so the dangers of separating your design from manufacture, which don't totally disappear, are largely overcome by your ability to have instantaneous communications.'

British Steel is contemplating a structural shift of a different kind, but one which echoes the purpose behind BAe's decentralization strategy: to make the organization as receptive as possible to the commercial stimuli of market demands. Scholey remarked in late 1988: 'At the moment, we have a very strong cost control system – it's probably one of the best there is. But costs are one thing; the pressures of the market are another. Whereas we've brought this much closer to the manufacturing base, the question is how much closer we can take it. The more we can organize the company into discrete business sectors, the more speedily we can do what I'm talking about.

'You could argue that we have been a top-down driven outfit, and that we've got to generate and increase the drive from the bottom up. As we are now, we are like a grand army and I say "wheel right" and so on. Maybe it should be more individual, and we want one bit to wheel right and the other bit to wheel left because they are all in different parts of the market.'

Scholey enumerated the profound changes that would have to be made if British Steel was to be thoroughly imbued with the market ethos. He called the process one of 'consolidation'. It would, indeed, be the culmination of the devolution drive that was started under MacGregor. He inherited the somewhat cumbersome group structure introduced by British Steel chairman Sir Monty Finniston in the mid-1970s. Finniston had formed five geographical manufacturing divisions as cost centres, with orders and sales made the responsibility of four product units and the subsequent overlap being co-ordinated by various committees – and Scholey, as chief executive. Faint antecedents of the MacGregor decentralization could be detected in the establishment of some subsidiary operations, including tinplate, stockholding and stainless steels, as profit centres.

Using the management consultants McKinsey, MacGregor went much further. He broke down the Finniston organization into a series of profit centre businesses, with the two biggest operations – general steels and strip mills – each made into an omnicompetent group embracing both manufacturing and commercial activities with a chairman apiece. The principles guiding this October 1980 re-organization – decentralization and delegation, individual manager accountability, management by exception via performance monitoring against agreed targets and a clear chain of command from chairman down the line – remained constant through the decade.

Eight years later, Scholey was looking at ultimate devolution. Eventually, every profit centre business might have its own bank account, while the parent organization became more of a holding company. And return on capital employed (ROCE) would become the basis of operation for the profit-centre businesses. Such arrangements are commonplace among diversified private sector companies. The difference in British Steel's case is that the group is, at least at present, basically a steel company – albeit one with an uncommonly wide product range.

Perhaps it is this 'purity' of concentration on one kind of business that has produced British Steel's exceptionally powerful manufacturing philosophy, a motive force which stands out from the general run in British industry. Scholey may not be an industrial Aristotle, but under him, British Steel dwells exceptionally on the potential for infinite improvement and makes the apparently abstract thoroughly relevant to commercial practice.

Maybe there is something about the steel industry and the perpetual motion of the steel making process itself – the blast furnace fires must never die – which encourages such an approach. It is not confined to British Steel. The same philosophy is articulated by Alan Cox, chief executive of ASW Holdings, which as Allied Steel & Wire was a pioneering joint venture between State-owned British Steel and private sector engineering giant GKN.

Formed in July 1981, ASW was the first of the 'Phoenix' joint ventures between British Steel and the private sector. It has proved well-named. When the company was created, it was losing £2 million a month. In 1988, it made pre-tax profits of £30.9 million. The previous year, it was bought from its original owners by its management and a group of financial institutions with British Steel retaining a 20 per cent stake. Less than nine months later, it was floated on the Stock Market valued at almost £100 million. Eight months later, its value had climbed to more than £155 million.

Cardiff-based, manufacturing a range of 'long' commodity products for the construction and engineering industries like rods, bars and sections, together with more downstream items like wire and reinforcements, ASW was in many ways a harbinger and pathfinder for British Steel. In the early days of its recovery, like British Steel, it sought to learn from overseas steelmakers – notably the Japanese Kobe and Kyoei groups – with whom it has forged a lasting relationship including visits by around 250 ASW managers and workers to Japan.

This cultural cross-fertilization has made a lasting, visible impression on ASW which is immediately evident at its Tremorfa steelworks in South Wales – where output increased two-and-a-half fold between 1981 and 1988. ASW's guiding light and inspiration is Cox, 51 years old in 1988, who has found his true vocation since leaving the corporate managerial hierarchy of turn-of-the-Seventies GKN. A charismatic and highly individual figure, Cox's vision of the challenge facing ASW has a rare objectivity. As a producer of essentially low-value products – nuts, bolts and screws – the group can only succeed against competition from low-wage countries by paring costs to the bone. At the same time, superior service and product quality will command a margin-enhancing premium in any market. That obvious fact makes ASW's particular experience relevant to manufacturing industry in general.

Cox knows that ASW has come a long way since it first turned to the Japanese for advice. 'At the beginning, we just said "Help". After 18 months talking, they at last agreed to come. Our management's own assessment of our potential was miles below what the Japanese were achieving with broadly similar kit. More than that, they were better than our top management thought we could ever be,' says Cox.

Something like a miracle has therefore been worked. In 1981, ASW was obtaining between 50 and 60 per cent of Japanese performance levels. In late 1988, Cox estimated that ASW was achieving 90 per cent of Japanese performance. And he was looking at that final ten per cent – the key that would open the door to true world class.

Cox could recognize the key: 'The difference between us and the Japanese isn't technology: it's the fact that their output is sustained at an excellent level the whole time. In our case, we achieve excellence a lot of the time but not the whole time. Therefore our average performance is less than excellent. This is the industrial product challenge.'

Cox also understands the components that make up that key to the attainment of Japanese standards: 'The Japanese are superb at revisiting subjects – energy consumption for instance. They will study it, go off and examine something else, then 12 months later come back to it. And you can't solve problems in isolation. You must look at the whole system. The business of constant improvement is like peeling off an onion: you get to smaller and smaller pieces. Because the whole system is coming more and more under control, you are able to measure more and control more. There is no end to the process, because it's an observable fact that, say, two in a thousand products don't make it and it's still an observable fact if it's one in a million products, and it can become one in ten million. The Japanese have that approach towards the quality of the product, the amount of energy used to produce it, maybe even towards the purchase price of the iron ore. If capital expenditure is required, all that does is alter the standard – and the standard keeps changing.'

So ASW looks at its business as a series of 'nerve centres'. 'If you can identify one area for attack, which in itself means that other areas are brought under control at the same time then you can concentrate on one thing and all the other factors improve automatically. It has taken management a long time to get hold of that idea, but now more and more people understand the process.'

ASW's role as a working model for British manufacturing industry is emphasized by the twin imperatives that follow from its manufacturing analysis. One is the need for sustained investment. As Cox remarks: 'You've got to be objective about the standards you set, but you have to spend a lot of time and money on being objective.' The other is the indivisibility of workforce and product quality – or cause and effect.

Use of statistical process control (SPC) – mainframe

computer-linked terminals monitoring plant processes to minimize product variation – can secure the consistency that both cuts costs and gains customers. British Steel's development of SPC has won the admiration of motor giant Ford, one of SPC's worldwide pioneers. ASW is expanding SPC through its plants.

In much of the private sector, the investment habit was lost during the recession and took a long time to recover thereafter. Natural concern to minimize risk combined with the post-slump takeover boom that appeared to make vulnerable any company which was not maximizing short-term profits growth. But British Steel and ASW were different: both effectively made fresh starts at the very outset of the decade but until very late in the 1980s, they were immured against the full range of market pressures – Stock Market as well as industrial market – that assailed private sector manufacturers. Therefore, they may have been able to breed a culture of constructive, long-term investment with sufficiently deep roots, by the time of their flotations, to absorb the pressures on public companies to show instant performance and instant reward.

Just how robust this balanced culture is will not be known until steel industry growth slows down or stops. At ASW, Cox has maintained that the basic assumption underlying group strategy has been to secure earnings growth even when the market is flat. His main pre- occupation is not transient market trends, but the persistent challenge of matching Far Eastern workforce quality.

'If the UK has one competitive disadvantage, it's in this area of education and training to maximize people's individual potential,' Cox said in late 1988. 'In South Korea, 99.5 per cent of the children stay in school until they are 18. The whole of the population is educated to a higher level. When you come to industry, you must have the ability to examine how things can be improved. If people haven't got the knowledge or taken the time to learn about it, you can't just say, "give me some suggestions".'

Because of the loss-making state of the businesses at ASW's inception, graduate recruitment had almost stopped and the company had to start building up a future management cadre almost from scratch. Apart from simple graduate recruitment, it started a sponsored scholarship scheme in which a school-leaver does a year with the company before going to university, and returns to ASW during university holidays. Higher up the scale, in 1983 ASW formed a 'fast track' management development group, comprising both graduates and existing employees nominated by their general managers. In the first two years of its graduate intake programme, ASW lost almost half the recruits at the end of their training period. Cox says: 'Because it was all so new, and they were coming out of their training, they were worried about whether they would get jobs. But that confidence level has risen as the new graduates can see their predecessors going into good posts.' In the four years to the end of 1988, only one graduate was lost out of the entire intake.

The problems of adjustment early on lay as much with the group as with the graduates. 'When you start bringing young people in and they've got this urge to go on and do things, it takes time for the company to be receptive to that. It takes time for people to realize that they have a contribution to make,' Cox comments.

Every aspect of the recruitment and training programme is stamped with characteristic professionalism and attention to detail. Previous-year graduates sit on the annual selection panel, while the number of those selected is governed not by a quota but by the quality of the candidate. New recruits are pushed hard, working on real projects with an impact on bottom-line profits at the end of the day. Some of those who join the management development group do not last the pace. Among the courses taken by those who do is one, introduced in 1988, on innovative thinking.

'These people should be harbingers of change,' Cox declares. 'You install new people; you make sure they don't pick up old cultural ideas. After four or five years, they should be reaching the top senior level below general manager.' ASW is a young company: in 1989, it sent a general manager to Harvard Business School for the first time. As a result of this investment in people, Cox says, 'we have got the management succession coming through'. Moreover, 'we have got the brainpower in the company now. We are solving problems we couldn't even have approached six or seven years ago.'

In late 1987, each ASW unit was asked to produce a long-term training plan. A year later as the expansion of ASW's on-site Cardiff training facilities demonstrated, the group began to gear up for its biggest task. It was preparing for a five-fold increase in the amount of training received by its 3,100 adult employees, with the aim of giving each one about two weeks' training every year – in line with that received by ASW's West German competitors.

After bringing ASW so far towards best international standards, Cox and his colleagues had concluded that only such a quantum leap in training could hope to produce a sufficiently skilled workforce to take the company the rest of the way. But the training effort would be worthless in isolation from changes in working practices and union co-operation to give ASW total flexibility in both employee training and deployment. In late 1988, as Cox determinedly sought to reach the agreements that would open this last, great door he commented: 'Our major task now is the training of the 3,000. This is the only way we can become world class – otherwise, I can't do it.'

Like Alan Cox, in October 1988 British Steel chairman Sir Robert Scholey attended the International Iron and Steel Confederation annual conference in Seoul and saw at close hand the training effort being mounted by the South-East Asian steelmakers. Scholey and his colleagues had not been idle. For British Steel, 1986 was not only Industry Year but Training Year, the launching pad for a sustained drive to raise the skill standards of its work-force – by encouraging employee self-improvement as well as management-led development.

David Grieves explains: 'You can only do so much with a Slimline management team. Therefore, the priorities of the early 1980s were really to get the productivity improvement and performance and results which would give some future to the business.

'Once we got a feeling that we were emerging like a great whale out of the water, we could then see a much-reduced labour force with more capital investment, technology, automation. We then came fairly rapidly to the view that the 50,000-odd people that were left really had to be of the highest quality. With some of the agreements of the last two years, we've built in the need for total quality performance and we have spent a lot more effort on identifying the content of jobs, the quality of people needed to do the jobs, and the means by which we could train people.'

British Steel has applied to training the same principles that infuse all its operations. It established a central training unit to ensure the quality of its training activities. In turn, the unit set up, in February 1985, an Open Learning development project both to encourage Open Learning courses throughout the company (video courses which any employee can take in private) and to develop Computer-based Training (CBT) and 'interactive video' training programmes. Interactive video, consisting of computer software which provides for two-way 'communication' between a video teaching programme and an employee, is being increasingly adopted, notably by large and multi-national companies. British Steel is a UK leader in the field, and has its own video-link course production unit based at the Scunthorpe plant. At one of its Tinplate works, an interactive video installation stands in the finishing department and can be used during workers' down time, 24 hours a day.

Worker receptiveness to these computer learning techniques has been demonstrably enhanced by the changing nature of steel making itself. The rapid post-strike move to automation and process control by workers seated in galleries above the 'shopfloor' monitoring operations on television screens – 'like the flight deck on a jumbo jet,' says Grieves – gave British Steel a flying start in CBT over companies in other industries.

British Steel needs all the advantages it can get, because of the UK's historic backwardness in vocational training. A study of British Steel (by Martin and Nicholls) found that while overall training spend in Europe was about 2.5 per cent of employment costs (0.5 per cent of sales), half British Steel's budget had to be spent on youth training while Belgian steel maker Sidmar can spend its entire budget on adult training, because its school-leaver employees have attended technical schools. Grieves remains sanguine: 'We don't look upon it as a handicap. I suppose you can look at it as a cost you are absorbing, but you are training your own. In South Korea, it is the other way round from Belgium: POSCO at Kwangyang provides a whole range of schools from kindergarten to senior.

'While the training cost is important, the process cost is huge. If your training can increase yield, productivity, speed of operations, quality, delivery on time; reduce difficulties; cut paperwork and improve customer relations – that's huge money.'

British Steel is believed by some observers to have secured – in one or two plants – the kind of total workforce flexibility that ASW is seeking. While both companies address the long-term workforce quality and malleability issue, they have immediate expansion prospects. Because of the European Commission-imposed system of production quotas, which was only abolished on 1 July, 1988, both companies entered the private sector vastly under-represented in mainland Europe. The continent should be fertile ground for them to bring to bear their low-cost production achievements and financial strength. But they have to find the right access.

On the one hand, British Steel must expand its distribution network in mainland Europe – easier said than done, because of the vested nationalistic interests on the Continent. For a time in 1989, it looked as if the company might be able to buy the steel trading business of Kloeckner & Co., which had been taken over by Deutsche Bank after it had suffered calamitous currency dealing losses. This dream deal would have enabled British Steel to capture in one fell swoop a complete West German distribution network. But the tantalizing prospect abruptly disappeared when Kloeckner was bought by the German industrial concern, Viag. British Steel, it appeared, would have to settle for a gradualist expansion of its distribution chain.

But through joint ventures in low-cost manufacturing countries, it was also aiming to build a manufacturing presence on the mainland. Such developments would form part of a trend outlined by Scholey in a speech to the Institute of Metals in London in May 1989, when he remarked on the formation by Japanese steelmakers of American joint ventures. Scholey made it clear that he believed international co-operation to rationalize and balance capacity represented the way ahead for the industry.

In terms of product, rather than geographical markets, evolution will to some extent carry British Steel naturally downstream from basic steelmaking into fresh areas where it can add more value to its products. A now-familiar example is in the growth market of coated steel, for which demand from the motor industry is notably increasing. Through a technological breakthrough to which British Steel is close, organically coated steel could be developed into semi-finished products which would do away with the need for a paint shop and could be delivered virtually ready for assembly in a vehicle.

Scholey is resolved that expansion will be in areas related to the company's steel and metals expertise, not in general diversification. 'It's best to go into those areas which we know something about, rather than to launch off into something we know nothing about and get a bloody nose. Some of our continental friends are diversified into areas that are not related to steel. We have got to think very carefully about where we have got to move; it is not something to indulge in lightly.'

Scholey's leadership of British Steel, which will provide corporate continuity into the new decade, is one of the most remarkable features of British manufacturing management. Aged 67 at privatization, he pledged to stay at the helm until he reached 70. By the time he retires, Scholey will therefore have been near or at the top of the company for almost 20 years. He was made chief executive in 1973, deputy chairman in 1976, CEO and deputy chairman in 1983 – and was finally appointed chairman, after 39 years in the steel industry, in 1986. There seems to be something about British Steel which encourages longevity: after the 1980 appointment of 67-year-old Ian MacGregor and his succession by 60-year-old Sir Robert Haslam, British Steel staff started to joke that by the year 2000 they would have the first centenarian chairman. Despite his age, Scholey killed the joke by the respect he commanded among employees as the first chairman to be appointed from within the industry since its renationalization 19 years earlier.

Nicknamed 'Black Bob' because of the black safety helmet he wore in earlier days, Scholey is a son of Sheffield steel – his father was a director of English Steel – who has been a steelman throughout his post-war working life.

His eventual appointment to the top job, after being passed over in favour of outsiders no less than three times (in favour of Sir Charles Villiers, MacGregor and Haslam), speaks volumes for the politicization of nationalized industries. Company politics are one thing. Westminster and Whitehall politics are something else again, being so far divorced from industrial needs and realities. By reaching the chair, Scholey had overcome long-held political and civil service resistance to his appointment. His close association with the tough management line during the strike had left a residue of Whitehall displeasure at the discomfort that inevitably resulted from such a massive dispute. He has never suffered gladly those he saw as being in error, and showed little respect for civil service management of the industry.

MacGregor's appointment caused a furore because it involved a secondment payment, or 'transfer fee', which could have amounted to £1.8 million (and actually came to about £1.5 million) to Lazard Freres, the New York investment bank where MacGregor was a general partner. But while he must have been disappointed not to get the job, Scholey recognizes the benefits of MacGregor's appointment: 'It was very fortunate for us, getting MacGregor, because the Government paid so much for him that the system had to stand back. With MacGregor, we started to operate more independently of the political whims.'

Scholey acknowledges that 'we have had less trouble with this Government than others'. Nonetheless, very close to the privatization itself there were still rumours that while British Steel management wanted the business floated at the earliest opportunity, the Government machine initially favoured waiting until 1990. Privatization in late 1988 was also Scholey's vindication: 'You have fantastic freedom to act as a private sector company,' he declared on the eve of the sale.

The remark reflected Scholey's free market beliefs, part of an open philosophy which added a dimension to the management character of the group. Scholey's breadth of vision might appear paradoxical given that his industrial experience is limited to steel. A curriculum vitae like that could have bred a confined, tunnel view, but in Scholey's case has clearly produced the obverse: a worldly and confident understanding grown out of comprehensive knowledge of his industry and all its angles.

Grieves likens British Steel to a surfacing whale, but Scholey reminds one more of the walrus – a wise, slightly awesome and immensely forceful personality who will expound readily on failures of management in the National Health Service and the BBC – two hobby horses regarded by his colleagues with wry and weary familiarity. More relevantly for manufacturing industry he also speaks his mind on the Government's slipping standards of inflation control: 'I had a go at Nigel Lawson about it a year ago,' he recounted in late 1988. 'We are learning to live with four per cent inflation; I was on about getting it down to 1.5 per cent or two per cent, because four per cent on our costs is £50 million a year. We want inflation down to West German levels.'

When a bout of unfounded pre-privatization speculation ran round the Stock Market that Japanese steel companies were preparing to pounce on British Steel shares, Scholey observed bluntly: 'One man's money is as good as another's in my book.' He welcomed the prospect that British Steel would have an international investor base: 'This is the way the world is going. I would have thought it was a good thing, because if the great shock horror in life is world conflict, the more you get linked together in commerce and business, the less chance there is of that kind of nonsense breaking out.'

That belief in the community of industrial nations has been fostered by the nature of the world steel industry itself, where a sense of fellow-feeling appears to have survived the trend to ever-intensifying competition more successfully than in other globally cut-throat industries. Grieves observes that 'although we are all competing with each other, there is a world brotherhood that does allow visits and exchanges and dialogue. It's a world process and our perspective is the world.'

Within British Steel, one senses a certain feeling that other UK manufacturers have lacked that global perspective and therefore failed to respond to the competitive challenge that it has presented. Scholey observes: 'All too often, there is an emphasis on our direct exports whereas really our strength should lie in our indirect exports from manufacturing products. From time to time we feel a little bit of disappointment that UK manufacturing has not got going as well as it might.

'What we've done, everybody else could do and should do. There is more tolerance of unemployment than might be supposed, and if you are going to sharpen up your manufacturing, you've got to face up to that. If the exchange rate moves against you, it's up to manufacturers to tighten up on their manpower utilization because we've got to export to live.'

One private sector counter argument would be that it is only thanks to massive Government subventions that British Steel has got itself into such enviable competitive shape. Certainly, the Government support has been massive – about £7.8 billion in the ten years before the company made itself self-sufficient in December 1985, plus the subsequent write-off of its accumulated deficit (British Steel Offer for Sale Prospectus, November 1988.) But since Government interference was principally responsible for getting the Corporation into such a mess, its later bail-outs are best seen as repairing self-inflicted damage. MacGregor told his first press conference: 'I went through a Japanese plant not so long ago ... you know, you could fire a gun through the thing and you wouldn't hit anyone – but it was turning out more steel than any of our mills.' Only after the political shackles were loosened in 1979 did British Steel bite the efficiency bullet, on its own initiative.

The great irony of nationalization concerns not money, but the huge home market muscle of the groups that the State created (or, in Rolls' case, took over). Few, if any, indigenous companies in the relatively fragmented and foreigner-penetrated British manufactured goods sector enjoy the scale of domestic market dominance wielded by British Steel, Rolls-Royce and – in aerospace and defence products – British Aerospace. British Steel holds the kind of home market share in the product areas that it covers that most companies which have spent their lives in the private sector can only dream about. In uncoated strip products, its 1987/8 British market share was 55 per cent; in coated strip, 67 per cent; in tinplate, 80 per cent; in sections and plates, 74 per cent; in stainless steel, 55 per cent; in tubes, 48 per cent. Its overall home market share of the products it supplies stands at 61 per cent. Compare that with Rover Group's under-15 per cent of the domestic car market.

The contrast with Rover is enlightening, because British Steel is everything that Rover might have been. Its huge home market share puts it at least on a par with every major European competitor national steel champion – Usinor-Sacilor in France, Ilva in Italy, the six major West German groups headed by Thyssen – while its profitability in 1987/8 far exceeded any of them. Every major continental European country boasts at least one significant, home-market leading, vehicle manufacturer – except Britain, where in 1988 Rover was third biggest behind the Americans Ford and Vauxhall (General Motors).

The reason for the difference, of course, is history. By the time Sir Michael Edwardes took British Leyland by the scruff of the neck (with Ian MacGregor urging him on from the non-executive directors' box), it was too late to recover all the ground lost by the company in the British motor industry. What is now Rover was unfortunate in finding itself in the front line of import penetration. Trapped in the British industrial decline of the 1970s, British Leyland was hit by all the weaknesses implanted by nationalization with no chance of enjoying its potential benefits. For benefits there were, as British Steel has already proved and British Aerospace can demonstrate in the 1990s. The size of the nationalized manufacturers, such a crippling liability in the 1970s when it simply magnified the flaws that riddled British industry, became a source of colossal potential strength in the 1980s when top management was given a freer hand.

That size and potential strength, not the fact that Government-financed life support ensured that the companies survived to reach the Stock Market, is the supreme irony of the privatization programme. It unleashed into the private sector massive groups which had emerged from the blatant government intervention that created them to take their place at the apex of Britain's manufacturing pyramid. They were the prime contractors. Below them stood the hierarchy of component makers and sub-contractors which constitute the industrial community.

The Thatcher Governments even conspired to preserve the companies' immunity as national champions – though the phrase was never made explicit. Article 43 of Rolls' articles of association states that 'it is a cardinal principle that the Company should be and remain under United Kingdom control'. As with British Aerospace, the Government stipulated that foreign shareholdings should be less than 15 per cent (though in 1989, the European Commission pressured Britain to raise the limit). In all three, the Government took a special or 'golden' share which could protect the companies against takeover after privatization.

But – and this is the final twist – if British Steel and British Aerospace had not been created by previous, interventionist governments, Thatcherism would not have invented them.

Rolls-Royce is a slightly different case. Tombs believes that its 1971 nationalization may not have been necessary: 'My own view is that nationalization didn't need to take place. The first RB 211 ran the day after nationalization, so the technical problems were over. There was a very understandable panic reaction to what was seen as a national crisis. Rolls-Royce going down was a bit like burning the Union Jack. If we had had the banks taking a longer view, then Rolls-Royce could have survived with a reconstructed balance sheet and it would not have been 16 years in State ownership. So there was something of a lack of vision at the time on the part of the financial establishment, and something of a chain reaction on the part of the Government. If somebody like that got into serious trouble today, the principal institutions would get together with the banks and sort it out.'

Whatever the truth of the matter, Rolls today is a far stronger company than it was even five years ago. A clear sign of its new confidence was given in February 1987, when the group abandoned a risk and revenue joint venture with General Electric in high-thrust engines which Duncan had concluded in February 1984. Under the deal, GE obtained a 15 per cent share in Rolls' 535E4 engine, designed to power the Boeing 757 mid-range jet with 40,000 pounds of thrust. GE thus secured access to a market which it had no product to service. In return, Rolls took a similar share in a big GE engine, with potential for more than 60,000 pounds of thrust. But it was GE which was in the driving seat. Without an agreement like that, Duncan believed, Rolls would have had to abandon the high-thrust market because it could not afford to develop an engine to satisfy it.

Just under three years later, the balance of power had shifted. Rolls abandoned the deal in favour of a more modest arrangement whereby it and GE would each act as a sub-contractor on the other's engine. Tombs noted: 'That original agreement was leading us nowhere.' Thanks to the 535E4, Rolls raised its share of the medium-size engine market from 20 per cent in 1978 to around 47 per cent in 1988 (Rolls-Royce estimate).

That position is exceptional, and Rolls remains very much the third player in the non-Communist aero engine industry. Nevertheless, it has succeeded in lifting market share generally. Since 1978, its overall civil aircraft engine market share has increased from about 14 per cent to a little over 20 per cent, and deputy chairman Sir Ralph Robins is confident of boosting that to 30 per cent by the early 1990s.

The cornerstone of its success has been the uniquely flexible design of the RB211, the engine that precipitated the 1971 crisis but has since spawned the 524 series of ever more powerful engines. What has made this possible is the engine's three-shaft design which, by placing compressors on each shaft, has allowed Rolls engineers consistently to upgrade the engine without incurring massive re-design costs. GE and P&W both use two-shaft engines.

Only at the very end of the Eighties did the original RB211 reach the limit of its almost infinite variability – and by then Rolls had started out on a £300 million project to build the RB211–524L series engine which would deliver thrust totalling between 65,000 and 70,000 pounds – a more powerful product than either GE or P&W possessed. Like the old RB211 generation, the new engine was based on a novel design centred on the so-called 'wide-chord fan', driven by a new low-pressure turbine which increases thrust and cuts fuel consumption considerably.

Rolls has continued to worry away at efficiency levels. In the two years after privatization, the workforce was trimmed by four per cent, sales per employee raised by ten per cent, manufacturing lead times cut to the point where an engine could be produced in a year, and stocks cut eight per cent (Rolls figures).

By being light on its feet – strong in innovation, highly efficient – Rolls aimed to hold its own against the American giants. Tombs acknowledged the difference: 'We have to use the rifle, rather than the shotgun.' One obvious threat from the Americans stands out, but Tombs commented in late 1988: 'If they did become more efficient, we would have a considerable problem. But they don't show much sign of doing so.'

At the same time, Rolls' size imposes certain limitations. The company will not capitalize research and development costs – that is, write them off against anticipated future sales – because that practice is what undermined its balance sheet in 1971. As a result, it has to fund R and D up front out of its cash flow. And its cash flow is not big enough to support a programme of the scale of the new RB211–524L project without Government aid to smooth out the cost burden. Rolls looked to the Government to loan it one third of the £300 million total cost, with repayments to follow from commercial sales. But the Government would not oblige, and sanctioned no more than £40 million in indirect aid. Consequently, Rolls settled for the second-best alternative of enlisting overseas partners to take revenue shares in the project. Japanese companies took a nine per cent stake; Rolls looked for a European partner to take another 11 per cent, bringing the total external interest up to 20 per cent or £60 million. The refusal of the Government to participate through launch aid meant that, as Tombs noted, 'by selling chunks of the project overseas, we diminish our foreign earnings capability'.

While Government policy was forcing Rolls to come to terms with this situation, the company was facing up to a corporate development challenge. For its longer-term health, it needed to broaden its business base away from the near-total concentration on aero-engines.

Its first target was Northern Engineering Industries, maker of power station turbines and boilers, electrical transmission and distribution equipment, and other engineering products like cranes and mining locomotives. NEI and its chairman Terry Harrison were well known to Tombs, who had worked for NEI's turbine company before the NEI group was formed. Rolls bought 4.7 per cent of NEI's shares and talks about a takeover of the company began – only to founder because the top price that Rolls was prepared to pay was thought too low by a majority of NEI's board. Harrison, who could see the advantages of becoming part of a larger group, favoured a deal. He and Tombs bided their time, and four months after the first talks failed, Rolls agreed acquisition terms with NEI in April, 1989. The deal at once reduced Rolls' bias towards aero-engines from about 90 per cent to less than two-thirds of the business. Further diversification was on the horizon.

Rolls' measured search for a broader engineering base was a reminder of the corporate immaturity that characterized more than one privatized manufacturer at the time of their flotation. However expert, and dominant, they were in their own, home fields, they were not fully rounded enterprises. Indeed, their frequent dominance of their home markets in a way pointed up a one-sidedness about these companies which confronted them, in the private sector, with the task of balancing, and therefore strengthening, their portfolios.

By far the most astonishing move of this nature was British Aerospace's 1988 takeover of the State-owned Rover Group. So well kept was the secret of the negotiations between BAe and the

Department of Trade and Industry that their first public announcement – on 1 March, 1988 – came out of the perfect flying conditions of a clear blue sky. Some clouds subsequently appeared – notably in European Commission insistence that the Government's proposed £800 million pre-sale aid for Rover be cut by £253 to £547 million – but 4½ months later, the deal was completed.

BAe paid the Government £150 million for Rover, but the other assorted benefits it received – including unused capital allowances and write-downs, which could be offset against tax, plus Rover's stake in the Leyland-DAF trucks joint venture that was floated on the Stock Market in 1989 – eliminated that nominal purchase price. Indeed, the abiding impression left by the terms and the manner of the deal – 'It all looked so cosy,' commented one industry analyst – was that the Government was paying BAe to take Rover off its hands. Certainly, it was not a sale – more a transfer of ownership.

For the DTI, it was second time lucky. After its first attempt to privatize what was then BL – Austin Rover cars, Land-Rover and the Leyland Vehicles trucks side – had been killed two years earlier by a hail of political opposition. Revelation of that attempt had been equally sudden, no-one having appreciated the Government determination, bordering on obsession, to be rid of BL. One BL manager close to the negotiations maintains that the DTI was guilty of excessive opportunism. The General Motors talks on the purchase of the non-cars business had been long-running and carefully developed. But the idea that the BL problem could be cured in one fell swoop, by the simultaneous sale of Austin Rover to Ford, was a latecomer which over-egged a denationalization pudding that was always going to be difficult for the country to swallow, because of the overtones of industrial Americanization. What doomed the masterplan entirely was the contemporaneous Westland crisis, which temporarily strengthened the influence of the Conservative backbenchers – several of whom, scenting major redundancies in their Midlands constituencies if the GM and Ford deals went through, vociferously opposed the disposal plans.

Two years on, hardly a voice was heard objecting to the BAe deal, however much of a giveaway it was. In the first moments after the deal was announced it seemed that the most likely objectors would be BAe shareholders, wondering what on earth their board was getting them into by talking over the weakest national volume car company in Western Europe. Instead, BAe shares jumped on news of the proposed deal – and jumped again as it was finally signed and sealed.

The BAe shareholders were quick to recognize the move as a remarkable piece of financial opportunism, guided by the astute hand of Professor Smith. Ever since privatization, British Aerospace's capital base had been viewed as being too small for a company with its range of activities – and notably, its exposure to the civil aircraft business. Now, the addition of Rover's assets at a stroke boosted shareholders' funds from £1 billion to £2.2 billion and increased stated net asset value per share from 420p to around 800p (actual net asset value was more than £10 a share, because of BAe's property reserves). A British Aerospace executive summed up the deal: 'It's a £700 million rights issue for nothing; that makes it our biggest achievement to date.' Smith averred: 'Other people must be kicking themselves for not spotting this opportunity.' He claimed that the acquisition surpassed BTR's takeover of Dunlop as the deal of the decade.

Certainly, the numbers were impressive. The deal catapulted BAe to second place in the British manufacturing league, behind only ICI, with annual sales in 1989 of about £8.5 billion. The new group had more than 100,000 employees. And because it coincided with Rover's return to (tax free) profits, it looked good at the bottom line. As for Rover, its chairman Sir Graham Day declared at the 1988 Birmingham Motor Show, several months after the deal was done, that it was 'good for this business, because the endless speculation – all of it utterly unfounded – about what was going to happen to us is now over.'

That was true, in the short-to-medium term. But the deal also raised a big additional question mark over BAe's future, as concern focused on the impact on the non-car side if Rover were to hit fresh trouble. Everyone in European motors knew that the industry was in line for a capacity shake-out as Japanese inroads into the market widened and lengthened. How would the none-too-secure Rover stand up to that? Rover's manufacturing efficiency was indeed far superior to BAe's – which was about the only piece of industrial, rather than financial, logic in the deal. And it had a bright, new marketing strategy in which volume market share meant much less than success in carefully targeted profitable niches along the car-making spectrum.

That strategy was intensely ambivalent. It made some sense, since the car market is becoming every more differentiated with the multiplication of customer segments. But it could just as easily have been manufactured out of sheer necessity to mask a continuing market retreat. What remained undeniable was that BAe had bought Rover when the car maker's strategy was completely untried. BAe projections for Rover's cash demands over the ensuing few years were hopeful, being put at less than £200 million a year. But at bottom, the deal had to be seen as an each-way bet by Smith and BAe. The terms left BAe with an eventual exit, should one be needed. One clause stipulated that BAe must not 'relinquish control' of Rover until at least five years had elapsed. BAe immediately took steps to tighten Rover's connection with the Japanese car maker Honda. Honda agreed to take a 20 per cent stake in Rover, and BAe had secured the company's future while confirming the extinction of the British-owned volume car industry. Meanwhile, it had acquired the extra leverage of a vastly-enlarged capital base.

Financial, not manufacturing, engineering was the prime motive of the deal. Both BAe's executives and the Stock Market reaction said as much. So did the Government's approach to what, despite Rover's Stock Market listing and 60,000 private shareholders, was effectively a privatization. Unlike other State disposals, however, it was a sad coming of age, 21 years after what became Rover Group was formed by the merger of British Leyland and BMC. For all its size and significance as a component customer, Rover had come to little more than a pile of assets fit to bolster someone else's balance sheet. For the group which had been the British-owned volume car industry, it was a melancholy epitaph.

An event which coincided with BAe's takeover of Rover emphasized how aerospace had superseded vehicle manufacture in Britain. A week before the Rover deal was finally done, BAe emerged as the lead contractor for a defence equipment order from Saudi Arabia which was the biggest such contract that Britain had ever won. Called Al Yamamah 2, the order covered a sizeable chunk of BAe's product range, including Tornado and Hawk aircraft, 146 and 125 executive jets and Rapier missiles, along with Black Hawk helicopters and – the largest single element – the construction of two airbases. The order was reckoned to be worth a mininum £20 billion, with at least half of that sum accruing to BAe. It promised to yield profits of around £100 million a year to the group, starting in the early 1990s and running on for years thereafter. BAe's chance only came because the American Congress blocked arms sales to Saudi Arabia – but the group seized its opportunity with both hands. Al Yamamah underwrote its military and Dynamics business – plus the Ballast Nedam construction side – for the foreseeable future.

BAe's prospects of achieving consistent profits from its civil aircraft interests remain in the lap of the exchange rate Gods – and in the almost equally problematical hands of the consortium which runs the Toulouse-based Airbus project. In early 1989, Smith entered talks about possible collaboration with Dr Edzard Reuter, chairman of Daimler-Benz, the West German vehicles-to-consumer durables group which had become BAe's European aerospace equal by taking a majority stake in Messerschmitt-Bolkow-Blohm. Since both companies have a vested interest in sorting out the chronically loss-making and virtually unmanaged Airbus operation, the Daimler purchase of MBB may open the door to an eventual solution. But with Aerospatiale of France the third main character in the Airbus menage, BAe has many more doors to pass through before that aspiration can be fulfilled.

The Rover deal may not have resolved all concern about BAe's balance sheet. One leading BAe institutional shareholder remarked after the takeover: 'BAe is still undercapitalized for the risky civil aircraft business, but not disastrously so.' However, as BAe approached the 1990s it was well positioned for further moves to strengthen its base further, both through international collaboration (there were joint venture talks with French group Thomson on missiles) and outright acquisition. The continued unquantifiability of the Al Yamamah bonanza cemented the impression that BAe was a case apart – that it would never display publicly the full panoply of the profits that it could make. 'BAe will never be allowed to make too much money,' commented one City analyst in 1989. Politics did not end with privatization.

CHAPTER SIX

LAYING NEW FOUNDATIONS

Among the papers in his desk at STC's London head office, chairman and chief executive Arthur Walsh keeps a City electronics analyst's report on Britain's second largest electronics group.

The circular, by Ray Bowden of stockbroker Fielding Newson-Smith, is dated October 1985. That was the month Walsh joined STC as chief executive after leaving the electrical and electronic giant GEC, where in 33 years of employment he had risen to the main board and headed the group's defence business Marconi, its biggest subsidiary.

The circular listed three possible scenarios for STC, whose shares had slumped to 72p from 300p just over a year earlier. The intervening period had seen the £411 million takeover of Britain's only mainframe computer company ICL, a disastrous rights issue which failed to staunch a calamitous cash outflow which was placing the group's future in severe jeopardy, and a consequent boardroom coup led by non-executive director Lord Keith which ousted incumbent chairman and chief executive Sir Kenneth Corfield, who had master-minded the ICL takeover but presided over STC's subsequent loss of cost control.

None of the scenarios was particularly welcoming. Either costs would be cut and conditions improve under the new regime led by Keith, Walsh and Walsh's right hand from Marconi, finance director Roy Gardner – in which case, said Bowden, STC could justify a share price of 90p. Or there would be a bid for the group, probably at no more than 80p a share. The third possibility envisaged cost cuts but no improvement in market conditions and a downturn in ICL's market place, which, Bowden observed, 'everybody knows is going to occur'. The circular concluded gloomily: 'The upside looks limited; the downside not. We counsel caution.'

Bowden's recommendation was understandable, given the fact that STC had recently reported an £8.7 million bottom-line loss in the first six months of its financial year – and was on the way to full year net losses of almost £54 million.

But he omitted a fourth scenario: that the new executive team, together with ICL's continuing strong leadership under former Texas Instruments man Peter Bonfield, would achieve so comprehensive a recovery that STC would not just be turned round, but set on course for international expansion. And that, less than four years on from October 1985, the share price of the group – Britain's second-largest electronics concern after GEC – would have climbed back past 300p to hit 380p.

In May 1989, when he succeeded Keith as chairman, Walsh noted that STC had completed one chapter in its development and opened another: 'We have cleaned the outfit, slimmed it down,' he commented. 'That phase has finished, and it is time for me to start looking where we go so that we don't reach what the City so blithely assumes is a plateau. I don't like plateaux: some go downhill fast'.

As it starts on this new ascent, STC carries with it many of the strengths and weaknesses, the hopes and fears for the new British manufacturing industry that grew from foundations freshly laid in the 1980s. Not only is it a major figure in the British electronics industry, whose general prospects of superseding many overseas competitors still look in considerable doubt, its existence is coeval with the 1980s industrial revolution. Despite the relative longevity of some of its component parts (ICL's origins go back to the post-war birth of a British electronics industry), the group was essentially a creation of the last decade: in June 1979, one month after Mrs Thatcher's election, STC's American owner International Telephone and Telegraph (ITT) sold 15 per cent of its wholly-owned British telecommunications equipment subsidiary in a public offer for sale which brought STC a Stock Market quote. Just over three years later, the umbilical cord with ITT was cut when the American group reduced its then 75 per cent STC holding to 35 per cent through a £210 million offer for sale which was 12 times over-subscribed.

The extent of the inchoate group's crisis three years after that is probably still not appreciated. Nor are the risks that were taken in the cause of saving STC, and the combination of good management and good fortune which rescued it. Before STC could approach maturity, the group came very close to terminal grief. In January 1986, when Walsh and Gardner were still wrestling with the simultaneous problems of cutting costs while building business for the future, they were hit by a bombshell. A major American bank, one of the big lenders to British industry in the 1970s, called them in and told them that it wanted to cease STC's line of credit in two months' time. Walsh and Gardner were aghast: if the bank had called in its loan, all STC's other banks would have followed suit. The company would have been sunk. Walsh and Gardner pleaded to be given time to repay the debt. The bank relented, and the group was saved. But the experience reinforced the new STC management's determination to win and safeguard its financial independence.

The experience with the bank may have been STC's closest call, but there were numerous other high-wire acts along the way to its salvation. Although Walsh says the recovery was fortunate in several respects, he and the new management team probably made their own luck.

Walsh was aged 59 when he was contacted by the firm of headhunters Goddard Kay Rogers, which had been employed by Keith to find a new chief executive for STC. His decision to leave GEC after so many years prompted all sorts of industry gossip, some of it to the effect that his appointment represented a further major extension of GEC managing director Lord Weinstock's dominance of the British electronics industry. Nothing could have been further from the truth. One sub-text of STC's revival under Walsh has been the group's emergence as a second British electronics manufacturing power, smaller than GEC but also more focused.

Walsh's parting from Weinstock and GEC, for a combination of personal and professional reasons, was not entirely amicable – though far from overtly hostile. STC was certainly crying out for a dose of the Weinstock cost-cutting medicine, which Walsh duly administered. STC's large head office in the Strand must have been a culture shock for Walsh: one manager described the office garage, which was filled with serried ranks of Jaguars, as 'looking like [Jaguar chairman] John Egan's benefit'. Walsh himself was told he could have any car he wanted. He chose a second hand vehicle, left by one of the directors who was departing as a result of the cost cuts that were now carried out.

The selection was characteristic. Walsh is a small, compact, immensely determined man who exudes a single-minded dedication to the job in hand which excludes all inessentials. He is so quietly spoken that in the first television interview after his appointment as chairman, viewers could hardly pick up some of his carefully-weighted words.

What he discovered at STC in the autumn of 1985 was an organization which had wandered far from the straight and narrow path of corporate efficiency and tight financial control that Walsh had trod at Marconi. 'STC was very centralized, but I as chief executive had no real control,' Walsh says. 'When I asked what the bank balance was, they didn't know and said it would take a month to find out. I was used to having the bank balance on my desk every day.'

There were three months left before the year-end, but managers' forecasts of results were continually changing. 'I'd never been used to that. The debtors and creditors and cash were simply not connected. The guy who paid the creditors did not know whether what he was paying for was real or not. Collecting the money was not being done either; it was not seen as the province of the units concerned.'

These colossal flaws were concentrated on the non-ICL businesses. ICL itself had recovered strongly from its own near-catastrophe in 1981, when it made a bottom-line loss of £133 million after massive corrective action was taken to reverse two years of rampant cost over-growth. The group was saved from financial collapse by Government provision of £200 million in loan guarantees – a rare and remarkable rescue by the Thatcher Government of an ailing private sector group, albeit a near-monopoly Government supplier. ICL was then managed back to success by a new team headed by chairman Sir Christopher Laidlaw, chief executive Robb Wilmot, finance director Robin Biggam and Bonfield. Sir Michael Edwardes succeeded Laidlaw in April 1984, but he, Wilmot and Biggam all left after the STC takeover four months later.

Walsh arrived to find ICL 'reasonably well run'. The rest of the group, however, 'was a collection of very diverse businesses including a very large components group, almost all of which seemed to be in some sort of trouble'. STC, says Walsh, 'was going in five different directions, which meant it was an opportunistic business'. The former head of one STC subsidiary put it more succinctly: 'Corfield simply could not say "No".'

The head office had to be sorted out, the sprawling portfolio of businesses had to be drastically pruned – and the group's organization had to be streamlined. STC's structure was such that the ineffective central organization was duplicated at business group level, and repeated again at individual company level: there were group chairmen and managing directors, and company chairmen and MDs, each with their own staffs.

Walsh and Gardner removed them all. They also abandoned the grand, eight-storey head office building fronting on to the Strand – much STC money appeared to have been lavished on buildings – and, again characteristically, moved to utilitarian, slightly cramped, single-floor premises in Maltravers Street, which backed on to the former headquarters. The physical distance between the old head office and the new was only a few yards; the corporate cultural divide between the two was enormous.

The most dramatic element of the new regime's departure from the old was in its identification of and concentration on a handful of core businesses. After examining the disparate portfolio, Walsh 'began to feel that whether we liked it or not, we were in the telecommunications business, including cables [STC was the world leader in sub-sea cables for telecommunication] and the data business through ICL. But that's all we could afford to be in, and I felt that if we concentrated our efforts on that, we might be big enough to succeed in something.'

This paring down programme proceeded with remarkable speed. Walsh and Gardner disposed of 19 subsidiaries in less than a year. These included the communications services company International Aeradio (AIL), which STC under Corfield had bought from British Airways for £60 million, and was now sold in various pieces for a total £75 million: 'AIL didn't seem to be terribly relevant,' comments Walsh. Foots Cray, the half-completed Kent site of Corfield's grand design to establish a £60 million factory to make standard semi-conductors, was restructured. Walsh wanted nothing to do with the cash-demanding, cyclical, volume microchip industry: 'A lot of money had been invested in Foots Cray, and the evidence was that it could become a white elephant quickly unless we could avoid it,' Walsh recalls.

In a neat and, he says, fortunate move, STC leased the plant to American group LSI Logic, which used it to make specialist microchips, and took a 17 per cent stake in LSI's British subsidiary from which STC could recover its investment in the project. It also guaranteed STC a supply of the semiconductors that it needed.

The most numerous disposals came in the variegated electronic components sector, a winnowing-out process which continued into 1989. Walsh simply did not see a need for products like capacitators and relays, and out they went. (STC's components distribution business, by contrast, has been retained and enlarged. Its cash generating potency has usefully counterpointed the more cash-demanding manufacturing businesses of telecommunications equipment and information systems.)

Also in need of focusing was STL Enterprises, the group's research operation, whose discursive range extended to the invention of flat-panel glass which held out the prospect of the flat-screen, wall-hanging television set. It was a nice idea, but there were a number of problems with it, including the fact that the screen was only black-and-white. Walsh overhauled the laboratory programme, concentrating it on the technologies that STC would need in the future.

It was one thing to decide that the group would concentrate on telecommunications, including cables, alongside the computer-based interests. But ensuring that it could actually compete effectively in the telecommunications areas was quite another matter, and called for an extraordinary degree of hands-on management by Walsh. 'To get the whole thing working, we had to go and educate the various parts of the business. We generally found things like the customer had gone away because our performance was dreadful.'

The biggest challenge facing the telecommunications side was to re-establish its battered credibility with its major customer, British Telecom. Failure to do that would have dealt a mortal blow to STC's chances of recovery. But at the start, the odds appeared to be against STC.

The group had to reverse a trend towards its marginalization as a BT supplier which dated from the October 1982 loss of its position as one of the three major developers – along with GEC and Plessey – of the new electronic telephone exchange, System X. As compensation for this loss, caused by BT's desire to streamline and accelerate the System X development, STC was guaranteed five years of orders as the sole supplier of the enhanced semi-electronic TXE4A exchanges, which STC had developed but which would be pre-empted by System X.

However, through its subsequent failings in product price, quality, reliability and on-time delivery, STC had not endeared itself to BT. It was no longer being invited to tender for telephone manufacturing orders, for instance. One industry expert comments: 'STC had to get straight the markets that it had messed up, and it really had messed them up. BT wouldn't come near them.'

Walsh rolled up his sleeves and went to work in a way that he had not done for years. 'I had to work through why there was interference on BT's optical line transmission systems (where STC had been losing orders), or find out why, when we put submarine transponders together, we blew up various integrated circuits. In the doing of that, you find out who is a manager who is concerned to make a contribution, and who is there for decorative purposes.'

But STC's comeback was achieved through more than merely putting the business basics right. That process established a platform, but without a high degree of calculated risk-taking it would have been worth very little. Its rehabilitation with BT was a crucial case in point. To get its prices down on the telephone making side, Walsh called in his managers and told them to study their purchasing policy, since bought-in materials accounted for about 80 per cent of the cost of a telephone. Walsh observes: 'Purchasing had been treated like a second-class citizen, but with a little effort they managed to bring the cost of materials down.' Then came the twist. The batch sizes that BT asked STC to bid for – usually around 500,000 units – were not big enough to give the group much leverage on its suppliers. So Walsh suggested that STC should bid for one million units, double the usual order, and use that volume target to get its price down through lower-cost supplier components. The move worked even better than STC had hoped: it came in as the lowest-price bidder, and BT eventually gave it an order for 1.5 million units. 'And we managed to make a profit on it,' notes Walsh.

That gamble, however, paled into insignificance beside STC's decision to bet its future growth prospects in telecommunications on winning the position of prime supplier for BT's new Flexible Access System (FAS). As with STC's strategy of concentration on two core businesses, the FAS decision was dictated as much by force of circumstances as by a carefully-weighted choice following dispassionate examination of all the options. STC's options, following its exclusion from the new System X generation of public switches, were distinctly limited.

But happily for the group, in timing and technology FAS coincided perfectly with STC's need for a genuine future growth market and its technical capability. The computer-controlled, optical fibre-based system, to be installed initially in the City of London, then progressively through the rest of the capital and in Britain's other major cities, embodied the shift in the fulcrum of the telecommunications industry away from the central telephone exchange towards the actual transmission network. The new key element in this transmission-oriented system was not the exchange but a digital (computer-controlled) multiplexer on the telephone subscriber's premises. This converted the telephone system into an 'intelligent network', the flexibility of which derived from the fact that its sophisticated computer control allowed capacity to be varied in line with demand –thus using the network far more efficiently than under the central exchange-based system.

Since its departure from the System X development consortium (and the failure of ITT's rival System 12 exchange) STC had already concentrated on the transmission side of telecommunications. STC engineers had developed the programmable multiplexer. But although STC and FAS seemed made for each other, Walsh and his team won pole position only after a nail-biting competition which wore many nerves to the quick.

Walsh took personal charge of the FAS programme, which in many ways marked the acid test of STC Telecommunications and the culmination of the new regime's 'management in detail'. Walsh says: 'STC should have put the money from the TXE4 orders into new products, and they hadn't. So very quickly, we had to invest a lot of money in transmission systems, take a risk, and go for it. Having put our eggs into this basket, we were determined that we would look after the basket. It was necessary for me to get right into this, because I didn't know who was good and who was bad.' A number of the managers in Telecommunications had to be changed, and several were replaced by ICL managers, notably Peter Gershon, who was appointed to head the Telecommunications side.

The changes came just in time, because when the group top management looked at the FAS submission that STC was going to send to BT, they thought that they had no chance of winning the City of London contract. BT, it was concluded, would not have understood what STC was talking about.

The group's bacon was saved by a BT decision to postpone the deadline for FAS submissions by three months. In the interim, Walsh sat down once a week with everyone involved in FAS. Among the radical – for STC – changes which resulted was installation of the practice of engineering the product down to a particular price, rather than simply designing it and thinking about its price later.

STC won the FAS competition, and in its relationship with BT began to improve. The FAS success encouraged other developments: STC's land-based optical fibre cable business expanded rapidly against long-established rivals like BICC, from a ten per cent British market share in 1985 to what STC claimed in 1989 exceeded 60 per cent of the market. By then, the group was looking forward to winning FAS-type orders in mainland Europe and growing optical fibre cable operations there. It was already developing an optical fibre cable making business in America, where it started to build a factory at Portland, Oregon in 1988.

Meanwhile, it received an unexpected windfall from TXE4A, with orders for further enhancements to the exchanges, which meant that TXE4A business ran on more than two years longer than had been originally expected. A barometer of STC's recovery in domestic telecommunications is its Monkstown, Northern Ireland factory where telephones and FAS equipment are among the range of products. When Walsh arrived, the plant workforce, once 4,500-strong, had been run down to 800 and the factory was due to close. By early 1989, the labour force had almost doubled to 1,500 and efficiency levels were high.

The FAS experience – potential disaster turned to triumph by intense, near crisis-management levels of effort – was mirrored in STC's submarine telecommunications cables business, the group's one truly international world-leading activity.

But sub-sea cables was very close to losing that lead when the new STC regime arrived. Its competitiveness was slipping in the face of the transition that it was having to make from copper to optical fibre cabling. Moreover, it was out of work. All but one of the entire top management of the business were changed. Without such wholesale reform, Walsh believes, sub-sea cables would never have got over the switch to optical fibre. But to survive and make that transition, sub-sea cables needed even more than that radical change. It took a huge gamble by Walsh and the new management to see it through into the new optical fibre era.

PTAT, the first privately built transatlantic telecommunications cable, was the breakthrough optical fibre contract that STC had to win. That order would give STC a prime position in the new generation of sub-sea cable construction. But the cables company's work famine meant it did not have the money to fund the development required to stand a chance of winning PTAT. There was one chance: if STC could win the world's last order for a copper cable link – which was to run across the Indian Ocean between India and the United Arab Emirates – that order would provide the cash needed for PTAT development.

Walsh and his team took a £12 million risk: in the six months after he took charge, STC went ahead and built the India–UAE cable – before the contract was awarded. Because the group could not guarantee that it would win the order, the construction cost of £12 million had to be written off against STC's profits. By building the cable ahead of the contract's award, STC made it likely that it would win simply because it could deliver off the shelf. The greater danger was that India or the UAE would discover what it had done: STC would have been over a barrel, forced to take the contract at a loss-making price. But the gamble worked. STC clinched the order, its secret remained safe, it made a profit on the contract which was ploughed back into the transatlantic cable work – and PTAT was won.

Sub-sea cables revived to prosper. The full measure of its

global supremacy became evident in late 1988, when it won the lion's share of a trans-Pacific cable between the United States and Japan. The Japanese took a minority share of the contract, but the suspicion remained that if competition had been entirely unbridled by national influences, STC would have won the whole thing. As it was, the group ensured that it would handle everything in the Japanese half of the cable save the actual landing of the cable at Miura in Japan – establishing a vital bridgehead in its Japanese competitors' backyard.

The survival of the cables business to achieve this signal victory was due to much more than its remarkable improvement in competitiveness. It had also to escape a cloud which overshadowed the whole group and its share price for much of the recovery period: the future of ITT's outstanding shareholding, by now reduced to just over 24 per cent.

The shareholding was just a small part of ITT's telecommunications operations, and in January 1987, ITT sold them to a newly-formed group, Alcatel, in which the French electricals giant CGE had majority control, with the Americans retaining a minority holding. STC mounted a vigorous and successful campaign to keep the ITT stake out of Alcatel, which would have squeezed the independence out of STC. Walsh and his team knew, for a start, that 'submarine systems would have disappeared down a hole' in Alcatel, because CGE already owned Europe's largest telecommunications cables group, Cables de Lyon.

By finding in the Canadian giant Northern Telecom a willing buyer of the ITT stake; by encouraging ITT to sell the holding to Northern; and by getting the agreement of ICL's technological partner Fujitsu of Japan to the deal, STC completed the most delicate balancing act of the recovery period. The uncertainty about the ITT stake was removed, while the Northern alliance, reinforced by STC purchases of Northern businesses in Europe, in fact promised to be mutually beneficial, giving the Canadians access to the British – and through that – the European – market while helping STC Telecommunications expand in North America.

Northern's stake (it actually held 27.8 per cent of STC, having owned some shares prior to the ITT purchase) inevitably aroused industry speculation that the group would one day take STC over. STC executives, however, are confident that this will not be the case.

It is not clear whether the agreement with Northern contains a provision barring a full offer for STC from Northern except in the unlikely event that another, hostile party, makes a bid for the group. The deal's most salient feature was its highlighting of the distinguishing characteristic in STC's recovery and growth: the way in which its new management made a virtue of necessity, deftly transforming apparently defensive decisions made by force of circumstance into springboards for genuine expansion which coincided with, or anticipated industry trends. Just as the exclusion from public exchange manufacture prompted STC's move into the big growth area of transmission systems, so the Northern agreement only came about because of ITT's determination to sell its shares, but put STC at one with the increasing moves towards international alliances in the electronics industry.

As a result, STC's strategy came, to outsiders, to be touched by a certain ambivalence. It was sometimes hard to tell where short-term pragmatism ended and longer-term vision began. To an extent, this external uncertainty was inevitable: not only was STC a young company, but its financial crisis meant that it had had to make a new start only a few years after first attaining independence. It was scarcely surprising that observers should be hazy about its identity, since that identity was still in the process of formation.

It was assumed, for instance, for at least two years after Walsh's arrival, that STC's major area of expansion would be defence electronics, of which the former Marconi duo of Walsh and Gardner had so much experience. What happened instead was that in 1987, STC's defence business actually ceased to exist as a separately defined sector, and its different parts were incorporated into the relevant communications and information system cores of the group. There, they remained a potential area of expansion, in line with the group's growth ambitions, but not – as STC's refusal to back Cable & Wireless's attempted bid for Racal in the early summer of 1988 proved – at prices the group regarded as excessive. Walsh and Gardner had a strong sense of value, and defence was not a dynamic growth area.

But defence was a minor point. Where outsiders most overwhelmingly and consistently identified ambivalence in STC was at the very core of the group's structure – in the relationship between the ICL information systems side and the telecommunications business.

As STC prepared to enter the 1990s, the future of this relationship was the central strategic issue with which it was confronted.

To a large extent, the doubts about STC's commitment to the union of ICL and Telecommunications sprang from the fact that it was the last and grandest design of the Corfield regime, predicated upon the belief in the 'convergence' of computing and telecommunications technologies. With STC's subsequent disasters, however unrelated to the ICL takeover, convergence became a dirty word, tarnished by the downfall of its chief proponent.

Moreover, the crisis in STC's pre-ICL business prevented early justification of the convergence strategy because it thoroughly disrupted the process of integrating ICL and the Telecommunications side. In immediate terms, this was no great loss: left to its own devices, ICL kept the group going during its time of trouble, producing pre-interest profits of almost £62 million in 1985, when STC as a whole lost £11.4 million before tax. ICL consistently generated more than half STC's sales and profits, right through to 1989.

The human traffic was similarly one way, with ICL managers being put in to run telecommunications businesses; and from its London head offices on either side of Putney Bridge, ICL continued to run its own television advertising campaigns, which did not acknowledge its position as part of a larger whole.

Although it never amounted to a reverse takeover, this ICL predominance unbalanced the group and presented Walsh, Gardner and STC's corporate development director Nigel Horne (whose analysis of electronics industry trends had inspired the ICL acquisition) with a convergence challenge which embraced not just technology, but corporate structure.

Gradually, the STC and ICL people made sense of their union. Management interbreeding was effected to form a community of approach, through company meetings and functions, and courses organized by the London Business School, which ICL under Laidlaw and Wilmot had used to change the way managers thought and acted after the group's near-failure.

A second major plank of the Laidlaw-Wilmot recovery, ICL's 1981 technological alliance with Fujitsu, which supplied the microchips for ICL's Series 39 mainframe computers, helped build into the new STC an awareness of the benefits to be gained from properly constituted international alliances.

When STC won FAS with a design in which Series 39 technology played a central systems management role, the quest for technical convergence in the group passed a milestone. It had been a long time coming, but as Walsh commented in late 1988: 'Telephone exchanges are beginning to look more like computers.' By then, too, ICL was selling STC Telecommunications' packet switches (which allow the transmission of 'packets' of data which can be personally addressed and directed and which make more efficient use of communications channels). ICL's software capability is of considerable use to the telecommunications side. STC sub-sea cables incorporate network management by ICL systems.

As he succeeded to the chairmanship in spring 1989, Walsh likened the relationship between STC and ICL to that he had built between GEC and Marconi. 'They are one company, just about. Marconi now feels part of GEC. And ICL feels part of STC, or STC feels part of ICL – which way round it is, I'm not sure. We keep the ICL brand name, which is well known and which we must not lose. But we do have a company which now works quite clearly together,' says Walsh.

The links that have developed between the two sides of STC may amount to convergence, but they constitute convergence by another name – or phrase. Walsh declares: 'I've got a company which works together, but I don't have to go into dogma to explain it.'

In STC's post-recovery stage, the pragmatism demonstrated by that remark has dovetailed both with the performance of the two sides of the group and with their requirements for longer-term development. ICL has for years defied the Cassandras who have been forecasting a halt to its growth (remember that stockbroker's circular in Walsh's desk), expanding by more than ten per cent a year from 1985 to 1987. Its sales growth slowed in 1988, but margin improvements still boosted profits substantially. The company, like the rest of STC, has honed its manufacturing processes to a fine leading edge, and its early 1989 move to concentrate on computer assembly at one site emphasized that there remained considerable scope to take overhead costs out of the business.

Underlying the operational efficiencies has been a more fundamental, and for British industry, archetypal shift in ICL from manufacturing to assembly. As the decade ended, this move was in turn being superseded by a change in direction of the business's central drive from hardware output to knowledge-based software development – just as STC's non-cables telecommunications side was looking to expand into the rapidly growing niche of Value Added Network Services (VANS), which literally add value to telephone networks by enabling them to provide new data-based services.

These elements, combined with the move to international manufacture of cables, made STC something of a storehouse for the constituents of British manufacturing's late 1980s industrial evolution. The sizeable dependence of its major businesses on the growth of the telecommunications industry on one hand and the retail industry on the other emphasized how the artificial barrier between manufacturing and services industry had been eroded by the decade-end. ICL, whose core strategy is based on the supply of information systems to five markets – retail, local and central government, manufacturing, financial and defence – can hope to gain important retail market share in America from the acquisition of the Brooks Brothers stores chain by Marks and Spencer, with whom ICL worked closely in Britain, and the Stateside expansion of Carrefour, the French hypermarket group which is a significant ICL customer.

The point reflects the one significant regard in which STC could not be said to represent all of British industry – only a sizeable part of it. For different reasons, the combination of STC and ICL created by Corfield and inherited by Walsh had negligible overseas business. Except for the sub-sea cables side, STC had to build an international base virtually from scratch.

In the case of the original STC businesses, this over-concentration on the home market stemmed directly from their provenance as the British offshoot of ITT's worldwide empire. ICL, by contrast, had simply chosen to stay in the home market where its near-domination along with IBM had guaranteed it a constant stream of business. Its safety-first policy paralleled that of the major British defence electronics groups, which had been constantly nourished by Ministry of Defence contracts at cost-plus prices.

Yet from Bonfield down, ICL in the late 1980s was extremely conscious that its market was now international. The group was one of the earliest proponents of Open Systems – the concept that computer manufacturers should allow the products of other companies access to their systems – and hitched its wagon early in the day to American giant AT&T's Unix operating system that rapidly became the industry standard for office automation. ICL was also in the vanguard of British companies preparing for the single European market, having established a special European Strategy Board in April 1988. In 1989, it broke new ground for a British company by starting a European 'milk round' of universities on the Continent to recruit French, Spanish and German graduates. And while its executives set about improving – or, in many cases learning – a European language other than English, the company initiated a pathfinding British university course combining the study of information technology with learning a foreign language.

ICL was starting from a small base. Of its £1.36 billion sales in 1988, no more than about 13 per cent, or £180 million, were in Europe. The group had established a sizeable bridgehead in French retailing and a strong niche in the American Do-It-Yourself stores market. But in August 1988, electronics industry analysts at securities house Warburg Securities estimated ICL's Dutch sales at about £45 million and its West German and Scandinavian sales at no more than £30 million.

West Germany was a major headache. ICL's operation there broke even in 1988, having lost about £10 million the previous year (Warburg Securities estimate). But the group's European aspirations would not allow it to withdraw from the market. As John Davison, head of ICL retail, commented: 'I can't have a sensible pan-European strategy which doesn't embrace the German retailers.' So ICL looked for potential acquisitions of systems houses in West Germany, to give it access to the local market.

STC's switch from domestic house-cleaning to overseas acquisition-hunting demonstrated that the group was entering a new phase. By the end of 1988, Walsh's daily bank balance statements showed that, despite consistently strong levels of capital investment, STC was in the happy position of holding £283 million in net cash. That was a further measure of Walsh and Gardner's success in staunching, then reversing, the cash crisis of 1985 when £185 million flowed out of the company in the first six months of the year.

From this now-sound financial base, at the turn of 1988, STC made its first significant acquisitions since Walsh took charge. Both were in the United States, costing a total $294 million. One expanded the Telecommunications side's VANS capability; the other lifted ICL to the position of world number three, behind IBM and its American fellow NCR, in the retail market for electronic point of sale (EPOS) terminals – electronic tills and back-office systems. The purchases were sound, tight, demonstrably logical moves slotting straightforwardly into the group expansion strategy – just the ticket for STC's first substantial steps into the overseas takeover business.

Convincing as they were, however, those acquisitions – and the further, generic purchases that were set to follow them – stood secondary to the much greater challenge stretching out ahead of the group: the imperative that its two core businesses secure their place in the new universe of global competition. With the Northern Telecom alliance, sealed by the Canadians' major stake in the group, STC appeared to have satisfied that need for a strong international connection in respect of its telecommunications operations, but only for telecommunications. Subsequent telecommunications alliances with French and West German companies established bridgeheads in mainland Europe. But Northern's disbelief in the convergence theory of electronics emphasized that its presence represented no solution for ICL.

So the ICL question remained. It was succinctly defined in July 1988 by Alan Rousell, the long-standing managing director of ICL's British business who was switched by Bonfield that year to the new post of operational head of the European Board. 'I believe that over the next two to three years, we have to have effected a major change in our position,' Rousell said. 'The sheer business of generating enough growth and revenue to finance our Research and Development is terrifying.

'There are about seven major European information technology suppliers. My personal view is that there will not be enough room for all of them. We are number six. We have to be in the top three.'

A FIGHTING CHANCE

ICL's obvious route to that top trio was a major alliance with another European IT group. The conclusion of many in the industry and outside it, who had forever suspected the new STC regime's commitment to ICL, was that the business would be sold outright. The Italian group Olivetti was known to harbour a long-held interest in buying the company, and was even rumoured to have offered £900 million for it.

But the sale of ICL would have left behind a very odd-looking STC, with a telecommunications business and a mountain of cash, which would be instantly vulnerable to takeover unless it had something big it immediately wanted to buy. It would also be the easy way out.

What STC was looking at, as it ended its eventful decade of independent corporate life, was the far more difficult trick of forming an equal partnership between ICL and one of the other IT majors, while obtaining management control of the new entity. To do that, Walsh and co. would have to walk a tightrope more narrow than all those they had negotiated successfully in the past. Such a joint venture would need the approval of Northern Telecom and Fujitsu – unless the deal actually involved Fujitsu: in mid-1989, it seemed possible that STC and Olivetti would link, with the Japanese company taking a stake in the joint venture.

Most fundamentally, STC would have to reconcile two apparently irreconcilable imperatives – the need to form a credible, fully effective partnership while ensuring that it did not strain too far the links between the parent group and ICL. To an extent, this conundrum is common to all joint ventures. But this time, the scale of the challenge will be enormous, because of ICL's relative significance to the STC group. The ICL solution will be a test case for British industry's hitherto unproven ability to manage and benefit from the international joint ventures that will proliferate in the 1990s.

Only once in the first three-and-a-half years of the Walsh–Gardner regime did STC's clear strategic lines appear crossed, and the resulting confusion fed rampant rumours about the group's intentions towards ICL and large chunks of the rest of Britain's electronics industry.

That was during seven days in early January 1989 that became the most extraordinary week-long period that British industry had experienced for at least 20 years, more remarkable even than the megabid first week of December 1985 with which the period between 9am on Saturday, 7 January and 2.30 the following Friday afternoon, 13 January, had a strong connection. One of the megabids proposed in December 1985 had been by GEC for Plessey; now a second GEC attempt to take over Plessey – this time in partnership with the West German giant Siemens – sparked off truly momentous events.

No takeover bid was launched during those seven days. But at more than £7 billion, the bid that was threatened would have been more than twice as big as the largest takeover attempt that Britain had ever seen.

The target was GEC itself, the giant of Britain's electrical and electronics industry. The prospective bidder was a £1 off-the-shelf company called Metsun, which announced its intentions that Saturday morning in a sparse, one-page press statement entitled: 'Possible offer for GEC'. The only other available details were that Sir John Cuckney, then chairman of Westland and holder of a string of other senior board positions, was Metsun's chairman, and that the company was being advised by the merchant bank Lazard Brothers.

The following Friday, a breathtaking seven days later, GEC's managing director Lord Weinstock – the man who created GEC in the late 1960s and had dominated it for two decades – cut the ground from under Metsun when he agreed a series of joint ventures with the giant American group General Electric and its formidable chairman, Jack Welch. Only a few hours earlier the same day, according to Metsun sources, Welch was ready to shake hands with them and back their bid for GEC. The following week, Metsun abandoned its bid attempt, but did not give up all hope of making another one. It packed up its tents, decamped from Lazards to Baring Brothers, and watched while the great upheaval in Britain's electronics sector continued, its ripples spreading outwards into mainland Europe and lapping upon the shores of world industry.

That Friday the Thirteenth was unlucky for some. But for whom? Even months later, a full answer to that question could not be given. It will be several years before the shape of things blueprinted in invisible ink by the events of that week becomes clear.

What was immediately apparent, when the GEC–GE deals were unveiled to the media at 2.30pm at a hotel just off London's Hyde

Park, was that one chapter in British industrial history had ended and another begun. The hotel fell inside a triangle formed by two other hotels, the Inter-Continental (occupied by Metsun people) and the Inn on the Park (where Welch took up residence), and by GEC's Stanhope Gate head office which had been the crucible of an amazing drama. Into that crucible over the four days and, for many executives and advisers, sleepless nights, had been pitched the whole future of Britain's electronics industry. 'You could have got killed in the rush of people passing confidential documents to each other between the three places,' observed one participant in the drama. 'It was like an Irish horse fair – except that there is a higher standard of ethics at an Irish horse fair.'

The fact that GEC was at the centre of this drama testified more simply than anything else to the extraordinary dominance of the British electrical and electronics industry by Weinstock's company. But it also said something about the nature and limits of that dominance. It was Welch – known as 'Neutron Jack' for the swathe he had cut through costs and jobs in GE – whose arrival in London the previous Tuesday morning proved the final catalyst for change.

GEC and GE had been negotiating for months on the central deal of the quartet – the formation of a jointly-owned domestic appliances company to expand the two groups' Hotpoint brand (and other products) into mainland Europe – as well as for some form of alliance in the fields of medical and power engineering equipment. Welch had become so exasperated with the failure to reach an agreement that, through London merchant bank N. M. Rothschild, he had begun to explore the possibility of making a hostile bid for GEC. Then came Metsun, and suddenly Weinstock was ready to talk, faster than before. According to one source close to GE, Welch's first reaction was to refuse to meet GEC's managing director. It took mediation in New York by a director of the Wall Street investment bank Goldman Sachs, who was acting for GEC but was a personal friend of Welch, to change Neutron Jack's mind. Welch flew into London, met Weinstock at his Stanhope Gate flat, talked again with him the next morning – and the ice was broken. Welch sustained the pressure, and concentrated everyone's minds, by not shutting the door in Metsun's face until the

GEC deals were done – a tactic which did not endear GE to people in the Metsun camp. 'GE are like hyenas,' commented one later. 'You have to kill the animal, but then they will eat as much of it as they can manage.'

Welch headed home so fast after the Friday afternoon press conference that you could barely see him for dust. But even before the dust settled, it was clear that GE was the one indisputable winner from the week's momentous events. Before them, the group had been a European outsider, hammering on the gates of a Community it feared would turn itself into a fortress which would raise its drawbridge against American companies. That would have been a colossal obstacle to GE, with its objective of being a global leader in all its chosen business sectors, but which despite its huge annual sales of more than $40 billion still had some way to go, notably in Europe, to achieve that aim.

As Welch implied, Metsun might have given GE the immediate leverage to effect the GEC deals, but the real impetus and urgency for establishing a bridgehead into Europe dated back to 16 November, 1988, the day that GEC and Siemens launched their £1.7 billion joint bid against Plessey. Less than six weeks later, Weinstock followed that move with a merger of its power generation, transmission and distribution equipment operations with the French giant CGE's Alsthom subsidiary, and the fat was in the fire. Welch declared: 'When one scours the papers, and one sees Lord Weinstock going down the path of a series of alliances, first with Siemens, then Alsthom one doesn't know where one sits. So one has to catch up here and see what the cards look like. If we couldn't reach an accommodation over the issues, we would have had to look at all the alternatives.'

That comment may have been a veiled threat, but it was also a back-handed justification of Weinstock's stunning strategic departure. Welch was not the only expert taken aback by GEC's Siemens move, which came after years when several of the joint ventures with which GEC had been most notably associated were ones which had fallen through. Earlier in the 1980s, GEC had negotiated long and hard for a significant stake in the West German electronics and domestic appliances group AEG, but its bid had been blocked by the German authorities. More recently, an agreement in principle for a merger of GEC's medical electronics business with that of the Dutch giant Philips had fallen through over nitty-gritty problems with the financial terms.

Weinstock shed no tears for the failures of the Philips talks: 'The whole thing went on for 11 months. You can get an elephant in that time, starting from the date of conception. It would have been a disaster for us to have done that deal.'

Weinstock said that what informed his Siemens alliance was the experience he had had with AEG. 'The reason we couldn't do things then was that we didn't have enough clout. That was why we bid for Plessey the first time. European industry understood very well what it was all about. And seeing that we were ready to do these things, to take this chance, made them willing to come and talk to us when conditions in the European market made it more appropriate.'

For Weinstock, the Siemens move was nothing less than the answer to the critics, industrial and financial, who viewed GEC as gripped by stasis in the 1980s. As Weinstock himself described it, 'the general perception is that we are a lot of layabouts sitting around here doing nothing much and just counting our money'. GEC had been famed for tight cash controls from its earliest days. It was the prototype for the financial monitoring systems adopted by many companies, although few went as far as Weinstock was rumoured to do. Legend had it that after the annual process of setting the monthly profit targets of each subsidiary, GEC's creator would extract from each subsidiary's manager 12 post-dated cheques made out to the set profit target, and place them in his desk. All the manager had to do was ensure that each month's profits matched the figure on the cheque.

But by September 1988 GEC's cash mountain had climbed to £1.24 billion and become the most abused landmark in British industry. It was seen as representing a GEC antipathy to risk-taking, a maximization of short-term returns at the cost of longer-term investment, a symbol of the loss of dynamism in Weinstock's industrial empire. While the cash mountain grew, GEC's share-price rating stagnated.

From the financial institutions which usually kept their own counsel emanated occasional cries from the heart seeking relief from the oppressive weight of lowly-rated GEC paper with which they were lumbered. In the mid-1980s, the Bank of England attempted to establish some forum in which institutions could co-ordinate action to revitalize the management of underperforming companies. As a first step, the Bank asked institutions to list the companies where they would most like to make a change. Top of the list was GEC. When David Hopkinson, the relatively outspoken head of the M&G fund management group, retired in 1987, he expressed a parting regret that BTR had not bid for GEC instead of for Pilkington.

That view was voiced about the time of growing, but unfocused institutional unrest over GEC. A year later, in the summer of 1988, a much more serious move started which took the line from an early stage that GEC needed not so much a change of management as a complete restructuring which would involve GEC's industrial competitors taking pieces of the business. That appears to have been the origin of the Metsun concept. But still no-one would take the lead and make the first move for GEC.

It was the GEC–Siemens joint bid for Plessey which threw the whole field open. Weinstock had intended that the bid should unlock many doors, but perhaps even he did not realize the extent to which he might also be opening Pandora's Box.

Sitting in his office shortly after making the joint bid for Plessey, Weinstock rejected once more the suggestion that GEC had been drifting in the 1980s, but that now its time had come again. 'GEC's time has always been,' he retorted. 'It's just that the City hasn't recognized it.' Nevertheless, a glance round the office made it superficially easy to conclude how the feeling had developed outside the company that GEC had lost its drive and vision while the man who built it up had been distracted by other interests. The office bore witness to Weinstock's passion for horse-racing: a portrait of the Derby winner, Troy, on the wall, the statuette of another Derby winner on his desk. The magazines on a side-table had a European dimension, but they were racing periodicals. Yet here was the man whose control of the company was embodied in his retention of the managing director's position: not for Weinstock the title of chairman with its connotations of withdrawal from shirt-sleeved, hands-on management. He created GEC; he ran GEC. The second Plessey bid, and the remarkable bout of GEC corporate activity which followed it through the string of joint ventures, showed that Weinstock was recalling the kind of form that led him, 19 years earlier, to tell Graham

Turner in the same Stanhope Gate offices: 'Some of us here have the feeling that we are engaged in a crusade.' As Turner explained, that crusade was the reform of the British electrical industry. Some of it, said Weinstock, had been 'a blot on national life'. (Quoted in *Business in Britain* by Graham Turner, Eyre and Spottiswoode, 1969.)

'Say what you like about Weinstock now,' came the observation in 1986 from one of the men who worked under him when he was creating the modern GEC in the 1960s, 'but he saved the British electrical industry.'

What made the GEC–Siemens bid for Plessey so evocative a turning-point in the history of both GEC and British industry were its echoes of the bid 21 years past in which Weinstock's GEC agreed a friendly merger with English Electric against a hostile bid for EE from Plessey, headed then as in 1988 by Sir John Clark. The English Electric deal, coming a year after GEC's takeover of AEI and only six years after Weinstock had become managing director of GEC at the age of 39, established GEC's lasting predominance in the British electrical, and later electronics industries. By 1988, it was Britain's fourth-largest manufacturer in sales terms (behind Unilever, ICI and Hanson – *Financial Times* Top 500 European companies, November 1988).

However, Weinstock's Euro-vision was partly driven by the stark fact that became abundantly clear when GEC was lined up alongside Siemens, CGE and General Electric: beside those giants, the group that bestrode its home market looked positively undersized. GEC's annual sales in the year to March 1988 totalled £5.9 billion. With annual sales of more than £17 billion, Siemens was almost treble GEC's size, while GE had sales in 1987 of £23.5 billion.

Except in medical equipment, which was dominated by its American subsidiary Picker, GEC also had a relatively limited overseas manufacturing presence. Only a quarter of its sales were made from bases overseas, as distinct from UK exports.

So Weinstock had very good reasons for joining forces with Siemens against Plessey, a move which opened up GEC, and by extension the whole British electronics industry, to international engines of change but also gave it a chance to harness their power for the group's future growth.

The bid and the deal with CGE that followed it threw GEC's

competitors into ferment. A prime mover in Metson summed up: 'The bid showed them that if they were ever going to make a move for GEC, it had to be pretty quickly.' GEC's British competitors (not to mention some of its customers and suppliers) did not like the bid and were worried about the additional muscle that GEC would gain in the home market if it were successful. Some of GEC's overseas counterparts or competitors – as Welch of GE testified – were concerned that they would be denied the opportunities created by Weinstock's deal-making. But there was also a certain respect for his initiative. 'Everyone has been talking to everyone else for months about what we might do, but he has actually done something,' commented one British company executive.

Britain's electronics island had indeed been alive with voices that spring and summer. Some had been proposing mergers – like that suggested by STC to Plessey some time before the GEC–Siemens bid. The inspiration for this approach remained unclear, but to round out its telecommunications portfolio STC clearly nurtured an inclination to get back into the public switching business from which it had been excluded in 1982, given a suitable opportunity. Its Northern Telecom connection offered one, long-term possibility of doing so – but the best and shortest route would have been to gain access to Plessey's half-share in the Plessey–GEC System X joint venture GPT (presup-posing that this would have been possible within the terms of the GPT agreement which gave either partner the option to buy the other's 50 per cent stake if control of that other partner should change). But in any case, STC's suit was rejected. Plessey found one core condition – that the merged group should come under STC's management – unpalatable.

Cable & Wireless's abortive plan to bid for Racal – motivated by C&W's ambition to get its hands on Racal's highly profitable Vodafone-dominated cellular radio business – and Racal's pre-dictable but totally successful defence, Vodafone's demerger and flotation, belonged more to the service side of the electronics industry, but was further indicative of the turmoil below its surface.

Further spice was added to the melting pot by a report on the British electronics industry, published in July by the National Economic Development Office, written by the American-owned management consultancy McKinsey (*Performance and Competitive Success. Strengthening Competitiveness in UK Electronics*). The central message of this study, which covered all the major electronics manufacturers except for Alan Sugar's consumer products company Amstrad (excluded because NEDO defined it as a designer and marketeer, not a manufacturer), was that unless they carried out sweeping changes in every aspect of their operations, the British companies would remorselessly lose ground to their overseas rivals until their survival would be in jeopardy.

McKinsey had quite a history of association with the British electronics industry. In 1964, the American-owned management consultancy had been employed by the Clarks to advise on the restructuring of the group. It was therefore somewhat ironic when the only captain of industry who reacted splenetically to the NEDO report was Sir John Clark. He called it 'a monstrous travesty based on a mass of generalizations.' His annoyance proved short-lived. After the GEC–Siemens bid was made, Plessey called in McKinsey to help with its defence.

McKinsey's report for NEDO showed that while the total British electronics market had grown from £8.3 billion in 1976 to £20.5 billion ten years later, the British companies' share of that market had slumped from almost half to less than one-third. McKinsey forecast that the market would expand further to £34.1 billion in 1991 – but that without major corporate reform by the British, foreign-owned companies would in 1991 dominate more than three-quarters of the British market.

Bill Pade, one of the McKinsey people responsible for the report, commented: 'There has to be a very significant reorientation if the British companies are going to continue to grow. They will require a different kind of leadership, different organization and skills. They have got to change very quickly because they are beginning to run out of time.'

The British, according to McKinsey, lacked overall strategic drive and co-ordination because they were too decentralized in their decision-making; lacked critical mass and therefore competitiveness in individual businesses because they were too diversified; lacked overseas penetration because they were too insular; and – a related point – suffered from limited growth potential because they were over-concentrated on the defence and telecommunications industries, where the outlook was for little or no growth. The only area where British prospects were identified as bright was in software, a growth sector exemplified by the information technology services company Hoskyns – though one in which the British faced tough competition from the French, whose government had promoted software services development. Moreover, McKinsey said the quality of the British component supplier base was seen as poor.

In contrast, the non-American foreign companies cited in the report – including Philips, Ericsson of Sweden, Japan's Sony, Olivetti and Thomson of France – had a far more international customer base. Only the Germans Siemens and Nixdorf were anywhere near as dependent on the home market and Siemens was so vast that in absolute terms it was much more well-spread geographically than the British.

Perhaps the most interesting point made by McKinsey concerned the relative degrees of critical mass and business focus. Only five companies out of 32 compared in the report were involved in five or more business sectors and yet had annual sales of less than £15 billion. Two – Lucky Goldstar and Samsung – were the nascent Korean electronics companies; the other three were British – GEC, THORN EMI and Racal. Both Philips and Siemens, and the Japanese duo of Hitachi and Matsushita were active in five or more sectors, but they all had annual sales of more than £15 billion. None of the American giants surveyed – including IBM, AT&T, Rockwell, and DEC – and no other overseas companies, were involved in more than four sectors, however large they were.

This picture was completed by a comparison of the relative degree of concentration by the British and various overseas groups on what McKinsey defined as 'core electronics businesses'. This inevitably subjective, but fascinatingly contentious analysis showed that in volume terms, only the core electronics businesses of GEC and STC matched in size those of the (smaller) overseas companies. And because of GEC's diversified nature, only STC of the British groups approached the overseas groups' combination of size and focus.

The report confirmed the central structural flaw in British

electronics: not only were the companies involved in electronics too thinly spread in their activities, but there were too many companies involved for the size of the industry. On top of this, McKinsey attacked the one apparent saving grace of the British companies: their high profitability. The British rates of return on capital employed in 1986 were the highest in the world, and their operating margins, almost throughout the ten years from 1976, were second only to the Americans. McKinsey's report observed that the substantial cash surpluses amassed by British companies over the five years to 1986 reflected not just this profitability, but also lower investment levels than those of the overseas competitors.

McKinsey declared: 'This positive cash balance developed largely as the result of the actions of a few UK companies which have steadfastly managed for stable short-term earnings gains. These companies apparently have found it difficult to identify attractive opportunities – or were simply unwilling to reinvest in their elec-tronics business at levels that would sustain rates of growth comparable to their non-UK counterparts.'

The paragraph named no names, but it read like an indictment of GEC. Indeed, by sheer definition – the fact that GEC dominated the industry that was the subject of the report – the whole McKinsey study implicated Weinstock's company above all for the failings it identified in British-owned electronics. Weinstock had little time for such synecdoche – 'What is an electronic?', he would respond to those pounding the patriotic drum for 'the British electronics industry'.

Nonetheless, GEC's influence was extraordinarily widespread: it seemed that anyone who was anything in the industry had some sort of connection, friendly or otherwise, with Weinstock. At STC, Walsh and Gardner had come from Marconi. The Clarks, Plessey's founding father and sons, were old adversaries; Racal's Sir Ernest Harrison had bought the defence electronics business Decca from under Wein-stock's nose; Colin Southgate, chief executive and later chairman of THORN EMI lunched with Weinstock regularly and accorded him a tribute in the group's 1987 annual report and accounts: a large colour picture of the opera-loving GEC managing director chatting to conductor Riccardo Muti on the balcony of Milan's La Scala opera house, illustrating THORN's music business. Nothing like that ever appeared in a GEC annual report. As for Amstrad, Weinstock had at one stage discussed with Sugar the possibility of his moving the company into GEC, with Sugar taking a position in GEC management. The notion apparently evaporated when Weinstock made it clear that Sugar's executive role would not be as wide-ranging as Sugar wanted.

GEC's focal point position in the British electronics sector therefore made it appropriate and perhaps inevitable that Weinstock should suddenly emerge, with the Siemens alliance against Plessey, as the catalyst for industry-wide change. The irony of this, after all the appearance of petrifaction at GEC, and the barely-veiled criticism of the group in McKinsey's report, was doubled by the joint venture's partial similarity to McKinsey's own prescription for a British recovery. 'The UK companies must ... commit themselves to attaining critical mass and global presence in a smaller number of sectors, identifying more aggressively where they will compete and where they will not,' the report had declared. 'To achieve critical mass rapidly, the UK companies will need not only to focus their investment, but also to build position through an increased use of strategic alliances and partnerships and if necessary through further merger or business portfolio rationalization. They must identify those technologies which they can develop themselves and, if they lack scale, develop clear strategies for attaining friendly access to required technologies.'

Not only was GEC's bid with Siemens for Plessey precisely this kind of strategic alliance, in defence (GEC's prime interest) and telecommunications (Siemens' main focus) but it would also help to remedy other British deficiencies identified by McKinsey. It would intensify both GEC's core electronics concentration and reduce the dispersion of British electronics capability. Plessey had itself worked hard to build overseas alliances –it had been about to conclude a deal in naval equipment with French group Thomson-CSF just before GEC and Siemens pounced – and had spent £500 million in short order buying defence businesses in North America and the British computer services and software systems company Hoskyns.

But with the new bid, GEC sprang a trap which, for all their dealing activity, Plessey's top management of Clark and managing director Stephen Walls could not escape; a trap which to a considerable extent was of their own making. It was a telecommunications trap, and it had been set the day in 1987 that Plessey agreed to merge its telecommunications operations, including System X and the American company Stromberg-Carlson, with GEC's own telecommunications business to form GPT. A deal between GEC and Plessey to combine their two separate System X manufacturing businesses had made obvious sense – but presented equally obvious difficulties. That was why negotiations for a deal had run, off and on, for years. Telecommunications was much more important to the smaller Plessey than to GEC – it contributed more than half Plessey's sales and profits – and Plessey almost certainly had a stronger telecommunications business, having invested heavily at its Edge Lane, Liverpool manufacturing site and bought and turned round Stromberg Carlson.

The most obvious deal was for Plessey to buy GEC's business, but GEC would not agree to that. The result was an impasse, which was broken suddenly, at the start of October 1987, by Plessey's agreement to an equally-owned joint venture which, it rapidly became apparent, would be headed by GEC's Telecommunications chief, Richard Reynolds.

Some observers believed that Clark's abrupt agreement to a deal in which the chief beneficiary was his long-standing rival Weinstock had as much to do with Plessey's boardroom politics as its corporate strategy. That impression was strengthened when the agreement was rapidly followed first by the resignation of Plessey's managing director Sir James Blyth, whose recruitment by Clark had bolstered Plessey's fight against the first GEC takeover bid, and then by that of David Dey, the man who ran Plessey's telecommunications business and had been appointed by Blyth. Blyth and Clark's mutual antipathy had been an open secret inside and outside the group. It could hardly have been otherwise, since the two had shouting matches in open hearing of Plessey staff. Now Blyth was gone and Clark, backed by Walls, then finance director and a prime mover in the GPT deal, was once more in sole charge of his inheritance.

There was another factor which almost certainly brought Plessey to the negotiating table where its internal politics came into play, and that was the sheer financial muscle of GEC. Plessey's telecommunications investment might have been higher, but GEC's size meant that it could exert enormous pressure in the British public switching market. This, the vindication of its cash mountain, combined with a ruthless competitiveness and ability to capitalize on any sign of weakness in a rival. In the late 1980s, these characteristics were demonstrated most vividly in power engineering where the group succeeded in driving into a corner the turbine generator-making arm of Northern Engineering Industries, its sole British rival in such equipment.

The GEC–NEI story is instructive. GEC's opportunity stemmed ironically from NEI's success, after years of trying to dislodge GEC from its entrenched position as the Government's favourite power equipment maker, in being nominated as prime turnkey contractor for a massive coal-fired power station project in India called Rihand One, which was backed by British Government aid. Unfortunately for NEI, the project turned out to be a poisoned chalice. Work on the station, which was being built at an extremely difficult and remote site, slipped rapidly behind schedule. Department of Trade and Industry officials, having chosen NEI in preference to GEC, felt their faces were being plastered with egg. Then a similar coal-fired power station project backed by a British soft loan package came up in China, at Yue Yang. GEC had already won a massive nuclear turbine generator order in China at Guangdong – a contract for which NEI refused to compete, despite Chinese requests to do so. The DTI actually put pressure on NEI to stay out of the way.

The incident offers a revealing insight into the strength of the influence GEC wielded within the DTI. On 21 May 1985, DTI official Dr Bob Dobbie wrote severely to Dr Bob Hawley, head of NEI's power equipment operations, reporting GEC allegations that NEI had provided the Chinese with price and technical information for a turbine similar to that required for Guangdong.

Dobbie declared: 'I have been instructed by ministers to inform you that if the Chinese should seek to use information provided by NEI in negotiations for the turbine generator island for the Guangdong project, we would make clear to them that GEC are the only UK contractor which has Government support in bidding . . . in this project.'

Ministers, said the letter, had considered 'the likelihood that any information provided to the Chinese would simply be used to bring pressure to bear on GEC's negotiating position, and thus reduce the overall benefit to the UK of any contract which might be won.'

Ten days later, Hawley replied. He expressed surprise at the letter, and protested most strongly: 'NEI has never jeopardized any UK opportunity for business, and your information on our conduct on Guangdong is incorrect. We have honoured our undertaking not to prejudice GEC's chosen instrument status [ie, the DTI's chosen bidder] despite overtures from the Guangdong Nuclear Joint Venture Company.' NEI had actually rejected a Chinese invitation to counter-bid against GEC, Hawley told Dobbie. 'I regard the allegations contained in your letter as damaging to NEI and I must ask you to inform ministers of the true position without delay.'

GEC's attitude on Yue Yang was somewhat different. A consortium of NEI and the cables group BICC's construction subsidiary Balfour Beatty was nominated by the British Government as the supplier, but because of the Rihand embarrassment NEI had to take a supporting role, despite its experience, to Balfour Beatty. Negotiations were proceeding when the Chinese asked GEC to put in a rival tender. GEC obliged. The Balfour Beatty–NEI group fought hard, and thought it had knocked GEC out of the bidding. But GEC recovered, and its British rival lost its grip on the talks. 'They went home for the weekend,' was the hard but not entirely inaccurate shorthand summation by one informed observer. GEC did nothing of the sort. The company negotiated through Christmas 1987 to win Yue Yang. The DTI interest in developments was, in stark contrast to Guangdong, conspicuous by its absence.

While the Yue Yang competition was still running, up came the contract for the second Rihand power station, again covered by a British overseas aid package. NEI's name was still mud somewhere in the DTI, so GEC displaced it as the Government's chosen turnkey contractor on the project. NEI subsequently recovered much of the time that it had lost on Rihand One, and all of the credit with the Indian Thermal Power Corporation that it had forefeited, but it was too late.

Meanwhile, the Central Electricity Generating Board, the power generation authority for England and Wales, invited bids for three new coal-fired power stations each with two units generating 900 megawatts apiece, the largest stations ever considered in Britain. The CEGB later effectively abandoned all three stations, but before then the design placing of contracts for turbines and boilers provided another demonstration of GEC's bidding power. GEC won all three turbine design contracts. One contract was placed first, then the other two simultaneously. The first competition was decisive. Although there was little between the two bids on price, GEC's design appears to have been superior in thermal efficiency, so GEC won. NEI improved its design and bid hard for the second slice of two, but GEC had seen it coming and anticipated its move. Precisely how it won remains unknown, but the best guess is that GEC took the orders at a very keen price. Although NEI won the boiler design contracts, the central lesson was clear: give GEC a trick, and you lose the game.

In agreeing to form GPT, Plessey may have made the same mistake. The company could acquire as much as it liked in other areas, but it had effectively given GEC a lien over its own destiny. Plessey could hope that opposition from Britain's Ministry of Defence, whose hostility to the first GEC bid had led to its veto by the Monopolies Commission, would neutralize GEC's GPT weapon. But from the moment that GEC came back with its novel form of attack, and made it clear that it was prepared to sell off businesses whose combination with GEC operations would create a monopoly supplier to the Ministry of Defence, Plessey could not rely on MoD protection.

What made GPT look even more of a trap was the pre-emption clause that the agreement contained, giving each party the pre-emption right to buy the other's half-share should it be put up for sale, at a price to be fixed by independent auditors. That locked Plessey even further into GEC's larger orbit.

The first thing that became clear after the GEC–Siemens bid was launched was the extent to which the GPT agreement restricted Plessey's choice of potential white knights – friendly counter-bidders. Weinstock reduced their number even further, of course, by GEC's series of alliances. The only way that Plessey could possibly turn the GPT agreement to its own advantage and against GEC was for a bid actually to be made for GEC. Then the GPT clauses would work in reverse, to Plessey's advantage. In the final analysis, that is probably how Metsun got off the ground. As a Metsun participant commented: 'The key was getting total control of GPT.' The problem was that, even after the GEC–Siemens bid, 'one got into this hall of mirrors, with everyone saying "after you"; "no, after you".'

When Metsun went ahead that Saturday morning and ran up its anti-GEC flag, backed by a £3.5 billion Barclays Bank loan facility, the only company that was obviously rallying round it was Plessey. Thomson, the State-owned parent of Thomson-CSF, was the next closest supporter, but all the others – GE, STC and, further away, AT&T, which would not enter a hostile bid arena – were far more problematical supporters, as very quickly became apparent. The Metsun announcement came the day after Plessey's launch of its main defence document against the bid, and just ahead of the week in which the Government was deciding whether to refer the bid to a Monopolies Commission inquiry. On top of that, Metsun was being advised by Plessey's merchant bank, Lazards – a fact which blurred Metsun's purpose, and which should, and could, have been avoided. The identification with Plessey's defence queered Metsun's claims that it was making a disinterested, utilitarian attempt to give GEC shareholders a better return on their investment than they were getting from Lord Weinstock.

That, indeed, was Metsun's intention. Instead of Metsun, the company was almost called 'Shareholder Value Limited'. It was intended to have a finite life, possibly 2½ or three years. It was neither a consortium bid for GEC, nor a management buy-in, although that was probably its closest approximation. Its idea was to restructure GEC. To this end, it would offer GEC shareholders one share in Metsun for each GEC share that they owned. Metsun would then maximize GEC's value by two means: parts of GEC – GPT was the most obvious target – would be sold to companies which had, as it were, pre-contracted to buy them. But much of the group would remain intact. Metsun would have a trustee-type of board consisting, it was said, 'of eminent and prominent people' headed by Cuckney. But this board would not run the group: that would be done by a new operational board probably comprising people from within GEC. Metsun's whole mission was to liberate GEC's assets and its management.

But if its appearance as an arm of Plessey's variegated defence tactics was one blot on Metsun's clean sheet, the liberation argument constituted a much larger flaw. Because liberating GEC's assets, and completely restructuring the group, was precisely what Weinstock was already doing. Why should GEC shareholders take that task away from the man who understood the group from top to bottom and hand it to a new and completely untried organization?

There was the paradox of Metsun. The move that had brought the long-waited bid for GEC to the brink of realization, the GEC–Siemens bid for Plessey, was also the corner-stone of Weinstock's very own reformation of GEC – a restructuring which negated the purpose that Metsun now had the chance to publish. The opening that the GEC–Siemens bid gave Metsun with one hand, it took away almost simultaneously with the other. The position was most succinctly expressed by GEC's share price, ultimately the key to everything. A Metsun insider commented: 'Getting GPT out and allowing some board changes at GEC could have been quite attractive when the GEC price was 160p.' But as soon as GEC and Siemens announced their Plessey bid, GEC's shares started rising – and went on going toward 250p. Metsun's only real hope, after abandoning its first attempt, was that the GEC–Siemens bid for Plessey would somehow fail and that a subsequent slump in GEC's share price would make the group vulnerable again.

Without that eventuality, Metsun still deserved more than a footnote in industrial history. Apart from anything else, its announcement prompted a reaction which revealed for the first time since Westland that the instinct to politicize British industry still lingered in some corners of the opinion-influencing community. Nothing had been heard from Michael Heseltine while GEC and Siemens were bidding for Plessey; but when a bid for GEC was mooted in which Plessey was clearly involved, Heseltine was immediately on his feet before the television cameras describing the dire threat it posed to British industry.

Quite why GEC should be free to make hostile bids for another defence company while being bid-proof itself was not clear. Perhaps it was the speculation that General Electric of America was also implicated in Metsun that so concerned Heseltine. That was certainly what impelled Lord Rees-Mogg, the former editor of *The Times*, who also occupied a non-executive seat on the GEC board, to inveigh against American predators in the columns of *The Independent*. When GEC's deals with GE promptly followed, Lord Rees-Mogg's arguments looked even more divorced from industrial reality than Heseltine's.

What Metsun also did was to turn a short-lived but intense spotlight on to Weinstock's joint venture strategy – acting in the process, at the very least, as an involuntary galvanizing agent in forging the GEC–GE deal. Metsun helped by its very existence to pose the key questions: where would the remarkable transformation of GEC lead the group? Would the changes benefit GEC shareholders? Would they benefit British industry?

By the time the deals with GEC and GE were sealed in spring 1989, and counting in the structure of the proposed Siemens partnership, Weinstock had placed almost half of GEC, in sales terms, into joint ventures. One immediate observation was that he was turning the company into an investment trust, with shareholdings in a number of different businesses. This was a rather exaggerated view, but it did hint at the abiding enigma at the heart of GEC's sudden switch into deal-making overdrive. Weinstock, it was pointed out, had been largely antipathetic to the idea of joint ventures for his entire working life. Why the sudden conversion? Weinstock responded that the strategic conception had always been present, awaiting the opportunity to implement it. Industrial Europeanization and globalization had now made it not just possible but imperative for GEC's continued development.

Inside British industry, there remained a counter-theory that the GEC managing director had taken pre-emptive action to thwart a possible bid for GEC. The alliance with Siemens was not the first move that Weinstock had made in 1988. It came more than three months after GEC had announced that it was reorganizing itself into eight major business groups. To some, that looked like the prelude to a potential demerger of the entire company. In the event, details of only two of the business groups – the two largest, Power Systems and Marconi – were announced. The restructuring was overtaken by the overseas alliances (though in the case of power systems, it could be seen as a necessary preparation for the union with Alsthom).

But if the joint ventures had achieved their aim and made GEC at least temporarily bid-proof, they immediately raised the question of how well they would actually work. Some Weinstock-watchers, who believed that what the GEC managing director wanted was to obtain maximum control for the minimum risk, or financial outlay, were doubtful that he would achieve that end. That analysis in turn raised a far greater imponderable: had GEC, in making the series of alliances, exposed itself to eventual takeover or break-up by one of the very partners it had found? Would GEC, in short, fall into the same kind of trap with which it had snared Plessey in GPT?

When this question was put after news of the Siemens alliance, Weinstock responded: 'It isn't necessary to be bought by Siemens. Neither they nor we have it in mind. This is a very flexible arrangement, and the flexibility is very important because we don't know how things will go. We'll see how we get on in seven years' time.' It was not clear whether that was a literal or a Biblical figure.

With the GE deals, and the sense that Weinstock had been

levered by Welch into agreeing at least some of them, the issue of GEC's future vulnerability recurred. The uncertainty was not stilled by the final form of the joint ventures, which excluded the original plan for GEC to take a minority 25 per cent stake in a European medical electronics company 75 per cent dominated by GE. That plan would have left GEC's American medical equipment business Picker, which was much larger than its European operation and competed with GE in its home market, out on a limb – a fact recognized by the eventual decision to minimize the medical equipment agreement.

One opinion within the industry was that proposal of a European medical equipment alliance had only been an afterthought to the domestic appliances and power equipment deals. But there was also a view that the change showed how Weinstock had managed to claw back ground he had given to GE under the intense pressure to which Welch had subjected him during that second week in January. Then, under the heat of the television lights at the Friday the Thirteenth press conference, Weinstock had given a superb account of his strategy. But alongside him, the laser-eyed Welch, a powerpack of a man who made his impact felt even seven rows back in the media audience, showed every sign of holding the initiative. Perhaps it was misleading, but the impression with which one left the conference was that Weinstock's negotiation, for all its undoubted mastery, had been ultimately defensive.

After the news that the 50–50 household appliances business would be run by GEC management, Welch told the meeting: 'GEC has insisted during all these discussions on control. So while we put the units together, we are betting a lot on GEC management.' He added, ambivalently: 'The one thing they haven't given us is the control of their destiny.' The destiny that some of those who know Weinstock well believe he has in mind is his eventual succession by his son and fellow GEC director, Simon. According to this view, Weinstock knew that the group had to change, so that things could stay the same. As the GEC that Weinstock built entered its third decade, it looked as if the group had taken a giant leap into an unknown that even Weinstock's Euro-vision could not penetrate. One senior pension fund manager, who had followed GEC from the earliest days of Weinstock's leadership, speculated: 'Twenty years ago, the reconstruction of British industry started with GEC. With its central financial controls and its emphasis on decentralization of management decision-making, it was the first modern company. Maybe it will now be the first to be deconstructed.'

CHAPTER SEVEN
THE GLOBAL CHALLENGE

The metamorphosis of GEC may have been the largest, the most sudden and, in terms of its consequences, the most unfathomable of the sea-changes undergone by British companies in the late 1980s – but everywhere, as the momentous decade turned into the 1990s, manufacturers were in the throes of further transformation.

Management structures were reorganized to make companies market-responsive rather than product-driven; a rash of disposals of 'non-core' businesses took place as companies concentrated their resources or sought to move their portfolio up-market into areas where they could add more value to raw materials. And a spate of acquisitions ensued, because one man's peripheral activity was another's core business or because companies wanted to expand geographically and acquisition was the fastest way to achieve that aim.

The fundamental motive force behind this extraordinarily widespread corporate upheaval was the drive to achieve competitiveness by attaining market leadership, or near leadership. In a growing market – like the market for automotive electronics – the race was to grab a place on the front row of the grid; if the market was big but relatively mature – as were many consumer product areas – a company might be third and still do well. But to be certain of success, it needed to be first or second, or it could find itself going nowhere. Only from a market position of command could a group generate the resources necessary to sustain profits and earnings growth. And to this new consciousness was added in many cases a new measure of competitiveness: the competition was no longer from domestically-owned manufacturers. It was going global.

Recognition of these new facts of industrial life yielded changes in corporate shape every bit as remarkable in their way as was Lord Weinstock's remaking of GEC. Under the leadership of a former ICI executive, Dr Brian Smith, the can-maker Metal Box, a member of the old British manufacturing establishment, changed its name to MB Group and gave up full ownership of the packaging business which represented 80 per cent of its sales to joint venture, CMB Packaging, with the French group Carnaud. The deal left the new MB to rebuild itself from a base of only two small operations, cheque printing and central heating.

An equally dramatic change in direction was made by TI Group, which had annual sales in 1986 of about £1 billion. Sales in 1988 were almost identical, at £959 million. But their source of those sales was radically different. In the space of two years TI sold operations which accounted for more than half its business and completely replaced them with new activities. The extent of the overhaul, which rapidly became a Harvard Business School-studied model of corporate restructuring, was not just remarkable in itself. It was a colossal symbol of change in British manufacturing industry. Its central feature was the sale for a total £238 million of TI's entire consumer products interests – Raleigh cycles, Creda and New World cookers, Glow-worm and Parkray heaters, Russell Hobbs kettles and Tower Housewares. The group also pulled out almost completely from the steel tubes business from which it had drawn its former name, Tube Investments. And it finally followed the path taken by other famous names, like John Brown, and abandoned machine tool manufacture. The move was particularly evocative, because only four years earlier TI had added to its existing Matrix-Churchill brands that of Alfred Herbert, one of the most famous names in the British industry's history which had become a noteworthy casualty of the economic recession and the advance of the Japanese machine-tool industry.

In their stead, TI bought specialized engineering businesses, particularly in America, establishing world leadership in mechanical seals and thermal technology (with vacuum furnaces for making industrial materials) and European and North American supremacy in small diameter tube (used in car brake and fuel lines and fridges among a variety of other products). The strategic change was all the more interesting because Chris Lewinton, TI's chief executive from

July 1986 and the man most responsible for its reorientation, had come from the consumer product industry having run the razor blade manufacturer Wilkinson Sword, later taken over by Allegheny International. Lewinton was a man with a mission statement. It read: 'TI's strategic thrust is to become an international engineering group concentrating on specialized engineering businesses, operating in selected niches on a global basis. Key businesses must be able to command positions of sustainable technological and market leadership.'

The City, which was unaccustomed to such mission statements, regarded TI's adherence to this one with initial amusement. But when Lewinton showed every sign of practising what he was preaching, engineering securities analysts sat up. In the process of the two-year change, TI also transformed its geographical business base from one which was 55 per cent-concentrated in Britain and 17 per cent North American into one where the British element was reduced to 25 per cent and the North American increased to 40 per cent. In common with other British companies, the challenge it then faced was to expand in the Pacific Rim during the 1990s.

Lewinton's rapid fulfilment of the mission statement, during which process TI smoothly overcame the 19 October Stock Market crash that threatened to disrupt one important acquisition, left some analysts in the City pondering whether TI's re-creation was not too good to be true. Certainly, simply by switching businesses TI did not automatically guarantee itself growth. Its true test would come in the 1990s.

Lewinton believed that a key psychological step in internationalizing TI was the closure of its Birmingham head office and its move to a London base a quarter of the size. But his central thrust was the analysis that TI had an engineering culture which made it unsuited for the marketing-dominated consumer product business. It should therefore switch from making end-user products like household appliances to complete concentration on manufacture of indirect engineering components. The change exemplified that undergone by other major British companies in the face of the emergence of global consumer product manufacturers. The withdrawal of THORN EMI from both 'white goods' kitchen appliances – sold to Electrolux of Sweden almost simultaneously with the TI disposals – and television manufacture (sold to Thomson of France) paralleled TI's move.

The Thorn sales were only part of a corporate restructuring even bigger than TI's. In less than four years, under chief executive and later chairman Colin Southgate, the group sold 60 (mainly manufacturing) subsidiaries. Instead of making white goods and televisions, Thorn set about building up a global business renting out electrical goods while establishing a world-scale music publishing and recording operation. Thorn's withdrawal from most manufacturing interests culminated in the 1989 sale of its defence electronics operations, althou Southgate stayed in lighting sources and fittings, Thorn's historic manufacturing business, and developed it into a world player. There was still a place for the British-owned consumer appliances company – Hepworth bought TI's Glow-worm and Parkray heaters, and Birmid Qualcast, later taken over by diversifying cement maker Blue Circle, acquired New World – but their status was one of local manufacturer. After the TI and THORN disposals, the only British household appliances group left with a chance of going global was GEC's Hotpoint – which beat Siemens in the bidding for Creda, but had next-to-no presence outside the UK until its union with General Electric.

The global route taken by a large chunk of Britain's manufacturing constituency in the 1980s was through component manufacture. TI's reshaping encapsulated the trend: as a white goods maker, it had competed against Electrolux. Now, through its small diameter tube business, it was a component supplier to the Swedish group.

In other companies, such corporate reorientation was more gradual but just as fundamental. A trend-setter was Smiths Industries, best-known in the 1970s for clock-making, which moved out of that business early in the 1980s. Smiths was left with only one small consumer business, in environmental controls. Otherwise, the group became dedicated to component manufacture. But here too, Smiths gave its portfolio a shake. It started the decade with a sizeable automotive parts operation, but pulled out of that in favour of higher technology, higher margin aerospace components, particularly avionics – aerospace electronics, including Head-up Displays, in which instrumentation panels were replaced by data projected on to the pilot's cockpit window. Despite establishing its credentials with the Seattle-based aircraft industry world leader Boeing, Smiths still had to secure its position as a global player, but it did just that in 1987, when it outbid GEC for the American group Lear Siegler's avionics operation.

Smiths' 1980s history touched on that of two other component manufacturers, Dowty and Lucas Industries, which approached the

1990s as prominent British figures in the twin drives for global presence and higher technology products. Like Smiths, Lucas started the decade with a wide exposure to the motor industry. It was also Europe's biggest aerospace components group, but in the lower-technology, predominantly electrical and mechanical engineering areas of actuation (for wing control) and power units. Smiths' way out of motor components was greatly smoothed by Lucas's 1983 decision to take over control of Smiths' dashboard instrumentation business. Had Lucas not been a willing buyer, Smiths would have closed the operation down. Instead, Lucas took 80 per cent of a joint venture, combining the Smiths' business with Lucas's own ignition electronics operations, called Lucas Electrical and Electronic Systems, with Smiths holding the outstanding 20 per cent – which it subsequently wrote off in its balance sheet when the venture proved a disaster. Its failure played a significant part in deciding the outcome of the contest inside Lucas between joint managing directors Tony Gill and Jeffrey Wilkinson over which would emerge as heir to the chairmanship. Wilkinson carried ultimate responsibility for the LEES decision. He left the company again in 1984 and Gill became chief executive, subsequently succeeding Sir Godfrey Messervy as chairman.

Gill's was the driving force behind the striking change of direction which Lucas then underwent. Through a combination of sales of historic Lucas motor component businesses and mainly American acquisitions of aerospace and, to a lesser extent, industrial companies, he reshaped the group's sales base. In 1984, 74 per cent of the group's £1.5 billion sales were in automotive; four years later, aerospace sales had been almost doubled while automotive had increased overall by less than ten per cent and accounted for 61.5 per cent of the near-£2 billion total. In 1987, Lucas pulled out of the lighting business that Joseph Lucas had founded as well as starters and alternators manufacture. Both businesses went eventually to the Fiat subsidiary Magneti Marelli. Lucas formed a joint venture in batteries with the Japanese company Yuasa and sold or closed other smaller parts of the group.

Although Lucas retained its base in the West Midlands, the moves constituted a major cultural break, removing lingering vestiges of the labour and quality problems which had plagued the group when it was seen as a local Birmingham employer. The group halted central pay bargaining, devolving negotiating power to its individual operations. At the same time, Lucas asserted its corporate authority over parts of the business which had developed a semi-independent identity: the name of its braking subsidiary Girling – the group's one truly multinational auto components company – was subsumed into a new Automotive Division as Lucas Braking Systems, along with three other 'systems' manufacturing units. The step may have been required by the new central strategic drive (similar action had been taken by Pilkington to collar the devolutionary tendencies of its Glasgow electro-optics and periscope subsidiary Barr & Stroud) but it nevertheless seemed an unfortunate loss.

The most dramatic event in Lucas's 1980s history, however, was one that never actually happened – and has never been revealed, until now. In mid-1986, the group – unquestionably vulnerable to possible takeover – considered a merger with GKN, Britain's other major motor components manufacturer. The idea is believed to have come from GKN, which had established a genuinely multi-national, world-leading position with its constant velocity joints (CVJs), which maximized efficient power transmission in front-and all-wheel drive vehicles.

Under Sir Trevor Holdsworth, GKN had already reshaped itself comprehensively, disposing of a string of activities – notably its steel interests but also commodity engineering businesses including nuts, bolts and screws manufacture. But the CVJ was approaching maturity, and GKN appears to have been looking to extend its automotive product range, as well as to anticipate the trends in vehicle design towards increased electronic controls and demand by customers for complete systems instead of individual components. There was obvious potential, for instance, in the union of GKN's driveshaft products with Lucas's anti-lock brakes.

A merger, which would have created an engineering group with annual sales of more than £3.5 billion, would almost certainly not have foundered on the Monopolies Commission opposition that sank GKN's earlier bid for AE, since there was no overlap between the two groups. But after studying the proposal, Lucas appears to have decided that a deal would have done little to enhance Lucas's own prospects. Lucas said no, and GKN – first under Holdsworth, then led by his successor, David

Lees – concentrated on developing suspension systems and its axles operations, as well as on expanding its industrial services interests and building up a defence business. In 1988, it took the major step of acquiring a sizeable stake in Westland, with a view to taking eventual majority control of the helicopter maker.

Industry insiders believe that Dowty, like the much larger Lucas, also considered a major merger in the mid-1980s. Dowty's suitor was none other than Smiths, then looking – before the Lear Siegler deal – to expand its aerospace operations. But, like Lucas, Dowty rejected the proposal and went its own way with, as the 1980s ended, increasing success. It was shaken out of its somewhat comfortable Cheltenham- based existence and into the realities of international competition by Tony Thatcher, its chief executive since late 1986. Thatcher's background was in electronics, and his application of that culture to what was a very traditional British industrial components manufacturer made Dowty a classic case of restructuring for the 1990s.

Through a combination of acquisition (particularly the £80 million takeover of information technology group CASE), disposal (notably of the group's long-standing mining equipment business) and organic development, Thatcher has moved the group away from lower-technology, lower-growth businesses, and into higher value-added, more knowledge-based activities with a global geographical spread. In 1982, Dowty's product portfolio was 90 per cent mechanical engineering and ten per cent electrical/electronic. Seven years later, the split was 50–50. An information technology division, embracing electronic office products such as electronic mail systems, was developed from nothing in 1985 to sales of about £200 million in 1989, more than 25 per cent of the group. In that year, the group's overseas business had increased to more than 50 per cent of total sales. Thatcher aims to take that proportion to 75 per cent by expansion in both the United States and the Far East, while making Dowty a £1 billion sales group by 1993.

Not that British manufacturing industry at the end of the 1980s was wholly given over to components manufacture. As Sir Francis Tombs observed: 'Europe has a lot to learn from the British conglomerates, with their emphasis on decentralization and local cost centres.'

And by the end of the decade, a successor to BTR and Hanson

appeared to have emerged. The rise of Williams Holdings, whose interests ranged from Crown and Berger paints to luxury car dealerships, and from specialist engineering to Rawlplug and Polycell DIY products, was in some respects even more remarkable than that of its two precursor conglomerates (or, as the phrase went, industrial holding companies).

Williams was, in a way, inspired by the Thatcherite industrial revolution and its growth has been synonymous with the 1980s revival. At the turn of 1981, in the midst of the recession, Nigel Rudd went to Hong Kong to see Brian McGowan. Rudd was a successful 35-year-old businessman who had been the youngest chartered accountant in Britain when he had qualified at the age of 20, and had made his money turning round a loss-making housebuilding contractor. McGowan, aged 37, was a friend and former colleague who had gone to the Crown Colony to work for the trading house Sime Darby.

Rudd told McGowan: 'Now is the time to get back into Britain. Industry is on its knees. Engineering is going nowhere. There has never been such a situation when share prices have been at such a discount to asset value. Let's have a go.'

The consequence was that in February 1982 they took a 51 per cent stake in Williams, a Welsh engineering company based in Caerphilly, which had lost almost £1 million the previous year, had sales of £6.9 million, net tangible assets of £2.1 million and a Stock Market value of £340,000. Seven years later, Williams was heading for pre-tax profits of about £160 million, on sales approaching £1.2 billion, had net assets of £280 million and was valued by the Stock Market at more than £800 million.

Rudd describes himself as 'a dealer, somebody who gets deals, thinks of deals' and McGowan as 'akin to the merchant banker, probably one of the best corporate finance people I've met in my life'. An early acquisition brought in Williams' Third Man – managing director Roger Carr. Carr, formerly a rising star in the marketing department of the giant computer group Honeywell, has played a key role in Williams' growth, initially as the leader of the group's post-acquisitions team – the hit squad that descends from black BMWs to sort out each company immediately after Williams has sealed the deal. Carr's role has widened to the point where, as Rudd says, 'it's now a triumvirate at the top of the business'.

A FIGHTING CHANCE

In 1988, almost two-thirds of Williams sales were made in the UK, with North America the group's major overseas market. But that will change as the single European market approaches. Rudd declares: 'Our aim before 1992 is to be the lowest-cost producer of any of our products anywhere in Europe. Then nobody can take the market, because we've got the margin. If you are the lowest-cost producer, you can influence pricing.'

Like BTR, the group does not stress volume: 'We use capital expenditure not to increase volumes but to get the costs down.' Williams, which already reckons to have attained lowest-cost status in Britain, has other articles of faith: 'A business can be anything in manufacturing, but it has to be number one or two in its market place because it has got to have decent margins on sales,' says Rudd. The emphasis on margins provides a built-in drive to avoid low-added value areas: 'We don't want to be a sub-contractor, making un-sophisticated products for Rover, Ford or whatever.'

Several precepts make Williams stand out from the corporate crowd. For one thing, in the marketing of its consumer businesses – which also include Swish home furnishings and Smallbone furniture – it has not joined the recent trend for companies to attach their name to the brands that are recognized by the public. 'They are discreet businesses. The managers will want to feel it's their business; sometimes they don't want to tell the customer that the business is part of Williams.'

Williams has another motive for not pushing itself as an overall brand: if it wanted to sell a consumer business, the task would be much harder and the price much less if the business was seen as part of Williams rather than a stand-alone branded operation. The thinking reflects another key feature of the group's remarkable progress: its acquisitions are always underpinned by deal-making prudence. No purchase is entered unless Williams can see an exit should something go wrong. Likewise, and exceptionally among British companies, the group has avoided entry into foreign, particularly American markets, through the direct acquisition of native companies. 'Hanson has got it right, but so many people get rolled over in the United States.'

Williams' rise through the 1980s was a model of sustained portfolio turnover to produce higher margins and higher quality earnings. None of the businesses the group acquired in its first few years remains. Surprisingly for a company whose growth is so identified with the mid-1980s takeover wave, by early 1989 Williams had never succeeded with a hostile bid. The closest it came was in its 1987 attempt to acquire the building and consumer products group Norcros, which escaped by the skin of its teeth after Williams had made its first bid also its final one and closed the offer well before the deadline allowed under takeover rules. Like any negotiation, normal takeover custom is for an initial bid to be followed by a higher one which runs on until the latest permitted moment. Institutional shareholders are notorious for delaying their decision until the eleventh hour. Williams almost certainly failed because a number of financial institutions took the view that they were being dictated to by an arrogant Williams management, and resolved to put the group in its place. Rudd acknowledges that: 'We didn't play the City game, because we felt the bid wasn't a game. We are a little bit wiser now, although we'd still consider the tactic of just going once.'

Williams appears unlikely to move far into the 1990s without making a large, hostile bid. The group's most significant quantitative and qualitative leaps forward in the late 1980s were actually two pairs of major acquisitions which displayed to the full its combination of astute industrial awareness, razor-sharp opportunism, successful development of City relations, and total self-confidence. The deals also threw interesting light on the difference between Williams and other, much larger British groups.

The first 'twin' acquisitons were the June 1987 purchase of Crown Paints for £285 million and the £133 million purchase of Berger seven months later, which took Williams from nothing to second in the British paints market behind market leader ICI. In 1988, the acquisitions together yielded more than £46 million in trading profits and more than £340 million in sales.

Both businesses were disposals by larger groups. Crown was sold in an auction by Reed International en route to Reed's departure from manufacturing industry to concentrate on publishing. It was a good deal – because of the cash that came in Crown's balance sheet, Williams' net outlay was reduced to £250 million. But what turned Crown from a good deal into a great one was the Berger purchase from the West German chemicals group Hoechst. Berger was third in the market under Crown, and its constant price-cutting had sliced

A FIGHTING CHANCE

Crown's operating margins to six per cent (Reed's American paints business was making ten per cent). Before it ever bid for Crown, Williams had a game plan in place. 'Our corporate strategy was that unless we went on to buy Berger, we would sell Crown to a continental company or to Courtaulds (a lesser player in the British household paint market, though a leader in marine coatings), so we would be left with the American paints business and Polycell.' In the event, Hoechst approached Williams after the Crown purchase.

Williams still had to fund the deal through some form of cash-raising shares issue, and how the group did so presents an object lesson in industry – City relations. The Stock Market was still in a state of intense nervousness after the 19 October share price crash less than three months earlier. For some time, Rudd and McGowan had kept close to the group's top six shareholders. Nevertheless, when the Berger deal came along and Williams went to securities house BZW, it was told that 'there is no way this can be done'. Williams wanted to raise £100 million. It decided to go to five institutions the day before the issue, and persuade them to underwrite £20 million apiece. With the quintet guaranteeing security as primary underwriters, the other institutions would all come in since they would not be worried about being left with rapidly depreciating shares. A complicating factor was that the issue would have to give existing shareholders 'clawback' rights – the right to take shares previously allocated elsewhere – so that their holdings would not be automatically diluted by the new issue.

Initially, Williams considered issuing convertible loan stock, but the idea was dropped after one major institutional fund manager told Rudd and McGowan that if he wanted loan stock, he would buy government securities. He agreed to take 20 per cent of a straight equity issue. So did three out of the other four major institutions Williams approached. The deal was announced the next day, other institutions came in as sub-underwriters and Williams' share price actually rose. No shares were left with the underwriters. 'It was a question of going along to people who were really committed to British industry and were keen to see the City do something after the October Crash,' says Rudd.

The institutions' backing of Williams was soon more than justified, because the Berger deal that started as a £133 million purchase ended with Williams paying a net £23 million for the company. Berger's Australian-based Pacific Basin operation, second in the market behind ICI and ahead of Crown but still a loss-maker, was sold to ICI for £52 million. ICI forgot its initial reluctance to pay the asking price when the possibility of an American company buying Berger Australia was raised. Williams sold a string of other Berger businesses. Meanwhile, Williams already held a 4.9 per cent stake in the British own-label paint and decorative products company A. G. Stanley. In a neat move, it added that stake to Berger's 20.4 per cent holding in Stanley, which was clearly vulnerable. A successful bid, completed in June 1988, came from the DIY group Ward White. It valued Williams' stake at £33 million. In less than six months, Williams had recouped £110 million of the £133 million Berger outlay.

The efficiencies Williams proceeded to wring out of its newly-created British paint operation contrast quite strikingly with the results from ICI's own paint business. ICI's paint sales are probably five times those of Williams, but its profits are only double the Williams total. In decorative paint, for instance, Williams concentrated production at one plant working round the clock; ICI has about five factories, many operating on a single shift.

However, it is probably in deal-making that there exists the greatest divide between the long-established pillars of the manufacturing community and the conglomerates that rose up in the 1980s to stand shoulder to shoulder with them. At one stage during the decade, one of Britain's biggest and most blue-chip names went to sit at Lord Hanson's feet to learn from his acquisition technique and, specifically, his method of handling the post-takeover disposal of unwanted companies.

Rudd draws this distinction: 'These big, older groups tend to analyze possible acquisitions to death. I buy on hunch. I can tell by walking round a factory whether a business is going to make money, I can smell it. Of course, you've got to go through the figures but at the end of the day it has to be done on intuition. Right at the crunch point, you've got to have somebody who says, let's go. I'm sure some of these long-standing big groups have a committee.'

By a similar token, Williams' other major, dual deal of the late Eighties highlighted not just the group's acute eye for an opportunity, but also its area of difference from Hanson. In November 1988, it paid

£331 million for the Pilgrim House Group, which was itself in the process of buying from Hanson's American arm the fire protection business of recent Hanson purchase Kidde. Pilgrim House was itself an archetypal late 1980s corporate restructuring case of a mechanical engineer moving into higher technology electrical and electronic engineering. In its previous incarnation as RHP, it had sold its then-core business, RHP ball bearings, to a management buy-out and then embarked on a merger with electronics group Burgess.

But all was not sweetness and light with the Burgess deal, during which problems discovered in a Burgess subsidiary changed the original merger terms and turned them into an effective takeover bid by RHP. That left relations between RHP's chief executive Roger Pinnington and Burgess's creator Bob Morton somewhat strained. The problems enlarged the window of vulnerability which the now-renamed Pilgrim House had entered in the course of its attempted transition, and that window opened wider still when Pilgrim's proposed £137 million purchase of the Kidde business was delayed by an American competition authorities' inquiry. Williams, which had bought a stake in RHP before the Burgess deal, saw its chance. Pinnington had a past connection with Rudd and McGowan, who had asked him during the Norcros bid to join Williams and help run Norcros if the bid succeeded. But there was no sentiment now. Rudd, McGowan and Carr do not believe in old times' sake. The perfect timing of Williams' move and the astutely-pitched offer left Pilgrim's board with little alternative but to recommend the bid, and stifle Pinnington's hopes of building an independent international group.

The Kidde purchase, as Williams recognized, was a marvellous deal. Combined with Graviner, it immediately gave the group world leadership in the high-growth area of aircraft fire suppression and detection. Kidde also brought major geographical expansion, in Europe as well as the United States. But one feature of the fire protection group showed the difference between Williams and Hanson: no capital investment had gone into the business under Hanson – it had been run for cash. Williams immediately set about making up for the missing investment.

The Pilgrim House deal carried Williams, that creation of the 1980s, over the threshold of the 1990s. It was an international business – 'It's the first of what we hope will be several businesses which will be world players,' said Rudd. And with Burgess's microswitch business in the group, together with the fire protection side, it took Williams significantly into electronics. The move emphasized Williams' differences from Hanson, with its concentration of basic businesses, and to a lesser extent from BTR, whose electronics business content was relatively limited. It also made the fundamental point that in the new decade, a conglomerate with component manufacturing interests will have to deal with higher technology than its holding company forebears. To support its further development, Williams will enjoy the immense cash flow from its paint business. The group knows that growth there will slow within the next two years, but the cash generation should be formidable.

But Williams will never, in the scheme of British manufacturers, be a high technology pioneer. As Rudd acknowledges: 'Basically, our businesses have to be cash-producing, so we aren't really interested in high-tech companies which require so much Research and Development and money going back all the time.'

BTR, of course, has much the same philosophy. That was partly what made its aborted bid for Pilkington such a potent conflict of approaches to manufacturing. For Sir Owen Green, Pilkington was essentially a *de facto* monopolist of the British commodity glass market. Pilkington saw things differently: it intended to build up its existing multinational presence in the glass business while at the same time moving the group up-market technologically. After the bid was over, chairman Antony Pilkington set a fundamental target for the 1990s: by 1995, 30 per cent of group business was to be in high technology areas.

If Pilkington is to reach that figure, it will depend heavily on the success of a sophisticated strategy for Research and Development which was developed in the late 1980s under the leadership of Sir Robin Nicholson. Nicholson had joined the group from his post as chief scientific adviser to the Government, a move which connected the national interest with the vital need for a significant private sector civil R and D effort. Frequent studies during the 1980s had demonstrated that British industry spent less on research and development than did its major competitors; that what it did spend was concentrated disproportionately (and, the inference was, unhealthily) on the defence sector, but most crucially of all, that because of inefficiency in the management of R and D, what spending there was was not sufficiently productive.

Nicholson's fundamental task when he joined the company was to put in place an R and D structure which would both increase Pilkington's investment in long-term research, and improve the efficiency of the overall R and D effort, then running at about £100 million a year. To an extent, Pilkington's unco-ordinated position was simply the result of a series of acquisitions made by the group in its moves both to extend its product range and to raise the technology level of its portfolio – in particular, its £361 million purchase in August 1987 of the American group Revlon's ophthalmic business. The acquisitions had left Pilkington with numerous R and D centres worldwide, duplicating work and resources.

The group did, however, have a deeper-seated problem which had surfaced during the BTR bid, when BTR accused the company of lacking direction in its R and D. Pilkington would never acknowledge that BTR might have had a point, but Nicholson did comment: 'About two years ago, we had to decide whether we should leave things as they had fallen, or do something slightly more logical.'

Nicholson's strategic decision was to make the group's R and D centre at Lathom in pastoral Lancashire the unit responsible for work with a timescale of between five and ten years from product conception to commercial introduction, while devolving to the group's operating subsidiaries development with a laboratory-to-market timescale of nought to five years. Many of the operating companies had never really done longer-term research because they were simply too small to invest in it.

'Our research activity was not adequate for a group with the technological base, size and aspirations that we now have,' said Nicholson. 'Bringing in this concept will substantially increase the amount of long-term research, raise its quality and value for money.'

As Nicholson appreciated, the implications of this strategic shift extended well beyond the frontiers of even Pilkington's far-flung multinational business. As it approached the 1990s, British industry required a larger cadre of companies willing to take the longer view, and to translate that outlook into a greater commitment to effective innovation. Nicholson was characteristically sanguine: 'As profits have recovered, the long-term investment culture has come very much alive. Two things are needed for it to be well-established: it has to be demonstrated that British companies which made this effort do better than the others; and people need to see that current profit levels are maintained. Then we will enter a virtuous circle in which high profits lead to new products with good margins.'

One notable foundation for this cause was the establishment later that year of CEST, the Centre for the Exploitation of Science and Technology, a private sector-funded body backed by numerous innovation-orientated British manufacturers. The idea of CEST, and much of the spadework in setting it up, was done by Sir Francis Tombs, in his role as chairman of the Cabinet Office's now renamed Advisory Council on Science and Technology.

It was no coincidence that T & N, the former Turner and Newall which Tombs had rescued, was making significant advances by the end of 1980s. The R and D effort was partly dedicated to supporting the group's drive to establish itself as a global automotive engine components manufacturer. At the same time, T & N was concentrating on building up a strong base in materials technology, to equip itself to compete internationally in the next decade and more. To an extent, its R and D commitment was born out of the necessity of finding substitutes for the asbestos-based products which had nearly brought the downfall of the group earlier in the 1980s.

After its late 1987 triumph in the acrimonious battle for AE, the group's R and D effort was automatically and substantially expanded. The bid's main theme was clear: T & N wanted AE so that it could transform the quality of its earnings and substantially dilute the impact of asbestosis-related damages claims, together with low-quality overseas and mining earnings, on its results. But a prime sub-text of the bid, different from the BTR-Pilkington affair but in its way just as potent, was attitudes to R and D. One principal AE defence against the bid was the claim that T & N would slash AE's innovation investment if it won.

The truth was more complex. AE was known for being run by engineers, and it was no coincidence that its Cawston House headquarters near Rugby also housed an extensive R and D centre. Tombs and his chief executive Colin Hope, however, believed that

AE's R and D effort had been both somewhat unbalanced – concentrating on piston technology to the neglect of other business areas – and not as efficient as it should have been. It was claimed that AE's operational managers frequently found themselves 'second guessed' and overruled on development projects by the AE top management.

After its victory, T & N retained Cawston as its R and D centre. But it set about making significant changes to the way the group managed its innovation investment. AE had levied a central charge for R and D. To establish a closer link between Cawston and the group's operating subsidiaries, T & N began the phased introduction of funding the R and D centre from a percentage of the royalties earned by the subsidiary companies from licensing their technology. At the same time, Hope reviewed the R and D budgets of all the T & N companies, deciding in some cases that companies were not investing enough. In what was seen as a temporary expedient to be abandoned once a long-term commitment to R and D had become ingrained, T & N's top management actually ordered some companies to spend more on R and D. What it did not do was to dictate what they should spend the money on. The companies' managing directors were simply told to work with Cawston to develop suitable R and D programmes. But at the same time, T & N aimed to establish a group-wide awareness of the importance of financial objectives. All senior and middle management were sent on a special Loughborough University course covering finance for non-financial managers.

Reforms like those carried out in Research and Development by Pilkington and T & N reflected the fundamental change in the level of performance achieved by important parts of British industry during the late 1980s. Elements like R and D had previously been viewed either in the rather abstract, uncritical light of being 'a good thing', by those companies with an R and D commitment, or largely ignored, by those companies without one. Now a proper, practical application of such elements to the commercial life of some companies was taking place.

Quality presented a similar case for treatment. Not just product quality, but quality in all aspects of the operational process, from boardroom to shopfloor. Like the United States, British industry had got the quality message almost 40 years after the Japanese, but at last it had arrived. Mike Fischer, founder-chairman of the Oxford-based computer manufacturer Research Machines, was an early British convert to the quality doctrine propounded by the American Joseph Juran, who, like his compatriot W. Edwards Deming, had been a prophet ignored in his native country but honoured in 1950s Japan. RM, best known for its school computers, with which it battled for market leadership against the Olivetti subsidiary Acorn, achieved striking reductions in its internal defect rates by concentrating on quality improvement. On one range of new products, the group halved its internal defect rates in the space of 12 months. At the same time, it was able to lengthen to three years the duration of its warranty guarantee because of the significant cuts in warranty costs secured by the quality drive.

The quality commitment of a company like Research Machines went far deeper than anything encouraged by the Government through the British Standard 5750 which became, for many companies, the official seal of their success in raising quality. Fischer had a of warning for them. BS5750, he said, was something of a snare and a delusion. 'It's a bit like if you are learning to shoot. BS5750 tells you where to position your elbow and your finger, and when to hold your breath – but it doesn't require you to judge whether you have hit the target. Most of the things BS5750 requires you to do you would have to do if you were trying to improve your quality – but it doesn't require you to do them in a way that actually improves quality: it doesn't close the loop.'

Fischer quoted the example of one company which had been 'BS5750'd for some time; it didn't improve their quality. It is an information and product control system, and that is a very useful framework for a Quality Improvement programme. But it doesn't really put any pressure on you or give you any guideline as to how much company resource to invest in taking that data and applying it to achieve quality improvement.'

The same message that the official Government standard was only a base camp at the foot of the quality mountain was delivered by the London-based management consultancy PA through its Total Quality Management system. Among the welter of quality-orientated programmes, TQM was one of the most widely disseminated. Ilford Photographic, part of the Swiss group Ciba-Geigy, was the first company to adopt TQM. The forklift truck maker Lansing Bagnall followed.

At Avon Rubber in 1988, Tony Mitchard called in PA to help install TQM. For Mitchard, the move to embed quality of operation into the core of the company was the vital next step without which all Avon's mid-1980s efficiency improvements could go for nothing. Unlike the efficiency drive, the Total Quality effort would not be an overnight sensation. As David Cook of PA noted, 'It's much easier to change people's language than their behaviour. The organizations which really understand TQM will say after at least two, and possibly as much as four, years that they are just beginning to get to grips with it.' Even allowing for management consultancy hyperbole, the point was made.

Mitchard likewise saw TQM as making a quantum break even from the management psychology that had seen through the efficiency improvements: 'We are typical of very many companies in that we've decided to tackle effects and not causes. TQM takes you back to sorting out the basics.' Avon called the project a drive for 'the permanent fix, rather than short-term palliatives'.

TQM is essentially an all-embracing focal point for the actions that British companies need to take if they are to match Japanese standards of 'right first time' performance and continuous improvement. The system essentially analyzes the performance of each component of a company and, using numerous individual projects as a spearhead, aims to improve enormously the quality of work in, and between, those departments.

Implementation of TQM requires total commitment from top management – as Mitchard gave it in Avon – but is rapidly extended to involve the whole workforce. Apart from anything else, it is a huge training and education exercise. At Avon, it involved teaching the whole workforce the kind of understanding of statistics which Japanese learn in school at the age of 12.

Mitchard said: 'What typically happens in Western industry is that somebody up at the top gets an idea that something should be done. He gets together some of his immediate colleagues and convinces them of the need to do it. Then, perhaps a few meetings are arranged; perhaps some posters are prepared and a special edition of the company newspaper comes out with the message: this is going to become a quality company. But the people in the middle who have got to make the thing work don't really know much about it. And what happens, of course, is that the tablets of stone come crashing down.'

Avon produced not one edition of its company newspaper, but a new paper, Avon Quality News. And Mitchard observed: 'TQM will have no end. It will be perpetuated for all the years to come, in one form or another.'

A somewhat belated convert to TQM was the luxury car maker Jaguar. In 1988, it called David Harding, a former Jaguar quality expert now working for PA on TQM, back to its Coventry headquarters to mastermind a company-wide drive to improve quality in Jaguar's operations. Harding's appointment came within a few months of Jaguar's recruitment as manufacturing director of Bob Dover, who had done that job with considerable success at Land-Rover.

The two moves highlighted the crossroads that Jaguar had reached, and the new turning that it was now taking. Through most of the 1980s, the company had been the supreme symbol of Britain's industrial revival, its big cat marque almost as potent a popular engineering icon as Concorde, and much more profitable. Jaguar was part of Britain's cultural heritage. The Oxford English Dictionary used the company to illustrate the meaning of the word 'marque'; In the United States, historically the group's biggest market, the product was a by-word: the plot of an episode in the Phil Silvers show centred on the efforts by Sergeant Bilko to buy a Jaguar. That, of course, was before the company's 1960s slump and its subsequent de-personalization under British Leyland. But it meant that, when the recovery came, it triggered a fount of goodwill in the United States. 'America loves a turnround,' said one of Jaguar's US marketing team.

And since America also loved Mrs Thatcher, Jaguar received a double boost. The company's chairman, John Egan, personified the successful Thatcherite executive, a local boy (from Rossendale Valley, Lancashire) made good through his own self-improvement and determination to succeed. Egan has no time for traditional British trades unionism. He once described Jaguar's shop stewards as 'existing in an absolute nightmare of fag-ends of Marxism, socialism and so on'. At the same time, after his knighthood in 1986, Egan commented: 'You see an awful lot of people who have got knighthoods who deserve them, and it makes you feel proud to be amongst such a group. On the other hand, I think we have to spend a lot more time allowing our meritocracy to develop. It is right and proper that people who run the country are people who have worked their way there. I don't really subscribe to the idea that inheritance should give you very much. It makes you wonder when you think that, even now, so long after the industrial revolution, the richest man in the country is still a landowner.'

Under Egan, Jaguar had recovered from the verge of closure in 1980, when its net losses exceeded £52 million on sales of only £166 million, or less than 14,000 vehicles, to hit a pre-tax profits peak of £121.3 million in 1985. On 6 August the previous year, the company went public in a highly successful privatization: valued at £297 million by an offer for sale which was more than seven times over-subscribed.

Profits slipped slightly but not dramatically to £97 million in 1987, when the company launched its completely new XJ6 saloon in Britain, known initially as the XJ40. But on Friday, 26 August, 1988, Jaguar announced that its pre-tax surplus in the six months to June had more than halved to only £22.5 million – and the Jaguar 'legend', as the company's advertisements had it, was suddenly shattered. Profits for the full year 1988 were also more than halved, to £47.5 million.

Two comments in particular from Egan at Jaguar's press conference on that Friday came from the heart. He told the media: 'I'm not concentrating on short-term profit. I never promised you I would. I never made that the prime goal of this company. I made the prime goal of this company long-term growth.' And: 'Maybe there should be a special place up in heaven for a chairman who gets everything right except the bottom line.'

The profits slump was caused by one basic fact: although Jaguar's sales had actually increased in the half-year by 14.5 per cent, its cost of sales had risen by 21.5 per cent. A sizeable part of that problem was the combination of a rising pound – lowering the sterling value of Jaguar's American sales – and a squeeze in the United States market for European luxury cars which meant that Jaguar could not recover its lower sterling sales through raising prices. But that was not quite the bottom of the story. And later during that press conference, Egan alluded to the fundamental reality: 'The plant productivity level was achieved with too much overtime. It depends which thing appears first on the priority list. If you've got a huge waiting list, that takes priority.'

What basically happened at Jaguar was that after a genuinely strong and sustained initial recovery abetted by good luck, adverse circumstances conspired to catch the company at its most vulnerable point since the initial recovery from near-extinction, thereby not just exposing its underlying flaws but accentuating them.

Jaguar's much-publicized revival under Egan had acquired Churchillian connotations. What was now the company's Castle Bromwich body plant had, during the Second World War, produced the Spitfires that won the Battle of Britain. Now Jaguar had been thrown back from the bridgehead for future growth established by the company's own D-Day – the launch of the new XJ6. For it was with the launch of the XJ6 that the great Jaguar revival went wrong. The new vehicle was vital to the company: it would account for about 80 per cent of total sales (hence the oft-repeated criticism that Jaguar was a one-product company) and was the first completely new Jaguar saloon for 19 years. But fate – and management mistakes – were present from the start.

First, the company failed to avoid the coincidence of biennial pay negotiations, both with the launch and the separate efforts to get the changes in working practices needed to obtain the 20 per cent productivity improvement that had been built into the design of the vehicle. (When Jaguar engineers stripped down the comparative Mercedes model, they found that, despite the new XJ6 improvements, the Mercedes still contained substantially fewer individual parts). The group took one bout of industrial action, related to the new XJ6 working arrangements but, to avoid another round of trouble over the pay claim, settled at a level somewhat higher than it had originally planned.

Jaguar therefore started the new XJ6 era with higher than intended labour costs which were not defrayed by the major productivity gains that it should have realized from the new model. This was not just because of worker resistance. At least one stockbroking analyst has suggested that some of the company's expensive new capital plant proved inadequate. The problem was compounded by the fact that the marketing effort for the new car was too successful for the company's own good. Demand for the new saloon was phenomenal, and waiting lists in Britain rapidly soared to over a year in some cases. Egan had always adopted a strategy of supplying one less car than there was demand for, but waiting lists this long were not quite what he had intended. And when the car was launched in the vital American market (which accounted for more than half total sales) the following spring, 1987, the waiting list problem simply piled up further. Jaguar's component suppliers could barely keep pace – at one point in the summer of 1987, at least one supplier was delivering parts to the company's assembly plant at Brown's Lane, Coventry by taxi. It was a novel, and costly, form of just-in-time delivery.

To try to satisfy this demand, because significant productivity improvements were simply not coming through, Jaguar hired more workers. Throughout the recovery years, the company had maintained a cautious policy of recruitment. One of Egan's articles of faith in his attempt to foster mutual management-worker confidence and common cause was to avoid redundancies. It was not until 1984, when output reached almost 33,500 vehicles, that the workforce recovered to the levels of 1980, when output totalled 13,800 cars. Now, however, Jaguar's labour force surged to about 12,700 – well ahead of the time when the company had anticipated reaching this figure. Egan insisted that the company should not compromise its training effort to get the new people on the line, but each new recruit added weight to the payroll.

The impact on Jaguar of the October 1987 financial markets crash, which destroyed the confidence generated by the great bull market, is hard to gauge. Jaguar was not like Porsche, the German luxury car maker whose sales went through the floorpan after October because of its dependence on Wall Street yuppiedom. Much of Jaguar's American clientele was 'old money'. But in February 1988, came the first sign that Jaguar sales were falling in the United States. There was some respite in March, but after that the picture darkened steadily through the late spring and summer. BMW and Mercedes were also hit. The message was clear: prices of European luxury vehicles, fuelled by the dollar's fall against the pound and the Deutschemark, had outrun demand which was now, in many cases, funnelling into the much-improved, and much cheaper top-of-the-range American models like Ford's Lincoln and General Motors' Cadillac.

Jaguar was able to keep its sales growing thanks largely to the continued consumer boom in Britain, with help from the much smaller markets of France (boosted by Jaguar's 1988 triumph in the Le Mans 24-hour race) and Japan. But its final output figure of 52,000 cars in 1988 fell well short of its original target of between 55,000 and 56,000. And in 1989, weakness in American demand meant the company was heading for a drop in output, or at best a standstill – its first since the start of its 1980s revival. The deceleration was dramatic. Less than two years earlier, analysts had been expecting output of almost 80,000 cars in 1990. The American sales fall produced one immediate, cruel irony: after a heated productivity dispute in April 1988, Jaguar had won workforce agreement to raise output to 1,300 cars a week, sufficient to produce more than 62,000 cars annually. Jaguar hit the 1,300 figure for one week. Then, because of the abrupt slump in North American demand, the company had to cut weekly output back to 1,220 cars.

The six-year trend of growth in the workforce, from its lowest point of 7,500 in 1982, was reversed by a decision not to fill most vacancies. That would lose about 1,200 jobs in three years. Jaguar remained determined to avoid actual redundancies, voluntary or otherwise.

Whether it would succeed remained an open question as the company approached 1990. But not quite as open as the biggest question of all: when Jaguar's protection against takeover, which had been written into its articles at the time of privatization, expired on 31 December, 1990, would the company immediately fall prey to a bid by a foreign car maker? The London and New York stock markets thought so – Jaguar's shares held a level in early 1989 which owed nothing to its actual trading prospects and everything to bid anticipation. Jaguar itself was examining possible ways and means of taking action to pre-empt a hostile bid.

One thing was certain: despite its fall from grace, Jaguar remained a potent symbol of British manufacturing industry. No longer, though, a symbol of manufacturing's resurrection; now a portent of the incompleteness and fragility of that once-marvellous revival. Was the attribution to Jaguar of so great a significance actually justified? Certainly, there was a nice parallel between the company's exchange-rate influenced fortunes and those of British industry (and indeed of the British economy), with the strong dollar of the mid-1980s, which helped restrain raw material prices, giving way to the weak currency of the late 1980s which helped fuel the rise in inflation.

But, with hindsight, what probably facilitated the vision of Jaguar as a metaphor for British manufacturing – and made this vision facile –was the company's simplicity for a manufacturer of its size (sales passed £1 billion in 1987). The product range effectively consisted of two cars (the XJ6 and the XJS). Jaguar's was more transparent an operation than others. And because of its dependence on the American market (Egan reckoned that whatever happened there, sales would always account for at least 40 per cent of the group total) it was also an extreme case.

That is not to diminish the importance of its setback as a cautionary tale. The problems it suffered are best seen as a classic cxample of the difficulty of converting initial recovery and short-term growth into the second, follow-up phase of long-term development. But that difficulty was caused by the highly particular nature of the company. The new XJ6 had to be a success: if it wasn't, the whole company could have gone down. And Jaguar was a marketing-oriented company. Above everything else, Egan was a great marketing man. What was neglected was the other fundamental: manufacturing and general operating efficiency. Hence the significance of the appointments of Bob Dover and David Harding. Their arrival heralded a strategic U-turn as Jaguar contemplated a more price-competitive American marketplace, where the Japanese manufacturers Toyota and Nissan were about to launch their first up-market vehicles. Part of the efficiency effort was a drive to cut costs by £50 million a year.

'We decided about six months ago that we had to change our

fundamental philosophy,' Egan rationalized in November, 1988. 'Up to then, we had a philosophy of growth. Clearly the golden share (protection against takeover) was going out of the window at the end of 1990, and we felt we should grow our way into being an extremely large company by then. It was also important because, when I started here back in 1980, the company wasn't a viable size. We weren't selling enough to generate enough money to have an engineering department big enough to design new cars. We felt that until we had 50,000 or 60,000 units we would not be a viable size. Having reached that figure, we decided six months ago that we had to start concentrating much more on cost-effectiveness, especially if we were going to remain competitive in the United States.'

That decision gave rise to fresh potential danger. Jaguar had already cut back its planned investment spend from around £130 million a year to £100 million; it could find itself short of cash to fund new model programmes, and therefore have to delay them. Its new XJ41 F-Type sports car was not now expected until at least 1994. At the same time, the arrival of the Japanese would not trespass directly on Jaguar's unique market niche – but it might compress that niche, squeezing Jaguar into a tighter corner of the luxury sector. Without sufficient cash to broaden the product range fast enough, the company might be unable to break out. Profits could be strong, but growth would be restricted.

Jaguar remained confident that it could avoid these potholes and eventually return to its now-abandoned target of growing at between ten and 15 per cent a year. 'In the long-run, we'll come back into those figures,' Egan said in November 1988. 'We might need a wider and richer mix of vehicles, but I would say that we would probably be able to resume the kind of growth pattern we were in before, when we have demonstrated to ourselves that we have got all of our management processes under control. Over the next couple of years, we must undergo enormous behavioural and technical change to become a world class player.'

While Jaguar's future remained uncertain, the company that made the luxury sweaters worn by many Jaguar drivers was providing a contrasting, and archetypal, instance of successful 1980s corporate development which also cast a revealing light on the British textiles industry. For most of the first half of the decade, Dawson International depended principally on sales of its famous cashmere and knitwear sweater brands – Pringle, Barrie, Braemar and the like – particularly in the home market, where demand from American tourists had a major influence. In 1986, Dawson attempted to join the great merger boom by agreeing a union with its fellow Scottish textiles group, the multinational Coats Patons. Coats was far larger, but Dawson was rated much higher by the City. Dawson's native fervour for the deal was not, however, matched by Coats. Two weeks after agreeing the Dawson merger, Coats abruptly pulled out of the deal and merged instead with Vantona Viyella to form Europe's largest textile group – Coats Viyella.

The deal was created by Vantona's managing director David Alliance, an Iranian-born entrepreneur who had lived up to his name by building a massive group through a series of agreed takeovers. Alliance, knighted in 1988, was a charismatically persuasive figure, and the merger with Coats looked a perfect fit: Vantona was concentrated in Britain, Coats had operations worldwide. Unlike Courtaulds, which it had now overhauled in size but which had been diversifying into speciality chemicals, the newly-created Coats Viyella was totally concentrated on the textiles industry, where it was now Britain's national champion. Alliance remarked that, while Courtaulds' chairman Sir Christopher Hogg had revived the group by sweeping rationalization, he had expanded more constructively. And he looked forward to turning back the tide of imports with products made in the UK.

But before Coats could use its balance sheet strength and total textiles commitment to expand further overseas, notably into mainland Europe, it and the rest of the industry were struck by the falling dollar that gave Jaguar such a headache. The Far East countries whose exports had made vast inroads into Western markets, including Britain, all had currencies pegged to the American dollar. As the pound strengthened against it, so imports in Britain mounted – and killed off, at least temporarily, all hope that Coats could spearhead a reversal of Britain's textiles trade deficit. Instead, in 1988 and 1989, the industry was hit by a new round of closures and job cuts which brought it almost full circle, back to where it had started the decade. This time, Alliance, too, had to rein back, though he remained characteristically ebullient. And the group's potential remained. It seemed indeed, that the setback might have caused a shift in the balance of power within the group so that for the first time since the merger, Alliance's great flair might be harnessed by Coats' discipline to the benefit of the company and its shareholders. The impression was confirmed when, in May 1989, Coats moved to take over Tootal. It was one more alliance, but the rationale for the deal was the cash-liberating combination of the companies' thread interests – an area where Alliance had previously shown little interest.

The Coats problems may have come as little consolation to the once-jilted Dawson (which with a determination characteristic of its chairman Ronald Miller pursued a claim for compensation costs against former Coats Patons executives) but they highlighted the success of Dawson's enforced strategy of niche-building. Dawson, too, had its problems. An American–Chinese attempt to start a rival cashmere business in Puerto Rico, exporting to the United States, may have collapsed ignominiously, but from 1987, Dawson did find Mongolian cashmere supplies of adequate quality increasingly difficult and costly to obtain. It also had to contend with the decline in American tourist business in Europe through the combination of the low dollar and fears about terrorist activity.

But the impact of this last factor in particular was mitigated by the steps Dawson was taking both to broaden and deepen its business base, both by product, geography and actual industry. On its cashmere side in Britain, the company widened its product range and, most significantly, took its first steps into retailing. The two moves were related, since Dawson had to ensure that its retailing move did not tread on the toes of the stores which took its existing products. Its first Pringle shop was opened in the Gateshead MetroCentre on Tyneside in 1988. In Europe, Dawson took control of its West German distribution network. And, most significantly of all, it moved into the key United States market by starting a cashmere retailing business in major cities, employing top designers to produce cashmere ranges, and meticulously targeting different segments of the market.

Dawson's translation of its core business into the world's largest luxury goods market came only after the group had spent several years learning about the American market from US acquisitions of other consumer product manufacturers. But these acquisitions, which brought Dawson major market positions in thermal underwear and shower curtains, were much more than stalking horses for cashmere sweaters. In themselves, they enabled Dawson to diversify successfully, both geographically and into other textile-based areas. No British consumer products manufacturer with ambitions to be an international force could be without a significant presence in the giant American market. Dawson built one in the 1980s. In 1988, more than half its sales were made in the United States.

The big question marks over British manufacturers' future at the end of the 1980s did not concern the niche-occupiers. In the course of the general industrial revival during the decade, numerous companies – usually in components, but also, like Dawson, in consumer goods – had found niches and were facing up to the challenge of expanding them internationally. Niche manufacturing, reckoned the managing director of one medium-sized and growing building and security products business, suited the British worker's psychology: 'The UK is not very good at volume; people don't have the attitude for constant repetition. But I'm quite comfortable with that. It doesn't mean that you can't be successful.'

In this bias towards niche manufacturing, Britain presented a striking contrast with the much smaller likes of Sweden, which had a limited component supplier population (and was therefore a notable customer of the British), but a remarkably high density of big multinational manufacturers: ABB, Alfa-Laval, Atlas Copco, Electrolux, Ericsson, ESAB, Sandvik, SKF, Volvo.

In 1989, the corporate finance department of one leading British merchant bank, preparing its bids and deals ground for the onset of the open European market, drew up a list of the largest European companies in each industry. Among them were few British companies. Indeed, Britain entered the 1990s with a paucity of world-scale companies in relatively few manufacturing sectors. They were in chemicals (ICI), gases (BOC) and pharmaceuticals (Glaxo, Beecham, Wellcome); and in alcoholic drinks (Guinness, Allied-Lyons). The Anglo-Dutch giant Unilever was Britain's solitary global player in non-alcohol consumer products. Grand Metropolitan combined manufacturing with food and drink retailing. To a large extent, however, these were industries where British manufacturing had been traditionally strong, as ICI's former chairman Sir John Harvey-Jones pointed out (*The Observer*, 16 April, 1989). The achievement here during the 1980s was to retain that world position.

As Harvey-Jones noted, it was in the industries whose failings had fuelled Britain's manufacturing decline that the real test of recovery lay. These sectors – metals, engineering, electricals, motors and aerospace, electronics, textiles, food – produced a number of world players in volume industries during the decade. The major manufacturing privatizations – British Aerospace, Rolls-Royce and British Steel – were three. APV was another; and, potentially, Coats Viyella. Pilkington gained in global glass-making strength through the decade. BTR dominated some of its 'volume' niches – by 1989, it was the world's largest valve maker. GKN held its multinational lead in the field of driveline motor components, able to switch sources of production on a global basis, winning business from the Japanese with major orders from Toyota and lesser ones from Honda, although that was a mature business.

But after them came the numerous major British companies which might have transformed their performance during the 1980s, but would confront in the next decade the final challenge of leaping from the ranks of significant international manufacturers into the realms of global competitors. So far, they had made it – but only so far.

Lucas, for instance, had moved away from low-value electrical towards higher-value electronic motor components and was aiming to do the same in aerospace and industrial sectors while reducing the relative overall size of its automotive business. At the same time, led by its manufacturing director Dr John Parnaby, the group had achieved exceptional progress for a British company in establishing Japanese practices and standards of operation in its factories.

But while attainment of Japanese levels of efficiency might be one precondition of global competitiveness, it was only one among many. In aerospace electronics such as microwave systems, the group had established a $100 million a year business in the United States. Yet it still had far to go to climb from the ranks of the sub-system producers to the top tier of prime contractor or sub-contractor. At the same time, there was real doubt among some industry analysts about

Lucas's ability both to achieve its aerospace and industrial electronics aims and to keep pace with the globalization of the auto industry. In Europe, Fiat's Magneti Marelli subsidiary and Valeo of France, owned by the Italian financier Carlo de Benedetti, were emerging in the late 1980s as major dedicated auto component groups alongside the longer-established companies.

Lucas was superior to them in the level of its technology, although West German group Bosch retained its world lead in electrical and electronic motor components. But the competitive battle was likely to gain additional intensity from the arrival of Japanese component companies behind the British operations of Nissan, Honda and Toyota, all established during the decade. In committing itself to the diversification of its business base, Lucas, it was feared, might be dividing finite resources to the point where it would start to weaken in motor components just at the moment when automotive electronics were becoming a volume market, heading for more than a decade of immense growth. This concern gathered strength in 1988, when Siemens entered the lists by buying control of the Bendix auto electronics business of American giant Allied-Signal, immediately establishing itself second only to Bosch in the European industry. Lucas formed a joint venture with the Japanese group Sumitomo in its American brakes operation, and, in a strategic re-think, it decided to concentrate resources on its 'vehicle dynamics' operations – including brakes and fuel injection systems. Engine management became a 'support' technology rather than a product which Lucas would seek to sell worldwide. Until this re-definition of priorities could show success, it remained only a partial answer to the questions about Lucas's commitment to (and competitiveness in) automotive systems.

Even a British company as demonstrably successful during the late 1980s as Cadbury Schweppes faced the end of the decade a considerable distance away (leaving takeover bid speculation aside) from crossing the divide between major international company and true world consumer products group. In confectionery, Cadbury abandoned plans to establish a worldwide manufacturing presence by ceding its United States business to Hershey in a licensing deal similar to that signed by Rowntree years before with the same company.

However, its principal global drive was in soft drinks, where it was the world number three.

The only restraining factor was that numbers one and two were Coca-Cola and PepsiCo, two of the biggest corporations in the world. Cadbury could grow with them – through major joint ventures like that with Coke in Britain or through bottling links with either company – and it could grow on the back of the expanding market, particularly outside America, for carbonated soft drinks. But to an extent, it could only grow on their sufferance. It had to tread carefully between the feet of the elephants, ensuring that it did not trespass on territory they claimed for themselves. And even as the number three soft drinks company, the limitations of Cadbury's global power were highlighted in 1988, when the group had to reduce the minority stake it had taken during a buy-out of American soft drinks company Dr Pepper. Cadbury's lucrative profit on the sale of the Dr Pepper shares, required by the buy-out lead investors, was compensation, but only compensation, for having to lower a stake which it would have preferred to increase.

The Dr Pepper situation was also a reminder of the wider implications for British manufacturers of the rise in America through the 1980s of the LBO, the leveraged buy-out. LBOs represented both an opportunity and a threat to British manufacturers. The opportunity was two-fold: first, as in the Dr Pepper case, buy-outs gave British companies the chance to acquire attractive American assets that would not otherwise have been available. But this opportunity did not come without its downside, particularly late in the decade when LBO prices has risen sharply. In late 1988, Avon Rubber was one of two medium-sized British companies which were looking to establish themselves in the key American domestic market and found the perfect fit in businesses which were up for sale. In each case, the acquisitions would have doubled the British outfit's size. But both openings were blocked by LBOs which bid a higher price.

The other opportunity arising from LBOs came later with a stronger sting in the tail. It was highlighted by the case of two major American components makers, both the subject of LBOs, each occupying good positions in their home market which a leading British company was trying to penetrate. First, the British company had considered trying to take over one of the Americans. But it abandoned the idea when it saw what was happening both there and in the other American business. Because of their need to meet the debt repayments incurred during the leveraged (debt-funded) buy-out, the companies were being starved of capital investment. Manufacturing processes which had been automated by the British firm were still being carried out manually in the American companies. They were going backwards technically. The Briton saw a great chance to use its competitive edge and take market share away from the Americans. The company's chief executive observed: 'Buy-outs are destroying American manufacturing industry.' His opinion, and that of other British executives, ran clean counter to the claims of LBO proponents that overwhelming evidence testified to the beneficial effect of LBOs.

But, as Britain approached the 1990s, there was a very real possibility that the LBO would cross the Atlantic. Financiers concerned at the spiralling American LBO prices – which peaked with the $24 billion purchase of RJR Nabisco by LBO kings Kohlberg Kravis Roberts against a rival buy-out bid – but with money to lend or spend were eyeing up the British market. Britain did not offer the American tax concessions on interest payments, but any reservation that induced could be outweighed by the volume of money looking for a deal.

Although there were British companies which, despite recession and revival, remained made to be broken up, their number was relatively small. And many British managements were not ready to join a buy-out of the company that in many cases they had built up, to see it broken up so that it could service its debt repayments. Consequently, at least one merchant banker who had been examining the LBO potential concluded that, in contrast to common American practice, if LBOs took off in Britain they would be on a hostile, not friendly basis.

The gathering swell of the LBO, together with the spectre that British companies which deserved to remain independent might be taken over by foreigners capitalizing on the openness of Britain's acquisitions market, meant the final test for industry's relationship with the City and the shareholding institutions.

After all the years of debate about competition and takeover policy, the exhortations for companies to talk frequently to the City and for the institutions to take a more consistent interest in the companies where they were investors, no conclusive resolution had emerged. Many companies had learned important lessons in communication, starting from the fundamental point that there was not one 'City', but several. Institutional fund managers did not swallow blindly the share buying recommendations of the securities analysts and salesmen. Indeed, the institutions had grown more distrustful than ever of the securities houses since Big Bang abolished the distinction between stock jobbers (the share wholesalers) and stockbrokers (the retailers) and created the new class of market-makers. As a result, institutions could never be sure whether a securities house share recommendation was motivated by objective analysis or the desire to 'talk one's book', motivated by the firm's market-making position in the shares of the company concerned.

Correspondingly, companies had started to bypass the middle men of the securities houses and talk directly to their institutional shareholders, or the institutions they hoped would become shareholders. A landmark in this trend was the December 1986 decision by GKN and its future chairman, the then-finance director David Lees, to stop attending stockbrokers' lunches. These lunches, a City institution in themselves, were organized by a securities house and attended by a company management on one side and fund managers from different institutions on the other. The standard and seniority of the institutional representatives varied wildly, to the annoyance both of the company and some of the institutional guests. Moreover, the company had no say in targeting particular institutions to which it wanted to talk.

GKN had had enough, and resolved to go direct to institutions – in the first phase, to its own shareholders, later to non-shareholders. The move was immediately, widely, and wrongly interpreted as a decision by GKN to stop talking to the City. Nothing could have been further from the truth. GKN continues to talk to the securities analysts, while once a year, Lees sees the top ten institutional shareholders individually, and the next rank of significant holders in groups of five or six. He reckons that as a result, GKN meets holders of between 50 and 60 per cent of its shares each year.

This move, quietly followed soon afterwards by several other major groups, was a harbinger of change for the good in the way companies handled their investor relations. It unquestionably narrowed the communication gap between industry and 'the City'. As the 1990s approached, not only was investor relations becoming an increasingly important aspect of the work done by public relations, but specialist investor relations businesses were being established. This trend held out the hope, however slim, that at some time in the future, the flaws in the market-based British industrial-financial complex might be erased altogether.

An improvement in communications between companies and their institutional shareholders was one route followed by David Walker in his pursuit of the Nirvana combining the best of the British system with that of Germans and the Japanese. Walker also looked for a rise in 'relationship banking', in which companies would form longer-term relationships with their bankers rather than going to whichever bank was offering the cheapest immediate funding deal (Bridge Lecture to the Worshipful Company of Engineers, 17 February, 1988).

But his more crucial, and potentially more intractable, quest was to identify ways to mitigate the financial institutions' view that takeover bids were the only effective means of removing an adequate management which was causing an underperforming investment. As Walker had pointed out, the bid bias of the British system was not so much a case of constant short-termism as of overlong-termism (institutions' general reluctance to use their influence to engineer management change) culminating in the final, short-termist solution (the takeover bid). Instead, said Walker, a means was required of facilitating 'graduated' intervention by institutional shareholders.

Walker diagnosed as a central problem the immunity of executive management to much external pressure: 'British management is less accountable than any in the leading Western countries. It does not have a supervisory tier as in Germany or Holland or, in most cases, an audit committee as is obligatory for companies quoted on the New York Stock Exchange.' Moreover, too few companies were willing to appoint enough non-executive directors, who could help increase this accountability. By 1989, Walker had come to the radical conclusion that a fundamental resolution of the company-institutional conundrum might not be possible without changes in company law to introduce two-tier boards. Above the board of executive management would sit a supervisory board of responsibility containing representatives of the financial institutions, who could bring pressure to bear on underperforming managements. It was an interesting notion, though some industrialists believed that it would evaporate as completely as had the 1970s Bullock report advocating the appointment of worker directors.

The 1980s therefore ended with the problem inherent in the relationship between British industry and finance – that its demand for constantly rising returns to shareholders was not as conducive to long-term industrial success as the relationships existing among many of Britain's overseas competitors, where comparative standstill performance was tolerated while market position was established – still far from resolution.

This fact might have mattered less had the one obvious potentially compensating force of a constructive industry-Government relationship found an even footing. Instead, Britain entered the 1990s with the relationship still tilted drastically towards the doctrine that allowing free play of market forces was the sole determinant of industrial success. It was a doctrine that left British manufacturing disturbingly out of line with its overseas rivals. It translated into the contrast drawn between Britain's 'level playing field' and those on uneven foreign soil. Contemplating prospects in the New Year of 1989, Sir Francis Tombs observed: 'Our problem is that we invented cricket.'

All the post-recession realization of the efficiency gains induced by the first Thatcher Government's refusal to reflate during the slump that it had itself inadvertently deepened had not really changed the terms of trade between industry and the politicians. Ministers talked of Britain's great economic revival. Yet on the ground, it appeared as if the Government still did not trust the new generation of management, which had helped bring about that recovery, not to relapse into the bad old, inefficient ways. In 1989, with pay settlements following the rising trend of inflation, ministerial calls for companies to stand firm against 'high' wage claims had the *timbre* of time immemorial.

Overseas, Mrs Thatcher remained a great personal promoter of British exports. She did not always bring home the bacon (on a visit to Turkey, she argued the case both for a new British-built bridge across the Bosphorus and for a military vehicle order, although neither actually materialized) but the commitment was there.

At home, too, came acknowledgement of the tough battle being fought by British manufacturing. Three years after the House of Lords report on British trade, which the Government had so pre-emptively dismissed, the Prime Minister told a Downing Street dinner for captains of industry in September 1988: 'Gentlemen, we have a balance of payments problem.'

But the hands-off industrial policy remained the same – only more so. Interventionism was applied in manufacturing at only two points: the privatizations, which were completed in 1989 with the sale of Belfast aerospace group Short Brothers, and the attraction of inward investment, notably from Japan.

The highly successful effort to persuade foreign firms to set up operations in Britain was the ambivalent epitome of Thatcherite industrial strategy. A few days in April 1989 highlighted the amazing success of this policy. First, Fujitsu of Japan announced that it was establishing a European semi-conductor manufacturing plant in County Durham. Then electrical motor components world leader Bosch of West Germany said that it had chosen South Wales to be the site of a £100 million alternator factory – its biggest-ever investment outside its home country. Within 24 hours, Japan's biggest car maker Toyota stated that it would establish its European manufacturing base with a £650 million plant in Derbyshire.

The Fujitsu, Bosch and Toyota projects were showcases for concerted, intense effort by, first, national Government departments, and then local authorities, to win the investments. One week before they were announced, the managing director of a medium-sized public company, fast expanding overseas, was diagnosing a continuing fault in Britain's industrial system: 'The trouble is that the UK has cells – industry, central government, local government, education. All are cut off from each other. In France, West Germany and the like they all work together, talk to each other.'

That contrast is exemplified by the strain of schizophrenia that ran through the 1980s manufacturing revival. It was the difference between the outsider arriving with a clean slate and the long-established insider trying to wipe its dirty slate clean; the difference between the new, 'greenfield' project and the old 'brownfield' operation; the difference between first coming and comeback.

For the Government, the two sides of Britain's manufacturing recovery were intimately related: the foreign-owned investments constituted the carrot and stick with which indigenous companies were at once encouraged and beaten into raising efficiency. And the policy was effective. It provided a new point of reference against which established British industry could measure its shortcomings and successes.

It was appropriate that the culmination of this remarkably sustained policy should be two major Japanese investments made within a week of each other when Lord Young was Trade and Industry Secretary. It was Young, as an adviser to the Department of Industry during the first Thatcher administration, who had played a key role in establishing the inward investment strategy. In 1982, he visited Tokyo for the first time, meeting all the Japanese high-technology groups and a number of the other companies. 'They all stated two things: the climate wasn't right – and they meant industrial relations, not the weather – and the standard of components supply wasn't good enough,' reported Young.

The surge of Japanese investment during the late 1980s gave proof positive that, although the Thatcher governments had not made strikes a relic of the past, they had banished the impression left by the 1970s that the British worker was unmanageable and inferior to his or her overseas counterparts. The absence from the overseas-owned plants of workforce representation by a multiplicity of trades unions pointed up another fact, as a Treasury paper observed in April 1989: 'The recent evidence suggests unions tend, in practice, to be associated with lower productivity in the UK economy.' (Economic Progress Report, April 1989.)

But if, as Young said in late 1988, the labour relations climate was now judged by the Japanese to be 'fine', the component manufacturers still had considerable scope to raise standards. 'The Japanese tell me that they are getting better, but they are still not good enough,' said Young. The way to attain zero defects and to eliminate poor testing was clear: maintain the pressure from the inward investors.

'What we've lacked in this country is sufficient competition,' said Young. 'If we had had that, we wouldn't have lost half our car sales. Most of British industry lost their way, as we lost our car industry. Now that we have domestic competition, it sharpens up our local manufacturing. We are seeing a tremendous improvement in the quality of component suppliers who are now having to manufacture for the rigorous standards of the Japanese. Now that is spreading, because indigenous UK manufacturers recognize they can get quality and will start to demand it. Nissan is having an enormous benefit for Rover.' This last was quite possibly true, though Rover did not always like to acknowledge the fact. Rover's former managing director Harold Musgrove hit the roof at one point, when Lucas was seen to be implying that Nissan's standards were more demanding than those of his own company.

Young also granted that there was a fine line between sharpening up the indigenous British companies by importing foreign competition, and driving them out of business. But he declared: 'I'm not convinced that that point has been reached.'

The final test of this judgment will not come until the 1990s, when many of the Japanese plants, notably those of the motor manufacturers, will reach full operating power, and – as seems likely – Japanese component makers follow their domestic customers into Europe.

Increased awareness of the close, vertical links that existed between the leading Japanese car companies and their prime, 'first tier' component suppliers (cemented in some cases by actual vehicle company shareholdings in the supplier) may have encouraged another highly significant 1980s shift which promised to be of great benefit to British industry. It was, however, a move which demonstrated that Young's analysis of Britain's past industrial decline was not entirely accurate.

It was not so much lack of competition which undermined the quality of the British car industry in the 1960s and 1970s, as the imposition of too much short-term, short-sighted pressure on the component makers by their Anglo-Saxon customers. By pushing constantly for the lowest price, and switching abruptly from supplier to supplier in the quest for the cheapest product, the original equipment motor manufacturers created enormous uncertainty and destroyed all incentive for the suppliers to invest in facilities providing long-term quality. In the process, of course, the British and American vehicle companies weakened their own product so that when the Japanese invasion came, they were ill-prepared to repel it. In the late 1980s, that adversarial culture was at last being superseded by the industry-wide trend towards single-sourcing concentration on fewer suppliers whose long-term contracts would encourage the creation of a virtuous investment-quality circle. The trend offered great hope for the future. The only doubt was whether it was just in time to counter the Japanese onslaught, or just too late.

The Government's unremitting drive to expose established British manufacturers to the (higher) standards of the greenfield plants was mirrored in another keystone of Government policy – established in the second half of the decade. The Ministry of Defence programme to open up equipment programmes to competitive tender was inspired by Michael Heseltine in his period as Defence Secretary and implemented by Sir Peter Levene, the head of the MoD's Procurement Executive whom Heseltine recruited from United Scientific Holdings at a private-to-public sector 'transfer' fee which recalled the MacGregor furore at British Steel.

Levene was every bit as effective as MacGregor had been. He set about phasing out the 'cost-plus' order system, and replaced it with competition for contracts; he shattered the old inner circle of British suppliers with whom contracts were habitually placed, and opened up competition to a host of companies which had been unable to break into the business; the new regime was so tough that companies nominated to design new products were not guaranteed the actual equipment manufacturing contract or that they would recover their front-end costs.

Levene's was a procurement revolution, and there could be no argument about the healthiness of overthrowing the cost-plus hierarchy. But like most revolutions, this one reached the excessive point where it threatened to do at least as much harm as good. By 1989, disquiet about the ramifications of the policy had spread beyond those members of the old guard whose opposition to the changes was predictable. Concern was being expressed even by companies which had gained access under the Levene reforms to defence contracts from

A FIGHTING CHANCE

which they would previously have been excluded. It was said that some companies would simply stop quoting for contracts, because they could not afford the risk of incurring expense but coming away empty-handed.

One highly experienced industrialist commented: 'Relations between defence companies and the MoD should not be confrontational, as Peter Levene has made them. There has to be greater co-operation and collaboration than exists at the moment, with all this concentration on economy and cost.' He contrasted the British adversarial approach with the intimate part played by the French Government in supporting its defence industry.

'There has to be a swing back towards the middle,' said the industrialist. 'Like so many things with the Government, it has been taken to extremes.'

There was the rub. In practice, the Thatcher revolution made no allowance for the fact that the 'new' model industry that it had itself created might not repeat the errors of the past. In defence procurement policy, this attitude was reinforced in particular by the Nimrod affair, during which more than one billion pounds was poured into thin air over almost a decade by a British attempt to turn the highly successful Nimrod reconnaissance aircraft and submarine hunter into the carrier of an advanced system giving early warning of any airborne attack. The combination of Nimrod's quite unsuitable design for such a role, GEC-Marconi's difficulties in producing a satisfactory software system, and frequent changes of specification eventually ditched the project (in 1986), and the MoD bought the already-operating Boeing AWACs aircraft under an agreement in which Boeing guaranteed to place work in Britain 'offsetting' the value of the contract. The final decision came years after an RAF report had recommended precisely this solution, with the twist that instead of an offset agreement (which was implemented in a somewhat specious manner) it suggested – quite feasibly at the time – that the aircraft be made in Britain under licence.

Nimrod left a huge scar on the Thatcherite Cabinet psyche. Thus, when two years later, in 1988, the MoD had to decide whether a British tank (made by Vickers) or an American one should be ordered to replace the existing but sub-standard Challenger model, a ferocious contest almost resulted in the Americans getting the

Government's vote. Levene and some other MoD officials vigorously backed the American case. When Vickers' chairman Sir David Plastow appealed to Mrs Thatcher, he was told that she was not going to be 'Nimrodded' into another disaster. No consideration was given to the fact that there was no similarity between the two cases. Not only was the Nimrod system completely untried and untested, the aircraft itself had never been designed to perform the early-warning function. The Vickers tank was based on a proven design by a company which had been building tanks since they were invented. After months of debate, a Cabinet meeting just before Christmas 1988 gave Vickers the contract, on condition that its tank passsed various 'milestone' tests over the ensuing 18 months. But the decision was a close-run thing. Some leading figures in the Ministry of Defence, paralyzed by their concern to avoid a repetition of the political obloquy caused by Nimrod, sat on their hands. Mrs Thatcher only approved Vickers after Lord Young strongly supported the company's case in Cabinet, arguing that to dismiss the Vickers tank would be to forego the chance of winning major export orders, since no overseas country would buy a tank which had been rejected by its own country's national army.

Despite the free market doctrine, interventionism was not entirely proscribed in Young's DTI. A signal case occurred in 1988, when Dowty was competing for the £300 million contract to win the main landing gear on the new long-haul Airbus A330/340 aircraft, the penultimate major civil airline project of the century. In alliance with the American group CPC, Dowty was battling against the French company Messier-Hispano-Bugatti (also partnered by an American, Monasco). Dowty's innovative product was more expensive, but also lighter, therefore more fuel-efficient and cheaper in the long-run. But Messier was being strongly supported by the French Government. Dowty, concerned both that it might lose the contract and that, if it won, its resources to compete against Messier for future contracts would be sapped by the disproportionate degree of State support enjoyed by the French, proposed that the DTI loan it £35 million to boost its bid, with the money to be repaid from the orders won. In what was a remarkable departure from its public posture of non-interventionism, the DTI eventually agreed to a £15 million loan package.

But Dowty's hard-won Government support was then whipped away by a Treasury refusal to approve the package. The message was unmistakable: the Treasury was stamping on any embers of interventionism in the normal course of business. The rigour with which this line permeated industrial issues was emphasized by the refusal of direct government aid for the high-thrust Trent engine.

Recourse to expedients like the reduction in Rolls' payments to the DTI in the cause of British manufacturing emphasized that for all the industrial revival of the Thatcher years, sparked by the leadership of Mrs Thatcher herself, Britain's system of government had not adjusted to the new dynamism in British manufacturing. In a way, this unresponsiveness proceeded from the same wellspring as the industrial revival itself: the monetarist economic strategy which, in its emphasis on cutting the rate of growth in public spending, reinforced the power of the Treasury over the spending Ministries. Sir Francis Tombs observed in late 1988: 'I remain convinced that the Treasury has to be tackled. We have a very unsophisticated Treasury system. The revenue accounting system of the Treasury lies at the root of many problems. The Treasury is geared to the annual budget, and not at all to investment for the future.'

Understanding of, and responsiveness to, the needs of British industry were not much nearer the heart of Government in 1989 than they had been before 1979. Industry had been successfully depoliticized, but Government – the politicians and civil servants – had not been industrialized. What were seen as the old corporatist bastions of interventionism – the National Economic Development Council, the DTI system of 'sponsorship' of sectors and companies, the concept of picking industrial winners – had been weakened or demolished. In their place, and in place of everything else that had persisted before 1979, was fostered the 'enterprise' culture. It bred entrepreneurs, and the winning entrepreneurs would pick themselves.

The industrial dynamism generated by the Thatcherite revolution was powerful. But was it enough? Even highly successful entrepreneurs could find the transition to systems-based businesses too great a step to manage. And at the level of big business, competitor industrial cultures were so different: Japan 'Inc.' was a vast working model of intense domestic competition but huge industry-Government co-operation; France remained dominated by State-owned giants with top managements made by political appointment. But the recurrent rounds of executive changes, potentially so disruptive, were underlain by a common industrial culture where businessmen and civil servants were not only united by their higher education in the Grands Ecoles, but frequently interchangeable. The United States, of course, was the great inspiration for Thatcherite Britain. But America's huge domestic market gave its companies immediate potential economies of scale that Britain's, at one-quarter the size, could never hope to gain. And the massive American defence budget provided a great, permanent reservoir of subsidy for private sector investment.

The 1990s would be a decade of accumulating pressure to compete with the resources deployed by giant foreign-owned multi-nationals. As Britain entered it, there remained an abiding concern that without a more sophisticated, constructive relationship between Government and industry, the country's manufacturing companies would lose ground to rivals whose industrial base provided such an alliance. Taking Government's hands off British industry because post-war hands-on interventionism had been so disastrous was a highly effective interim step on the road to manufacturing recovery. But, to sustain that recovery over the longer term, something more creative than total non-involvement had to be put in place.

There were sporadic calls by industrialists (Sir Peter Parker, Sir Trevor Holdsworth) through the decade for the establishment of some forum or system of communication between Government and industry, where detailed issues even relating to individual companies could be discussed. These were not a plea for fresh political interventionism in industrial decision-making, but a proposal for giving industry an effective voice at the heart of the decision-making process. Tombs commented: 'We almost construct a barrier between the economy and government, partly through the background of politicians, partly through the educational background. Gradually, the Government has adapted a little by setting up joint advisory bodies where industrialists are represented. Industrial voices are becoming louder. That's one way to bridge the divide. We have to go through a phase where discrimination applies. That's difficult for politicians, because their civil servants know nothing about it. But it's crucial that we do, because at the moment the gap between the economy and Government is still enormous'.

As the 1980s ended, Government non-involvement still reigned. At the European Commission in Brussels, the Community-wide standards that would apply in the free European market were being hammered out. Eleven of the 12 EC countries had a Minister on the standards committee. The only exception was Britain. One British industrialist commented: 'They are leaving it to the British Standards Authority, which is fine except that ultimately, it just hasn't got the resources to argue a comprehensive case.'

For want of a Government-industry partnership, British industry's battle for long-term success could be lost. But every problem could not be laid at the Government's door. There were other concerns as industry entered the new decade. At Weir, Ron Garrick assessed the 1980s manufacturing record: 'If someone had come to me in 1978 and said, "Ten years from now this is where it will be", I would have said "You are off your head". We are offering better reliability, quality which is at least equal to our competitors, on-time delivery performance, lead time which is quicker, and back-up service which is second to none. We will be there first.

'The worry I have is that the Eighties are forgotten about, that people feel that the Eighties are a memory, that we should look at things differently. It was a salutary lesson for people in the company. The fact that it happened was really horrible. But I don't want to forget it quickly, because it drives an awful lot of our thinking now, and a lot of our day-to-day activities.'

The first real test for British industry's collective memory came in 1989, when rising inflation incited pressure for larger pay increases while demand growth slowed under the weight of higher interest rates. For the first time since the end of the recession, British companies would be unable to make up in volume-driven productivity growth what competitive ground they had lost through earnings increases which far exceeded those in their overseas competitiors.

Avon Rubber came clean in June 1989, when it told the Stock Exchange and the world at large that it had agreed an eight per cent pay settlement – double what the company had originally budgeted. Avon would not be able to recover all that increase from customers by raising prices, the company said. It would take the impact of the pay deal on its profit margin.

Avon remained committed to its long-term drive for competitiveness. Indeed, said Derek Hudson, head of its tyres business, the pay rise was made with that strategy in mind: 'How can you demand from your workforce that they extend themselves to Total Quality, and go on accepting no pay for change or flexibility, if you then have an unsatisfactory pay settlement and a dissatisfied workforce?'

But the inflation-induced rise in unit costs that would follow from higher pay increases, like the rumblings of industrial action by the AEU, the engineering workers' union, in pursuit of a shorter working week, were sharp reminders that the revolution of the 1980s had not called into being a completely new world, unfettered by all the competitive handicaps of Britain's industrial past.

Garrick also testified to the lost strategic capacity in British manufacturing that had not been replaced. Weir now has to buy sophisticated steel forgings in Italy, because it cannot get them in Britain. For variable speed gearboxes, it has to go either to Germany or to Hitachi in Japan. In the British motor industry, there is now no independent domestic manufacturer of vehicle transmissions. British manufacturing may have become component-orientated, but there are sizeable lacunae in its component range.

The extinction of British-made capital goods like these contributed to the rising trade deficit in manufactures, which formed the largest element in the mounting overall British trade deficit of the late 1980s. The deficit constituted a clear and present threat to confidence in Britain's currency, but not perhaps as fundamental and long-term a danger as it may have appeared. Its unprecedented size was partly produced by a freak, and by a peculiarly detrimental economic combination: the surge in British industrial investment and the peaking of the consumer boom fuelled by government economic laxity, which, while certainly benefiting British manufacturers, had pushed Britain's demand growth rate way out of line with those of its competitors. It sucked in quantities of the consumer and capital goods that British companies no longer made.

The alarm generated by the deficit was a backhanded rejoinder to those who claimed that British manufacturing industry's future was immaterial since it now comprised so small a proportion of British employment and national output. The deficit reinforced the argument that while the service sector could generate employment, it was manufacturing's vastly superior foreign earnings potential which would create most wealth in Britain.

The major issue as the decade ended was that raised by the trend towards multinational manufacturing. In the global age, when in order to grow, companies had to establish a presence worldwide, the term 'British manufacturing industry' was in need of sharper definition. The combination of British investment overseas and the Government's outstandingly successful policy of attracting foreign companies to invest in Britain held out the prospect that a far larger proportion of manufacturing than ever before in this country would not be British-owned.

This likelihood was reinforced by the multiplying instances where, under the increasing pressure of globalization, British companies ceded ownership of operations to overseas groups. The fork lift truck company Lansing Bagnall, as great a byword on the shopfloor as Hoover was in the home, was taken over by Linde of West Germany, the industry leader. Vickers sold its lithographic printing plates subsidiary Howson-Algraphy, a rare example of a British company with a truly global presence in a market niche, to the American chemicals giant Du Pont. Howson was a good third in the industry, but intensifying competitive pressure both to expand its product range and to withstand a mounting squeeze on prices demanded the support of more resources than Vickers alone could lend it. The company could have been put into a joint venture, à la Metalbox, but Vickers rejected the option. Howson went for £250 million, a handsome price but one which also embodied the long-term value of the company to an owner strong enough to hold its ground against the German, Japanese and American competition.

Foreign takeovers of British companies had happened since time immemorial, but the Lansing and Howson disposals represented a new departure. These were businesses which had been in the vanguard of the post-recession drive for total competitiveness: Lansing was the first British-owned company to adopt PA's Total Quality Management system, and Howson followed it as an early convert to TQM.

Did the expanding foreign ownership of British manufacturing companies matter? For some, the distinction was academic.

One of Industry Minister Kenneth Clarke's last acts before he moved to the Department of Health was to assert that the nationality of a company made little difference if it was bringing jobs and therefore wealth to Britain. On one level, this contention was irrefutable: better to have foreign companies generating employment in Britain than somewhere else. Yet while the accelerating pace of inward investment in the late 1980s represented international recognition of Britain's industrial revival, the acknowledgment contained a certain ambivalence which hinted at the limitations of that revival.

Bosch's £100 million alternator factory investment in South Wales in 1989 was a notable pointer. First, it showed both how high German labour costs had become and how low British labour costs had fallen: the average cost of a German worker (at 1987 figures) was DM32.70 an hour – nearly twice the British level of DM17.60 an hour. (*Wall Street Journal*, 30 March, 1989.) Bosch's labour costs would therefore be almost 86 per cent lower in South Wales than at its Stuttgart plant. But Bosch's overall cost saving in coming to Britain would only be 15 per cent – German productivity was still so superior to British that it made up 70 per cent of the difference.

Bridging the productivity gap stood out as the ultimate challenge facing British industry in the 1990s. That meant total productivity – not just output per person, but productivity in the sense of quality, innovation, cost-effectiveness. Achievement of that objective required much more than mere cash for capital investment. Ultimately, it demanded higher quality in management and workforce. Numerous 1980s studies, notably by NEDO and the National Institute of Economic and Social Research, highlighted the gulf between Britain's training effort and the far greater commitment embedded in its major competitor countries. Behind and before training, however, stood Britain's education system, so long antipathetic to the interests of industry which, for its part, had remained largely ignorant of and uninvolved with schools and universities.

The 1980s saw encouraging steps to close the divide between the two worlds. Part of that progress was due to the Government's efforts to make universities more efficient and business-conscious institutions while reforming the schools through the introduction of a national curriculum and changes to the system of examination and assessment. But there was also a growing number of independent initiatives to foster a creative relationship between school and industry. One such was Education 2000, which was backed by City and industry organizations and started life in 1985 as a pilot project in six Hertfordshire schools. Its aim, through various mechanisms including temporary release of teaching staff to work in industry and the widespread use of information technology, was to foster flexibility and all-round competence in young people while engendering in the community a united view of what education's objectives should be. As the decade ended, Education 2000 was poised to expand the project throughout Hertfordshire and into other areas of Britain.

Back on the factory floor, the Bosch investment said something else about the nature of the new manufacturing in Britain. The vehicle component involved, alternators, was a high volume, low added value, commodity-type item. It was not the sort of product on which to build an industrial renaissance. It was not the sort of plant which recognized anything in Britain other than its use as a low-cost peripheral site for an industrial power, on a par with the developing countries of the Far East where Bosch was putting some of its other manufacturing operations. In its own small way, it emphasized how far Britain still had to go to build a high-productivity, high-value, high-wage economy like West Germany's. British industry would not get there via satellite factories like that of Bosch. To stand a chance of realizing that elusive vision required a critical mass of internationally competitive British companies whose decision-making and intellectual property – the masterkey to global success – would be home-owned.

In late 1980s Britain, the will was there: 'In the next three years, we are going to take international markets and we are going to do it without holding people's hands unless we can find advantage by doing so,' declared Arthur Walsh of STC. At Avon Rubber, Tony Mitchard vowed: 'By the mid-Nineties, anyone who has not substantially improved their quality standards will wither on the vine. We aren't going to be one of those companies.'

In March 1989, the National Economic Development Office took stock of British manufacturing industry's 1980 performance. NEDO concluded that: 'Supply-side changes have had some effect on trade performance. Most noteworthy here is the turnround in the UK's relative productivity growth, but systematic evidence of

supply-side improvements enhancing the UK's non-price competitiveness has not yet emerged. . .'

Down on the shop floor, the phrasing was different but the
message was the same. There, among the German, Japanese, Italian
and American machine tools, visitors could often spy a banal and
yellowing sticker with a catchpenny adage which succinctly conveyed
the condition of British manufacturing industry after its most
momentous decade for almost 200 years. 'The impossible we can do
tomorrow,' the familiar slogan said. 'Miracles take a little longer.'

BIBLIOGRAPHY

TAKEOVERS, Ivan Fallon and James Srodes, Hamish Hamilton, 1987.

BUSINESS IN BRITAIN, Graham Turner, Eyre and Spottiswoode, 1969.

THE STRATEGY OF TAKEOVERS, Anthony Vice, McGraw-Hill, 1971.

ALL OUR WORKING LIVES, Peter Pagnamenta and Richard Overy, BBC Publications, 1984.

THE ENEMIES WITHIN, Ian MacGregor with Rodney Tyler, William Collins, 1986.

BACK FROM THE BRINK, Michael Edwardes, William Collins, 1983.

THE RECKONING, David Halberstam, William Morrow, Bloomsbury-Brit., 1986.

CREATING A COMMITTED WORKFORCE, Peter Martin and John Nicholls, Institute of Personnel Management, 1987.

INDEX

financial markets 16
Finden–Crofts 47, 51
Firestone 73
Fisher, Peter 75–6
Fitzgerald, Lou 49
food industry 110
Frazor, Sir Campell 38–40

Garrick, Ron 93–7
GEC 2, 14, 90, 100–1, 122, 214–232
GKN 137–8, 238, 266
Goodrich 73
Goodyear 73
Green, Owen 26–32, 44, 46, 49, 54–71

Hanson, Lord 111
Hanson Trust 26, 67, 100–1, 103–115, 131
Harvey-Jones, Sir John 2, 15–17
Heath, Edward 8, 18
Heseltine, Michael 20, 22
Hodgson, Sir Maurice 40–2
Hogg, Christopher 18
Howe, Sir Geoffrey 4,5,11

ICI 2, 15, 16, 27, 66
ICL 196, 199, 208, 210–13
Imperial Group 100–115
Industrial Reorganization Corporation 8, 28
Industrial Society, the 1
Industry Year 1
inflation 3–6, 17, 19, 28, 36, 87, 268
interest rates 4
interventionism 2, 8–10, 20, 23
investment 144
investor relations 116
Iron and Steel Trades Confederation 8

Jaguar 8, 35, 252–8
job cuts 154
Johnson Matthey 41
Joseph, Sir Keith 8–9

Kearton, Lord 18
Kent, Geoffrey 104
Khomeini, Ayatollah 3
King, Tom 7

labour costs 4, 62, 78, 80, 87
Labour Government 9
Labour Party, the 7
labour relations 7, 84–5, 87, 89
Laker Airways 88
Lawson, Nigel 12, 13, 87
Levene, Sir Peter 272–3
leveraged buy-outs 264–6
Lord, Alan 36, 39, 41
Lucas Industries 236–8, 262–3
Lygo, Sir Raymond 155–163

MacMillan, Harold 9
management 72–3, 77, 79–83, 87, 89, 98, 114–5, 233, 250–2
Maxwell, Robert 148
McKee, Davy 14
McKinsey Management Consultancy 221–3
McIntosh, Sir Ronald 146–7, 149
Mechanical Engineers, Institute of 14
Michelin 34, 38, 73
miners' strike 9
Mitchard, Tony 73, 76–8, 81–3
monetarism 4
money supply 5
Monopolies and Mergers Commission 101, 129, 135–8

Nabisco 106, 125
National Coal Board 18, 108
National Economic Development Office 3, 11, 14
Nestlé 122–139
Nicholson, Sir Robin 246–8
Nissan 10, 53, 68
non–interventionism, doctrine of 1, 20
North Sea Oil 2, 4, 17, 69

Office of Fair Trading 137
oil price 3
Overseas Trade Report 17

Parkinson, Cecil 9
pension funds 115–7
Pilkington 56–7, 59–60, 65, 69, 115, 120
Pirelli 33–5, 38, 73
Platt, Robert 1